The Bedford/St. Martin's Textbook Reader

Ellen Kuhl

Bedford/St. Martin's   **Boston** ◆ **New York**

For information, write: Bedford/St. Martin's, 75 Arlington Street, Boston, MA 02116 (617-399-4000)

ISBN: 0–312–40432–8

Acknowledgments

Bedford/St. Martin's gratefully acknowledges the following sources of the textbook chapters reprinted in this book: "Human Resource Management," Chapter 12 (pages 348–83) of *Exploring the World of Business,* by Kenneth Blanchard, Charles Schewe, Robert Nelson, and Alexander Hiam, Worth Publishers, 1996; "Stress, Health, and Coping," Chapter 13 (pages 536–69) of *Psychology,* Third Edition, by Don H. Hockenbury and Sandra E. Hockenbury, Worth Publishers, 2003; "Public Relations and Framing the Message," Chapter 12 (pages 422–51) of *Media and Culture: An Introduction to Mass Communication,* Updated Third Edition, by Richard Campbell, Christopher R. Martin, and Bettina Fabos, Bedford/St. Martin's, 2003; "Interactions in Communities," Chapter 44 (pages 792–813) of *Invitation to Biology,* Fifth Edition, by Helena Curtis and N. Sue Barnes, Worth Publishers, 1994; and "America through the Eyes of the Workers, 1870–1890," Chapter 18 (pages 650–82) of *The American Promise: A History of the United States,* Second Edition, by James L. Roark, Michael P. Johnson, Patricia Cline Cohen, Sarah Stage, Alan Lawson, and Susan M. Hartmann, Bedford/St. Martin's, 2002.

Preface

It's no secret that reading is an essential skill. Reflective, thoughtful engagement with written texts is key not only to college success but also to just about everything we do outside the classroom. Basic skills courses—and the books designed for them—do much to familiarize students with the elements of critical reading. But knowing the skills is not enough. To become effective readers, students need practice. College textbooks pose a special challenge. By necessity, they stuff a lot of information into a relatively small space. Writers and publishers typically provide tools and features to help students digest that information, but those features take getting used to. Students can easily become overwhelmed by the narrative text, and the tools meant to help with comprehension can themselves cause confusion. Recognizing this, *The Bedford/St. Martin's Textbook Reader* encourages students to practice their newly acquired critical reading skills with just the kind of textbook materials they will encounter in their college courses.

Each of the reader's five units presents a textbook chapter drawn from a discipline students are likely to encounter in college. The five disciplines represented here are business, psychology, communication, biology, and history. The chapters and the questions accompanying them progress from easiest to most challenging, allowing students to work their way up to a fairly demanding critical reading level. To help capture and maintain students' interest, a single theme—work, an inherently interesting topic relevant to all students—connects the parts. Rather than force students to read unrelated materials out of context, the chapters' varied perspectives on work—from the concerns of modern human resource managers to a historical interpretation of nineteenth-century workers' struggles for better job conditions—encourage students to make connections and provide them with information they can apply to their own lives.

The Bedford/St. Martin's Textbook Reader provides extensive materials to aid students' understanding of and engagement with the textbook readings.

Before the readings. Each unit begins with an introduction that provides an overview of the discipline it covers. The introduction then discusses the textbook itself and the chapter's topic and explains the key textbook features (such as headings, graphics, and summaries) that students need to understand to read the chapter successfully. It ends with a quick overview of how the chapter fits into the work theme.

Following each introduction are three prereading questions ("Preparing to Read the Textbook Chapter"). The first question encourages students to think about how the chapter material applies to their own lives and experiences, the second helps them understand the function of a key tool the authors have provided to aid learning, and the third ties the chapter to the overall work theme.

After the readings. Each chapter is followed by three sets of questions that get students comfortable with the kinds of questions most commonly found on college quizzes and tests:

- Ten "Practicing Your Textbook Reading Skills" questions test the discrete skills covered in most college reading courses and call students' attention to the textbook elements that aid reading. The reading skills addressed by these questions progress in difficulty from understanding vocabulary in the first chapter to interpreting arguments in the last.

- Twenty-five "Testing Your Understanding" questions (five true or false, ten multiple choice, five definitions, and five short answers) follow the chapter organization and ensure that students comprehend the textbook material.

- A "Making Thematic Connections" question encourages students to reflect more deeply on the chapter topic and to connect it with issues covered in other units of the reader. This question can be used for class discussion or for writing assignments.

Other assistance. *The Bedford/St. Martin's Textbook Reader* also provides a glossary that defines the key concepts used in each of the units. An answer key at the back of the book lets students check their work. The answer key includes the page numbers of the relevant sections of the chapters, so if students get an answer wrong they can review the material from the textbook chapters.

The Bedford/St. Martin's Textbook Reader will spark students' interest while helping them to become more critical and successful readers. We hope that it will be the start of a productive and rewarding engagement with reading for college and beyond.

Acknowledgments

As I put this reader together, it was my extreme good fortune to work with some of the very best people in college publishing. I am grateful to Joan Feinberg, the president of Bedford/St. Martin's, and Karen Henry, editor in chief, for putting their faith in me and giving me the opportunity to write a book. Marcia Cohen went out of her way to help obtain the textbook chapters, and Brita Mess came to the rescue more than once. Arthur Johnson did double duty, not only as a top-notch production editor but also, for a while, as de facto development editor. His grace and his dry sense of humor made writing the book fun. All the same, I was delighted when my friend Beth Castrodale came on board as editor. She's the best kind of editor a person can hope for: gently honest, generous with compliments, helpful, and flexible. As if trading e-mails and jokes with Beth weren't enough, fate smiled on me and gave me the peerless Barbara Flanagan as copyeditor. I couldn't have asked for a better group of people to work with.

Thanks also to Brian Wheel, Bedford/St. Martin's marketing manager, and to Gertrude Coleman of Middlesex Community College, Mary Sulzer of Lorrain County Community College, and Jim Early of Doña Aña Branch Community College. With input from Bill Davis and Tom Kling, they helped to identify what this reader needed to be.

Finally, I am deeply obliged to Maurice Scharton, late of Illinois State University, for seeing in me something other than an editor. It was Maurice who first suggested, with a gleefully wicked sense of subversiveness and a characteristic twinkle in his voice, that I could also write. How I wish he were here to see that he was on to something.

Contents

Business

"Human Resource Management"

Introduction

The study of business is a practical one. Students take business, marketing, and management courses to learn how companies operate, how competition works, and how employees and bosses can do their jobs most effectively. But take a look at the stock market and you'll quickly see that the world of business changes constantly—sometimes subtly, sometimes drastically. Because of this, businesspeople and scholars seek to understand changes and find ways to solve problems and increase companies' earnings. They study individual businesses and industries not only to identify what works but also to propose new ideas and theories that managers (and employees) can apply to their own business practices.

Exploring the World of Business, by Kenneth Blanchard, Charles Schewe, Robert Nelson, and Alexander Hiam, is an introductory textbook for new students of business. The authors are professors and businessmen who aim to teach their readers by sharing real-world experiences and examining the ideas that come from those experiences. The chapter reprinted here, "Human Resource Management," looks at an element of business that is crucial for any company's success: its employees. Human resources departments are responsible for finding and keeping the best people to work for a company. You may be familiar with the hiring role of human resources, but you may not be aware that companies also pay close attention to the kinds of benefits their employees want and need, how to train workers and keep them happy and productive, and what changes and emerging employment practices they can adopt to improve their business.

As you read the chapter, you'll see that the authors have taken great care to help you understand it. Notice, in particular, the "Learning Goals" listed at the beginning of the chapter and the notes in the margins that help you find the information you need to achieve those goals. Also in the margins, you'll find definitions of the key terms discussed in the text. Figures (such as

This unit's textbook reading comes from *Exploring the World of Business* by Kenneth Blanchard, Charles Schewe, Robert Nelson, and Alexander Hiam, Worth Publishers, 1996, Chapter 12, pages 348–83.

flowcharts) and tables throughout the chapter present information visually to make it easier to digest. And finally, review materials at the end of the chapter summarize what's important and encourage you to apply the information to a specific example.

The authors also provide a handful of examples separate from the main discussion: The "One Minute Manager" that opens the chapter shows a student discussing a career question with her professor; the question and possible answers to it are examined in more depth later in the chapter. A "Skills Check" box provides practical advice for job hunters. Two "Doing Business" sections show how particular companies applied human resources ideas in their business. And, toward the end of the chapter, an "Ethics Check" feature explores an issue that many companies struggle with: whether or not fifty-somethings should step down. Be aware that although boxed features like these interrupt the text physically, you don't need to stop reading the main discussion to read a feature exactly where it appears. Finish the main discussion first and then go back to the example to see how it relates. Or read the examples first. With practice you'll find what works best for you.

Understanding human resources practices should improve your chances of being hired the next time you look for a job. Learning about benefits and why companies provide them might even help you negotiate for better benefits in a current job. In another chapter of this reader you'll learn about stress and coping; pay attention to how this business chapter addresses that topic. Remember, too, that business changes constantly. The history chapter that closes this book discusses job conditions in America more than a hundred years ago. As you read this business chapter, then, think about how things might have been different, and how they might continue to change.

Preparing to Read the Textbook Chapter

1. Have you ever worked for or interviewed with a company with a human resources department? What were your experiences with it?

2. The authors of the chapter you're about to read refer to the practices of many well-known companies. Businesses they mention include Nike, Pratt & Whitney, Microsoft, Toyota, Federal Express, Hallmark Cards, Ford, General Electric, General Mills, Business Wire, and AT&T. Why do you think the authors provide so many examples?

3. Think about a job you have held recently, or a job you're hoping to have in the future. What do you expect from a job besides money? What can and should an employer do to improve your job satisfaction? Why should an employer do those things?

CHAPTER

[Handwritten margin notes:]
What is Human Resource?
Why is Human Resource *important?
the Administration of the Dept. or company
because they are responsible for
all the employee's hiring, payroll,
benefits, transfers, etc.

Human Resource Management

In this chapter you will learn what human resource management is and how it attempts to match the needs of the organization with the talents of individuals who work for, or want to work for, the organization. We will examine how recent trends affect the way businesses manage their human resources, and how those trends affect employees' careers. We will look at the human resource processes for finding, hiring, training, and compensating employees.

The material in this chapter will help you in two different ways. By understanding the employer's perspective on human resource management, you may learn to be a more valuable employee. And by understanding the hiring process, you may learn to be a more successful job candidate. After reading this chapter, you will be able to reach the learning goals below.

Learning Goals

1. Explain the functions of human resource management in relation to the changing work force.
2. Identify and describe the components of human resource planning.
3. Identify the various sources of job applicants.
4. Describe methods of screening and testing potential employees and identify two alternative hiring procedures.
5. Describe the three forms of employee training and explain how employee performance is evaluated.
6. Discuss various paths in career development.
7. Identify the two forms of compensation available to employees today and describe the types of cash compensation.
8. Differentiate between fixed and flexible benefits.
9. Discuss the use of flexible work schedules and leaves to increase employee satisfaction.
10. Outline the various ways in which employees can change status in an organization.

349

Changing Needs for Changing Times

"I really need your advice," Joanna said as she walked into the One Minute Manager's office. "At least my best friend Emily does. She just finished her B.A. with a specialty in advertising. She's been offered work with a really good advertising agency, but she wouldn't be a regular employee. They want her to freelance on a big project they're doing. Should she accept their offer or continue looking for something on staff?"

"Emily has to decide for herself whether this is a good opportunity, Joanna. But I can tell you this much: Workers who are not full-time employees are now so common that they have a special name—the "contingency work force." According to a recent article in *Fortune* magazine, more than 40 percent of the CEOs at Fortune 500 companies use contingent workers, and the same number believe they'll be using more of them in the future.[1] It's a good way for the business to cut costs because it pays workers only when it needs them, and it doesn't have to pay for benefits, which can be very costly. Using contingent workers also helps a business to be flexible—it can grow and shrink quickly, without hiring or firing in-house staff."

"I can see why the company likes the arrangement," Carlos observed, "but why should Emily be interested in it?"

"Many contingent workers like the freedom and independence of hiring on for only one project. That way, they can try out the company without making a long-term commitment. If Emily and the agency like each other, the arrangement might become a permanent one. But even if it doesn't, temporary work can be a great way to gain experience or just have some income while looking for a permanent job."

"That sounds like a good deal for both parties," Joanna said.

"It can be," the One Minute Manager replied, "but only if both parties understand the ground rules. The company has to realize that Emily won't be as committed as she would be if she were a full-time employee. And Emily has to understand that the company's commitment is also limited, and she probably won't get paid sick days, vacation time, or health insurance. Contingent workers also have to pay their own Social Security taxes and file quarterly income taxes. Many people don't like those conditions."

"I'll be sure to tell her," Joanna promised. "My guess is that she'll take it, though, because she looked a long time before finding this opportunity. Thanks for the advice!"

Managing Human Resources in Today's Business Environment

Throughout this text, we have looked at many different businesses as they pare down layers of management, outsource, hire part-time workers, and introduce new technology to increase productivity and reduce labor costs. All these strategies help businesses to compete by cutting costs and permitting flexibility, so that they can respond rapidly to customers' changing needs. But necessary as these strategies are, they can bump headfirst into another important organizational need—finding, hiring, training, and motivating employees who can function as empowered members of work teams, pursuing organizational goals at a level of high productivity.[2] Add to this the dynamics of an increasingly diverse work force, as described in Chapter 11, and managing human resources becomes a constant challenge.

Human resource management is the process of ensuring that a business has an adequate supply of skilled, trained, and motivated employees to meet the organization's objectives. In this chapter, you will see how human resource managers work with other managers to research and forecast employment needs. You will learn how they help develop programs for hiring, training, evaluating, compensating employees—and, when necessary, for laying off employees or firing them. In some businesses, human resource managers have become adept at tailoring their techniques to the needs of the **contingent work force**—part-time, temporary, and self-employed workers who do not conform to the traditional model of the 9-to-5, full-time employee. You will also see how human resource managers must stay in touch with legal and ethical issues to ensure that the businesses they work in treat employees in acceptable ways. First, though, we review some of the trends that have made human resource management so challenging in the current business scene.

The Changing Work Force

In 1987, the Hudson Institute prepared a report, *Workforce 2000*, for the U.S. Department of Labor.[3] It has been nearly a decade since that report, but its predictions have held up well. Here are some of the predicted changes and some current findings:[4]

- *Labor shortages will occur.* Growth in the labor force will fall sharply, from 2.9 percent to 1 percent per year as fewer new job entrants join the work force.
- *Jobs will require developed skills.* Half of all jobs will be service, technical, or managerial positions that require college degrees. At the same time that the number of eligible skilled workers is expected to diminish, employers will increasingly demand more highly skilled and trained employees.[5]
- *Most available workers will be unskilled.* Each year, 700,000 students drop out of high school, and an equal number are functionally illiterate. In Los Angeles, for example, nearly 4 out of 10 students quit school, and in Chicago the dropout rate is 46 percent. As Michael Godfrey, the head of the Los Angeles dropout prevention program says, "You wind up having an unskilled labor force. That forces businesses to leave L.A."[6]
- *The work force will mature.* Nearly half of all employees will be at least 40 years of age. Almost 44 million Americans will be over age 60, and more than half of all families will be two-*pension* households—both members will have retired.

✓ **human resource management**
Ensuring that a business has an adequate supply of skilled, trained, and motivated employees to meet the organization's objectives.

✓ **contingent work force**
Part-time, temporary, and self-employed workers who do not conform to the traditional model of the 9-to-5, full-time employee.

1. Explain the functions of human resource management in relation to the changing work force.

- *Many more women will work outside the home.* More than 60 percent of all working-age women will have jobs. Women now represent 47 percent of the work force, and women with children under age 6 represent the fastest growing segment of the work force. According to a report by the Federal Glass Ceiling Commission, created by the Civil Rights Act of 1991, 57 percent of the work force are women or minorities or both. However, white males still hold 97 percent of top management jobs.[7]

- *Minority and immigrant workers will be a larger portion of the work force.* Six in 10 workers will be members of minority groups or immigrants. Nearly two-thirds of working-age immigrants will join the work force, many of them better educated than new work force entrants born in the United States.

- *The percentage of workers in the contingent work force will increase.* Part-time, temporary, and self-employed workers now represent more than 25 percent of the civilian work force. This share is expected to increase to 33 percent by 2000. In a survey of 266 young professionals earning an average of $37,500, 38 percent say their most important personal concern is marrying and having a family. And 50 percent say their favorite activity is spending time with family and friends. A decade ago, surveys showed most young professionals' top priority was work, not family.[8]

Contingent Work Force

Placing "just-in-time workers" like these stock clerks is a growing business for employment agencies around the country. In fact, many agencies are actually taking the place of traditional employers by training their job candidates in business skills, placing them in jobs, and offering them benefits such as health insurance.

At the time of this writing, the future of affirmative action programs is uncertain as politicians and elected officials pare back government spending and programs. But one thing is sure: Diversity is a permanent part of today's work force and of the management and ownership of small businesses, as we saw in Chapters 6 and 7. These changes reflect the growing diversity of the country as a whole, and smart businesses will be sure that their work forces understand and offer service to the many diverse groups that represent the current flavors in the melting pot of America.

The Need for Increased Productivity

Companies—including those that are successful—are seeking to reduce their costs in order to compete more effectively, and labor costs are one of the largest fixed expenses in a company's budget. As you saw in Chapter 10, many companies are improving production processes and retraining employees using total quality management practices. Other companies find it necessary to reduce the number of permanent, full-time employees. Downsizing to eliminate employees—even entire layers of management—requires that the remaining employees become more knowledgeable, productive, and empowered. Advances in technology also allow businesses to operate with fewer, more specialized employees.

Strategies of Flexibility

Business strategies that increase an organization's flexibility enable it to respond rapidly to changes in the environment. As we saw in Chapter 9, one such strategy is *outsourcing*, contracting with outside organizations for one or more business services. A growing number of businesses outsource marketing analysis, accounting, manufacturing, and other functions. Data services firms such as Ceridian Corp., headquartered in Minneapolis, Minnesota, and Automatic Data Processing, Inc. (ADP), of Roseland, New Jersey, specialize in processing payroll for other companies. The popularity of ADP's payroll processing services is evident: Each year the company distributes paychecks to some 16 million workers and issues more than 30 million W-2 forms.[9]

Another trend in the ongoing quest of American business for greater flexibility is the use of more part-time employees. The use of part-time employees makes it much easier for a company to schedule workers around peak periods of demand, and it creates a larger employment pool upon which to draw. For example, Federal Express Corp. accommodates wide daily swings in work volume at its Memphis, Tennessee, branch by using only part-time employees below the level of supervisor. And at Novations, Inc., a management-skills assessment company located in Provo, Utah, almost all test scoring is done by part-time subcontractors, at times including up to 40 or 50 subcontractors, depending on the company's needs. Novations has found that this flexible, part-time work force is even faster and more economical than automated computer scoring.[10]

Some companies consider **employee leasing**—purchasing the long-term services of a worker from another company—to be a good option. Texas Instruments Inc. leases about 15 percent of its employees, and nationally the number of leased employees is now more than a million.[11] Besides saving money that would otherwise be paid in benefits, leasing allows a business to avoid the commitment of time, paperwork, and expenses associated with recruiting and maintaining regular employees. In many cases, firms that lease employees to other firms recruit and screen the workers, administer payroll and other compensation, and conduct formal performance appraisals. Freed of these administrative tasks, a company can reduce its overhead and concentrate on the tasks that will bring it more business.

Although these trends affect all companies to some degree, most human resource managers perform the traditional functions of planning for the future labor needs of the business, hiring new employees, training and developing employees, determining equitable compensation and benefits, and reassigning and terminating employees. Let's turn now to the first of these, human resource planning.

✓ **employee leasing**
Purchasing the long-term services of a worker from another company.

Human Resource Planning

2. Identify and describe the components of human resource planning.

Recall from Chapter 8 that planning is one of the four functions of management.

Human resource management—like all management—begins with planning. Managers in various departments work with human resources to anticipate specific staffing needs, which then become a detailed plan. This planning process, depicted in Figure 12.1, consists of research, forecasting, and job analysis, which includes drafting job descriptions and job specifications.

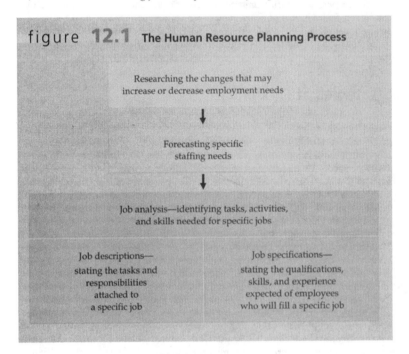

figure **12.1** **The Human Resource Planning Process**

Researching the changes that may increase or decrease employment needs

↓

Forecasting specific staffing needs

↓

Job analysis—identifying tasks, activities, and skills needed for specific jobs

| Job descriptions— | Job specifications— |
| stating the tasks and responsibilities attached to a specific job | stating the qualifications, skills, and experience expected of employees who will fill a specific job |

Research

Human resource managers collect information on upcoming changes that could affect the business's labor needs. Such changes might include the business's growth plans, new products and services, or developing problems. For example, Pratt & Whitney, a manufacturer of aircraft engines, recently decided to move its operations from East Hartford, Connecticut, to Georgia to reduce its operating expenses.[12] A move of this type requires that human resource managers work with other managers to develop plans for transporting personnel who plan to move along with the company and for recruiting, hiring, and training workers at the new location.

Research indicating dramatic economic or market changes permits human resources to make creative plans to head off trouble. Alpine Banks of Colorado suffered dramatic customer losses during the recession of the early 1990s. With the closing of two of the area's largest employers, customers moved out of the area and revenues dropped dramatically. Additionally, Colorado passed legislation allowing national bank corporations to purchase Colorado banks—increasing competitive pressures on small, locally owned banks.

Alpine Banks's management had observed, however, that a large Latino community had grown up around the area's ski resorts during the preceding decade. With this knowledge in hand, the bank made a concerted effort to attract Latino depositors by hiring bilingual employees. The human resource department of Alpine Banks placed Spanish-language help-wanted ads in the local newspapers, and it asked its Latino employees for referrals of potential employees. Ultimately, the bank hired 25 bilingual workers and was able to sign up hundreds of new depositors as a result.[13]

Forecasting

Forecasting takes a close look not only at a company's labor needs but also at sources of labor supply. Highly skilled technology workers, such as computer programmers and laboratory researchers, often cluster around regions where their skills are in high demand, such as northern California's Silicon Valley. Other regions of the country have different kinds of high-skilled, specialized work forces. For example, Michigan has an extensive pool of machine operators and New York City is world famous for its financial specialists. But even within such areas, labor supply and demand change constantly, and businesses must deal with these frequent and hard-to-predict developments.

In many areas there is a serious mismatch between labor and jobs. Much of the world's labor, skilled and unskilled, is found in developing countries. At the same time, most of the growth in the need for labor is generated in the cities of the industrialized world. This mismatch is triggering massive relocations. In some cases, people follow jobs. The greatest relocation involves young, well-educated workers flocking to the cities of the developed world.[14] But employers are also migrating. Jobs with a high labor content, such as clothing and footwear manufacture, are relocating to less-developed nations as manufacturers contract work out to low-cost labor markets.[15]

Job Analysis

The human resource department prepares job analyses of individual positions throughout the company. A **job analysis** is a general overview of all aspects of a particular job. This information is gathered from those within the organization who understand the tasks involved in each position and the degree of authority, responsibility, and accountability the worker has for accomplishing those tasks. For example, a job analysis of an administrative assistant position would specify the technical and social skills the prospective employee should possess, such as word processing skills, attention to detail, a pleasant manner, and the ability to work under pressure. It would also describe the administrative assistant's responsibility for accomplishing certain tasks and the authority delegated for doing those tasks. It would probably also list the other people within the company with whom the administrative assistant would interact. Many firms develop these documents for all company positions and maintain them on file, whether the position is to be filled immediately or not.

Once the job analysis is completed, a job description and job specification are developed from it. These two tools are used to locate appropriate job candidates and subsequently to judge their performance on the job.

Job Descriptions

The basic output of any job analysis is a **job description**—a statement of the tasks and responsibilities of a particular job. In the case of an administrative assistant, the job description might list such responsibilities as drafting correspondence, typing reports, maintaining a database, routing interoffice mail, and answering department phones. Notice that these are all statements about job tasks, not about the skills of the person who will perform them.

 job analysis

A general overview of all aspects of a particular job.

job description

A statement of the tasks and responsibilities of a particular job.

job specification

A statement of the qualifications, skills, and previous experience a person needs to perform a given job.

job requisition

A request for hiring submitted to the human resource department.

Job Specifications

A **job specification** is a statement of the qualifications, skills, and previous experience a person needs to perform a given job. Whereas the job description focuses on tasks and responsibilities, the job specification focuses on the skills and abilities of the person who will perform those tasks. A job specification for an administrative assistant might include familiarity with the WordPerfect software package, the ability to type at a minimum speed of 40 words per minute, and possession of a high school diploma and one year's work experience in an office. Figure 12.2 contains a sample job description and job specification.

The job specification helps employers decide how well a candidate's qualifications measure up to the minimum needs of a position. This is far easier to do for some requirements than for others. For example, one can easily determine whether a person has graduated from college; it is far more difficult to figure out whether a candidate has leadership qualities or the ability to work effectively as a team member.

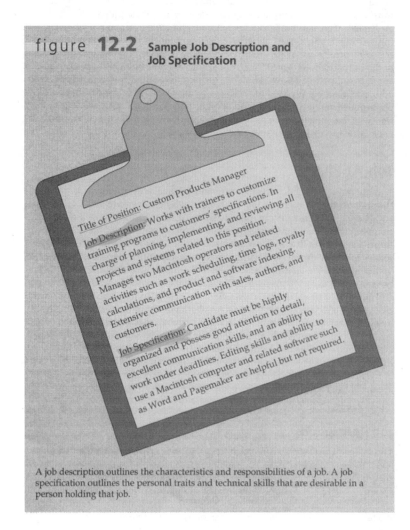

figure **12.2** **Sample Job Description and Job Specification**

Title of Position: Custom Products Manager

Job Description: Works with trainers to customize training programs to customers' specifications. In charge of planning, implementing, and reviewing all projects and systems related to this position. Manages two Macintosh operators and related activities such as work scheduling, time logs, royalty calculations, and product and software indexing. Extensive communication with sales, authors, and customers.

Job Specification: Candidate must be highly organized and possess good attention to detail, excellent communication skills, and an ability to work under deadlines. Editing skills and ability to use a Macintosh computer and related software such as Word and Pagemaker are helpful but not required.

A job description outlines the characteristics and responsibilities of a job. A job specification outlines the personal traits and technical skills that are desirable in a person holding that job.

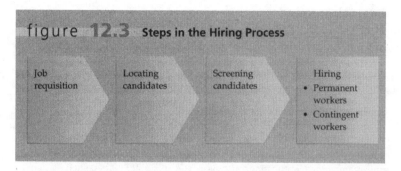

figure **12.3** **Steps in the Hiring Process**

Job requisition → Locating candidates → Screening candidates → Hiring
- Permanent workers
- Contingent workers

The Hiring Process

The hiring process begins when an employment need is identified, perhaps because an employee has left the company or a new contract creates a need for more employees. For instance, Eagle Bronze, Inc., a metal-casting company located in Lander, Wyoming, identified a need for trainees when demand for its products suddenly surged.[16]

The first step in finding a new employee is taken when a department manager or line supervisor submits to the human resource department a **job requisition**—a request for hiring—ideally, one based on a job specification developed in the planning process. The human resource department then begins work to locate a small number of qualified candidates. In most companies, the human resource staff screens candidates and provides information about applicants—such as test scores, resumés, and applications—to the manager who will do the actual hiring. Figure 12.3 outlines the steps in the hiring process.

Sources of Job Applicants

Sources of job applicants are almost as varied as types of applicants. To some extent, the kind of position being filled determines where a request for applicants will be placed. Managers may seek applicants with little or no experience for an *entry-level* position, such as receptionist or mailroom clerk. The pool of applicants who could fill these jobs is very large. Other openings, such as mechanic or financial systems analyst, may be limited to applicants who have many years of experience and can perform well with minimal training. Suitable applicants for such openings may be hard to find and will tend to command higher salaries. In most cases, however, employers look inside the company before moving to outside resources. Table 12.1 lists typical sources of new employees.

table **12.1** **Sources of New Employees**

Internal	External
Job postings	Local newspaper ads
Employee referrals	Campus recruitment
Walk-in applications	Private employment agencies
	Public employment agencies
	Professional associations
	Professional journals

Internal Sources

3. Identify the various sources of job applicants.

The first place most companies look for qualified applicants is inside the organization. Company employees have well-known work habits and performance records, and they are already familiar with many of the people, products, policies, and procedures of the organization. In addition, hiring from within is a tremendous morale booster for employees, who see that they can move up in their companies. Atlas Headwear, Inc., a Phoenix manufacturer of military and sports hats, has a firm policy of promoting from within. With a predominantly Asian-American and Latino work force, in which 80 percent of workers are women, Atlas Headwear's management team is a microcosm of diversity.[17]

Job Postings A **job posting** is a notice advertising available positions within an organization. Job postings are displayed in public places, such as department bulletin boards and company newsletters, where all employees have access to them. Sun Microsystems, Inc., of Mountain View, California, publishes a weekly listing of all openings along with the job description and specifications for each position. The company encourages all employees who feel they are qualified to apply for openings that interest them.

At the former Pacific Northwest Bell, now a part of US West, Inc., based in Englewood, Colorado, a computerized job-skills bank is used to help match employer needs with employee skills and interests. Any employee may choose to fill out a detailed profile of his or her skills, experience, and job preferences, including relocation preferences. The company's computerized personnel database adds existing information about the employee to that profile, including job history and training. Once a week, the human resource staff checks current job openings against the database. When a potential match appears, the human resource department notifies the employee and asks whether he or she is interested in the available opening.[18]

Employee Referrals Another valuable source of new hires is the **employee referral**, a current employee's recommendation of friends or acquaintances. Referrals have a high probability of success, perhaps because they already know something about the job and the company from the employee who refers them. Many employers pay a "finder's fee" to employees if their candidate is hired.

GB Tech, Inc., of Houston, Texas, used employee referrals to quickly recruit a work force of highly skilled workers. The company, which supplies information systems support to the federal government, had no real track record of performance. It wanted a pool of seasoned retirees who would lend credibility and strong staff credentials to the fledgling operation. According to Gale Burkett, GB Tech's chair and chief executive officer, "We were concerned about whether we would be accepted because we were still a fairly new company."[19]

The company started its recruiting effort by placing ads for candidates. Once a few applicants were hired, they were asked to contribute the names of other skilled workers who might want to work for the firm. Eventually, GB Tech hired 10 formerly retired workers and placed 70 others on a list of available candidates. Partly as a result of GB Tech's use of employee referrals and the success of its new workers in identifying and winning new business opportunities, employment has grown since 1990 from 14 to 415 workers.

External Sources

✓ job posting
A notice advertising available positions within an organization.

✓ employee referral
A current employee's recommendation of friends or acquaintances.

If internal sources fail to produce an appropriate candidate, the company will broaden its search by advertising in local newspapers, distributing job specifications to various employment agencies, or recruiting on college campuses. Government regulations may require public advertising if the firm receives taxpayer money, for example, in the form of a grant to a university or a contract with a defense contractor.

Employment agencies are especially helpful in locating hard-to-find applicants with advanced or specialized skills. Private agencies charge a fee for successful placements. Some charge the company for their services; others charge the job applicant. It is in the applicant's best interest to read the agency's contract closely and to be sure the responsibilities and obligations of both parties are clearly stated and understood. Important points are who pays the fee, how much will be paid, and whether the agency has an exclusive right to represent the applicant. Such issues can become major problems if applicant and agency disagree at some later time.

Federal job services and state employment development departments also operate employment agencies, but their services are free. Eagle Bronze, mentioned earlier in this section, knew that its remote location would make it more difficult to find qualified job candidates. To overcome that challenge, the company's human resource department consulted with the Wyoming Department of Employment, which identified potential job candidates at the local Wind River Indian Reservation.[20] Federal and state services are easily found in the government listings of the local phone directory.

Many large corporations and educational institutions also operate free *job lines.* These prerecorded telephone announcements list openings, brief job descriptions, and application information. Job lines may be listed in local phone books, or applicants can call the human resource department of particular organizations for their numbers.

Although numbers are down from the 1980s, many large employers recruit on college campuses. Microsoft Corp., for example, visits 137 campuses, some up to four times a year. In a recent year it reviewed more than 120,000 resumés, held face-to-face interviews with 7,400 students, and hired 2,000 of them.[21] At Howard University, the historically African-American college in Washington, D.C., approximately 400 companies recruit employees through the placement office. Senior executives of Mobil Corp. and Ford Motor Co. make regular visits to the campus.[22]

Screening Candidates

Job applicants usually submit a resumé and cover letter to introduce themselves to a firm that has a job vacancy. A **resumé** is a brief summary of an applicant's relevant experience, ideally one or two pages in length. The cover letter highlights experience that particularly qualifies the applicant for the job and provides information on contacting him or her.

Individuals selected from the pool of applicants are usually called for an interview and tests, which in large firms are administered by the human resource department. There they are required to complete the company's own application form, which asks standard questions that enable the human resource employees to determine the candidate's experience level. The form also requests salary history, references, and other necessary information that will help in evaluating the candidate.

Employers almost always seek additional information through employment interviews, which are personal meetings with the candidate. Candidates may be interviewed by several individuals in the organization, including a manager, a human resource specialist, and potential co-workers, all of whom question the applicant about his or her skills and experience and answer any questions about the position and company. The most promising applicants may be asked to return for a second or even a third interview. For a look at some questions frequently raised in interviews, see the skills check entitled "Careful What You Say—Your Job May Depend on It" on page 360.

4. Describe methods of screening and testing potential employees and identify two alternative hiring procedures.

✓ **resumé**

A brief summary of an applicant's relevant experience, ideally one or two pages in length.

skills
check

Careful What You Say— Your Job May Depend on It

While a resumé gives a potential employer a glimpse of your experience and qualifications for a position, the interview is where a potential employer really gets to know you. The more prepared you are for an interview, the more confident you will be and the better impression you will make on your interviewer. The following questions and statements often appear on interview forms.

- Why should I hire you?
- Describe your educational background.
- What was your favorite course in school? Why?
- Describe the previous jobs you have had, beginning with the most recent.
- Why did you leave your last job?
- Most jobs have positive and negative qualities. What were some of the negative qualities of your last job?

- Describe something you did that was not normally part of your job.
- Do you like working with figures?
- What do you see yourself doing in five years?
- What starting salary do you expect?
- When can you start?

By practicing your answers to these questions, you can raise your chances of being one of those selected for the final cut. But remember that you are also interviewing the employer. Take time before your interview to think about what you want to know about the job, the company, and the people you would work with. Then concentrate on phrasing your questions gracefully and tactfully.

Source: Robert B. Nelson, *The Job Hunt* (Berkeley, Calif.: Ten Speed Press, 1986), pp. 45–46.

Employment Testing

A specified skill level is an essential requirement for some jobs. In such cases, the human resource department (in larger firms) or the department with the job opening administers skills tests, which can sometimes be elaborate. For instance, Toyota Motor Corp. observes candidates for auto assembly jobs on a simulated production line before making the final selection. Other firms test candidates on their ability to use computers for word processing, data organizing, or financial recordkeeping.

Many businesses give applicants more general tests, some of which attempt to obtain a psychological profile. Although the ability of such tests to predict performance in a particular job has been questioned, their use reflects the desire of human resource managers to reduce the risk of hiring the wrong person. Travel agency Rosenbluth International, with 27 offices scattered throughout the Middle Atlantic states, uses psychological tests to screen out "freeloaders, political animals, and egotists," according to Rosenbluth's chief executive.[23]

Questions of fairness in employment testing have recently been a source of significant controversy, much of it centering on charges of cultural bias in favor of white American males. Those who question the validity of employment testing argue that the tests measure education, culture, and achievements, rather than aptitudes. These critics question whether test items accurately reflect the abilities of African Americans, Latinos, women, and others whose traditions differ from those of traditional white male-dominated culture. As researchers investigate such inquiries, many companies continue to rely on employment tests for help in making hiring decisions.

Hiring Employees

The applicant who makes a good impression, is eager to have the job, and seems qualified and likely to fit in with the existing staff will probably receive an offer—*if* his or her references check out. The hiring firm will ask the candidate's referees—former supervisors or other individuals who can attest to the applicant's skills and aptitude—for assessments of his or her performance and character. A bad assessment at this point can derail the chances of a candidate who is strong in all other areas, and a good reference can improve the chances of a candidate who previously did not seem so strong. Reference checks are also used to verify information on the application form.

If all goes well, an oral and then a written job offer will follow. That offer may specify that a medical exam is required. It typically specifies a **probation period**—an initial trial period, often of three to six months, in which newly hired employees may be terminated if their job performance is unsatisfactory.

Throughout the hiring process, many decisions—where to recruit, what to look for in potential employees, even how to describe the job—are strongly influenced by government regulations. Table 12.2 lists the legislation that has had the most profound effect on human resource management—especially on the hiring process. Note especially the restrictions designed to prevent discrimination in hiring. Each year, many candidates file lawsuits to overturn job actions based on discriminatory practices related to gender, race, disability, age, weight, and other personal characteristics.

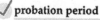 **probation period**

An initial trial period, often of three to six months, in which newly hired employees may be terminated if their job performance is unsatisfactory.

Chapter 4 discusses laws that relate to employment practices.

table **12.2**   Legislation Affecting Human Resources

Law	Year	Effect
Equal Pay Act of 1963	1963	Grants men and women the right to earn equal pay for equal work.
Title VII of the Civil Rights Act of 1964	1964	Prohibits discrimination in employment on the basis of national origin, race, color, sex, pregnancy, and religion.
Age Discrimination in Employment Act (ADEA)	1967	Prohibits job-related age-based discrimination against people of age 40 and over.
Vietnam Era Veterans Readjustment Assistance Act	1974	Requires companies that sell goods and services to the federal government to make special efforts to employ Vietnam War veterans.
Employee Retirement Income Security Act of 1974 (ERISA)	1974	Regulates the operation of employee benefit plans.
Immigration Reform and Control Act of 1986.	1986	Prohibits the hiring of illegal aliens and requires employers to verify that employees can legally work in the United States.
Americans with Disabilities Act (ADA)	1990	Prohibits employment discrimination against qualified people who have disabilities. Employers are required to make reasonable accommodations to help people with disabilities to do their jobs.
Civil Rights Act of 1991	1991	Grants the victims of intentional discrimination the right to jury trials; created the Glass Ceiling Commission, which reports on the representation of women and minorities in the nation's work force.

Source: Practical Guidelines for Lawful Supervision (Walnut Creek, Calif.: Borgman Associates, 1992), pp. 3–6.

Hiring Contingent Workers

The process described so far is, with some variation, standard in most companies. But a new hiring process is beginning to compete with it, one that starts with a call to a temporary employment agency for the contingent worker described earlier in this chapter. This new entry path lets managers and fellow employees get to know the temporary worker. If the person has the right skills and gets along well in the company, a formal hiring process can be started to bring the worker in as a full-time employee. This new approach is highly flexible because the business does not commit to hiring anyone.

Robert Snelling, Jr., chairman of the 275-office Snelling Personnel Services, explains that, "from standing in for people out sick or on vacation, or helping out during peak and seasonal work periods, [the use of contingent workers has] become a way of running a business in a businesslike fashion."[24] In the past, temporary employees typically filled routine, easy-to-learn jobs like typing, but now highly skilled temporary employees fill many professional jobs, too. On an average workday, more than 1.5 million people work as temporaries in U.S. businesses. In the average year, 6 to 7 million people will take on at least one temporary job. Many remain in the contingent work force, but a majority of them eventually become full-time employees.[25]

Training and Developing Employees

In the early 1990s, President Bill Clinton expressed a hope that American businesses would increase spending on employee training to 1.5 percent of the combined cost of employees' salaries and benefits. Motorola, Inc., is way ahead of this target, spending more than 4 percent of payroll, or $150 million in 1995, to educate its 132,000 employees. Companywide, Motorola offers 600 different courses to its workers at 14 different locations worldwide.[26] "Motorola University," the company's Schaumberg, Illinois, training facility—and the heart and soul of Motorola's training program—is as large as most of the schools attended by the readers of this textbook! The average 36 hours a year of training that Motorola provides each employee has helped it cut costs by more than half a billion dollars a year. Over the course of three years, the company reported $30 in productivity gains for every $1 spent on training.[27]

The importance of training to productivity and competitiveness led the MIT Commission on Industrial Productivity—a team of prominent Massachusetts Institute of Technology (MIT) economists, scientists, and engineers chartered in the late 1980s—to conclude that increased worker training was essential to continued growth of the U.S. economy. Unfortunately, the commission also concluded that "there seems to be a systematic undervaluation in this country of how much difference it can make when people are well educated and when their skills are continuously developed and challenged. This translates into a pattern of training for work that turns out badly educated workers with skills that are narrow and hence vulnerable to rapid obsolescence."[28] To overcome this problem, businesses like Motorola, Inc., Corning Inc., and Federal Express Corp. invest in three key areas: employee training, employee performance evaluation, and career development.

5. Describe the three forms of employee training and explain how employee performance is evaluated.

Employee Training

Employers conduct all sorts of training activities to improve their employees' knowledge and skills so that they may better do their jobs. For example, at Motorola University, factory workers can enroll in a 12-hour program that includes

CHAPTER **12** Human Resource Management **363**

Training and Developing Employees

In the fast-growing travel services industry, ongoing classroom training and periodic retraining are necessities for maintaining competence on the job. Here a teacher assists a travel agent during a training class.

training in basic math skills such as fractions and graphs. And senior managers have the opportunity to participate in a computer-based strategic game that simulates numerous real-life problems, including factories that burn down and customers who go bankrupt.[29]

Training is especially necessary for the newly hired. Managers often hire inexperienced employees because they are easier to find, have an unbiased perspective, and can be paid less than more experienced candidates. But, these employees lack some of the skills they need to do their jobs. In addition, as managers come to trust their workers and to delegate more tasks, authority, and responsibility to them, training needs increase. As a training manager at Motorola explained, "Ten years ago, we hired people to perform set tasks and didn't ask them to do a lot of thinking. If a machine went down, workers raised their hands, and a trouble-shooter came to fix it. . . . Today, we expect them to begin any trouble-shooting themselves."[30]

As businesses hire more temporary or contract workers instead of permanent ones, training becomes a critical issue. A steady supply of new employees means an ongoing program of training to maintain a constant level of competency on the job. Of course, old hands also benefit from training, which can help motivate employees by giving them new skills in problem solving, teamwork, and quality improvement. But whether directed at full-time employees or contingent workers, training usually takes one of three forms: employee orientation, on-the-job or classroom training, or retraining.

Employee Orientation

Nine out of ten mid- to large-size companies have their new employees spend part or all of their first day on the job in **employee orientation**, training that brings new employees up to speed on how the business and its industry work. The orientation teaches new employees about the company and its products, policies, and procedures, and it introduces them to their co-workers and supervisors. A good orientation program covers five basic areas:[31]

1. The function of the organization and the new employee's specific department, providing the big picture of how his or her job supports the organization's overall objectives

2. The employee's specific role in the business process and how his or her job relates to other jobs in the company and serves the customer

✓ **employee orientation**

Training that brings new employees up to speed on how the business and its industry work.

3. The resources available to support the employee, including what supervisors and co-workers are like, how to contact the supervisor, whom to speak to about particular problems, and what manuals or team leaders to consult; many companies appoint a specific sponsor for a new employee.

4. The employee's rights, such as the right to file a complaint or to spend a specific period of time becoming familiar with a job before performing it without close supervision; training also focuses on employee responsibilities, such as satisfying customers, contributing to teams, and searching for new and better ways of working.

5. The specific activities involved in the employee's job and any training and development that the company offers to help employees improve their skills, qualify for promotions, or change careers

Chapter 1 discussed six important new business strategies: flexibility in business formation, management innovation, employee development, increased customer focus, improved control systems, and creative financial management.

A good orientation program promotes positive work values and gives employees an understanding of how their work fits into the business process. Particularly in businesses that use new strategies such as those outlined in Chapter 1, orientation introduces new employees to special aspects of this strategy as it applies to their work. For example, employees may receive special training in problem solving as a part of a team, or in enforcing the company's ethical practices in contacts with customers and suppliers.

At Federal Express Corp., all efforts to improve customer service are based on a people-service-profit philosophy. New employees are taught that keeping the company's employees happy comes first, that this policy allows FedEx to provide superior service to its customers, and that good service allows the company to make sufficient profits to sustain itself.

At Kelly Services, Inc., a Troy, Michigan–based contractor of temporary workers, more than 600,000 workers fill temporary jobs in the offices of approximately 185,000 client companies each year.[32] Many work far from the support of supervisors at Kelly Services and so, to clearly communicate that Kelly stands behind them, the firm offers a toll-free Help number that workers can call when they need advice or are having trouble.

On-the-Job and Classroom Training

The most common form of training is **on-the-job training**, in which employees learn by doing a job or by receiving one-on-one instruction—usually from a manager or co-worker—in how to do a job. Often employees apply this learning immediately to tasks for which they are responsible.

Classroom training is more formal and is conducted by the company's training department or a training consultant. Advanced techniques such as interactive computer training and role-playing exercises are now common in the classroom training of many businesses.

In the past, most training needs were met simply through on-the-job training. Now that new skills, technologies, and strategies often have to be learned, the training process is more involved. On-the-job training is still used, but often it is complemented by other activities. Whatever form it takes, effective training follows six steps:

1. *Adequate preparation.* Employees should be told how the training is expected to affect their performance.

2. *Show and tell.* Whenever possible, effective training uses demonstrations, not just explanations. A trainer—either a supervisor or a classroom trainer—might display how a machine works while describing its use, for example. Or the trainer might show the types and formats of reports used by administrative assistants within the company.

3. *Practice.* Because most learning takes place by doing, employees should attempt to perform required tasks as soon as possible. Some tasks can be

✓ **on-the-job training**

Training in which employees learn by doing a job or by receiving one-on-one instruction—usually from a manager or co-worker—in how to do a job.

CHAPTER 12   Human Resource Management   **365**

doing business

Washington State Ferry System Invests in Diversity Training

The face of the American workplace is changing. Since the 1960s, women and people of color have made tremendous strides in gaining acceptance by American businesses. According to some predictions, white males, formerly the majority workers in the American work force, will soon make up less than 40 percent of all U.S. workers. This is a fundamental change in the nations' socioeconomic structure, and many businesses are seeking ways to soften the transition. For some, the answer is training in diversity awareness.

Before the Washington State Ferry System instituted diversity training, there were numerous complaints by African-American workers of racial bias, and female workers complained that they were being harassed by their male co-workers. Faced with mounting lawsuits, the management of the largest ferry system in the United States committed itself to spending $1 million on an extensive training program that would reduce the number of incidents of racial bias and sexual harassment among the system's 1,500 employees. Through a series of lectures, role-playing exercises, and videos, employees were encouraged to consider the diverse perspectives of their co-workers and to be sensitive to their needs. Workers were trained to call African Americans "people of color" and to refrain from calling women "ladies" or "gals." Also banned were such words as "geriatrics" and "yuppies." According to Alice Snyder Hunter, who ran the diversity

training program along with her husband Jeffrey Hunter, "We had to start with the basics, diversity 101. We had a list of what you could and could not say, because these people did not know the basics." In addition, African-American workers reported that they were treated with increased respect and female workers said male co-workers were less likely to tell them jokes with sexual content.

The road has been a bumpy one. Resistance among employees—especially white males—has been high. Although sexually provocative calendars have disappeared from the workplace and sexist and racist jokes are no longer told openly, many employees resent being given orders on what to say or how to behave. Says Marcia Morse, one of the first women to be employed by the Washington State Ferry System, "There's a huge backlash. Tons of anger." Experts contend, however, that this kind of reaction is to be expected and that, with time, the negative attitudes can be turned around. In an case, it is in the interest of the employer to make the effort. The workplace is changing, and companies have to keep up with that change. So far, the ferry system has paid out $1 million for its diversity training program. That's a high cost, but not as high as the $1.6 million it paid out to settle lawsuits alleging bias.

Source: Timothy Egan, "Teaching Tolerance in Workplaces: A Seattle Program Illustrates Limits," *New York Times*, Oct. 8, 1993, p. A18.

practiced on computer-based simulators, devices that imitate the experience without the high cost of failure. This technique has been applied to a wide variety of situations, from preparing a spreadsheet to living in and operating a space shuttle.

4. *Manager observation.* Employees need to be monitored on an ongoing basis, especially after training. Training is more effective when managers take the time to observe employees and comment on their behavior.

5. *Praising progress or redirecting efforts.* Learning depends on bringing both progress and mistakes to the employee's attention. Praise does wonders for inducing repeat performances of good work. Managers should also redirect employee efforts when performance is not up to par.

6. *Integration into work routines.* New learning should be integrated into the employee's work activities. The employee's work should then be reviewed with his or her manager to make sure that what the employee learned in training is being applied correctly.

A final form of training that is occurring both on the job and in the classroom is **diversity training**—training in awareness of and respect for individual, social, and cultural differences among co-workers and customers. For the story of how one company invested in diversity training, see the doing business box "Washington State Ferry System Invests in Diversity Training."

 diversity training

Training in awareness of and respect for individual, social, and cultural differences among co-workers and customers.

performance appraisal

A periodic written evaluation of an employee's performance compared with specific goals, which are often stated in a performance plan.

career development

The process of planning and coordinating the progress of employees through positions of increasing responsibility within an organization.

Retraining

In the past, only employees in technical jobs or jobs with frequent changes in responsibilities received retraining, but today most employees need to be retrained every year or two because of technical advances and new business strategies. Retraining provides employees with a chance to update their skills and knowledge and to remain valuable to the company.

Partly in response to the ever quickening pace of technological change and its impact on workers, Motorola plans to double its training budget to $300 million annually by the year 2000. After this plan is implemented, every worker will receive 80 to 100 hours of company-sponsored training.[33] Motorola management firmly believes that, in order to keep up with changes in technology and the marketplace, training must be an integral part of the company's strategy.

Hallmark Cards, Inc., of Kansas City, Missouri, the world's largest greeting card company, offers continuous retraining. Camera operators who once prepared color photos and illustrations using photographic printing processes have been retrained in new skills that allow them to achieve the same results using computer scanners. To keep all its workers busy, Hallmark uses workers where they are most needed. Ray Smith, age 52, is a cutting machine operator who works as a custom card imprinter, painter, or modular office assembler, according to the needs of the work load. At headquarters, manufacturing workers may work in the kitchen of the company cafeteria during slack times, but they still earn factory wages. As Hallmark CEO Irv Hockaday observed, "Through all kinds of economic cycles and market cycles, we have found ways to keep people; often by retraining them."[34] Retraining is a good way for businesses to invest in employee development and at the same time use their employees' new skills to increase company flexibility.

Evaluating Employee Performance

Direct evaluation of employees is the responsibility of their managers, not of the human resource department. But human resource managers design the evaluation process, including the evaluation forms and schedules.

One of the most frequently used tools is the **performance appraisal**, a periodic written evaluation of an employee's performance compared with specific goals, which are often stated in a performance plan. Many companies conduct performance appraisals annually. Human resource departments typically keep these appraisals in employee files for future review in case of promotions, dismissals, or other purposes. Some companies conduct performance appraisals by having mangers and their employees complete identical forms outlining the responsibilities of the position and evaluating how they were handled. This is followed by a conference in which the two discuss any differences of opinion.

A relatively new form of appraisal reverses the usual procedure by having employees evaluate their manager's performance. According to one survey, these upward appraisals were in use at 12 percent of U.S. businesses in 1993.[35] Federal Express uses this method in its annual leadership survey. Employees rate the extent to which they agree or disagree with such statements as "I feel free to tell my manager what I think," "My manager helps us find ways to do our job better," and "My manager lets me do my job without interfering." FedEx managers who receive low scores have to improve by their next performance appraisal.[36]

Career Development

6. Discuss various paths in career development.

Career development is the process of planning and coordinating the progress of employees through positions of increasing responsibility within an organiza-

CHAPTER **12** Human Resource Management **367**

tion. The burden of career planning and development has traditionally fallen on the employee. F. Wade Bates, director of human resources at Nabisco Foods, observed in 1992 that "the company can't be the only one responsible for career planning. . . . An individual has to take charge of his own career."[37] This attitude is changing. Many businesses are finding that establishing a learning organization requires nurturing employee expertise. In such businesses, the human resource department helps employees grow and take on jobs of greater responsibility and higher pay within the company.

Part of career development is specifying a **career path**, a succession of jobs that employees may hold as they move upward through an organization to positions of increasing responsibility and pay. The career of Lee Iacocca, who retired a few years ago as president and chief executive officer of Chrysler Corp., illustrates such an upward path through an organization.

After graduating from college, Iacocca signed on as an engineering trainee with Ford Motor Company in 1946. After a few years he left engineering for sales and, in 1953, became assistant sales manager for the Philadelphia district. In 1956, Iacocca was promoted to sales manager for the Washington, D.C., district and in 1960 became vice president and general manager of Ford Motor Co. In this position, he developed the popular Mustang and Cougar models. Ten years later, Iacocca became the president of Ford, a position he held until Henry Ford II fired him in 1978. Iacocca then moved to Chrysler, where he was credited with saving the company from financial disaster.[38]

Many companies define standard paths by which an employee can rise within the organization, such as from administrative assistant to coordinator to office manager to department supervisor to manager to associate director and finally to director. Alternatively, career paths can be unique to the individual, as was the case with Lee Iacocca, whose path reflected both Ford Motor Company's needs and Iacocca's particular abilities. For many employees, career development includes company-sponsored programs such as job rotation, succession planning, and mentoring. Other employees contribute to their own futures through networking.

Job Rotation

Job rotation is the practice of moving employees through a series of jobs for set periods of time to give them an understanding of a variety of business functions. U.S. firms are increasingly using job rotation, and businesses in Japan and Germany have had it in place for many years. By rotating jobs, employees acquire broad experience and abilities that enable them to deal flexibly with varied production tasks, unpredictable problems, and changing technologies.[39]

Part of Ford Motor Company's ambitious plans for what it calls Ford 2000—a corporate restructuring aimed at making it the world's leading auto manufacturer—includes job rotations for managers. And in Japan, many manufacturing firms place every new employee on a production line job for some period of time. The underlying philosophy is that all employees need to understand right at the outset that production is the stage at which value is truly added to the company's products. Also, Japanese managers tend to believe that problem solving is the most important part of any job. Hence, solving increasingly difficult problems is the most meaningful career path at many companies, even if the employee's job title does not change.[40]

Succession Planning

Succession planning is a formal evaluation to determine which employees within an organization are capable of future moves into key positions. If planning fails to identify such people, the company can select a few individuals and prepare them through special training, job rotation, and other techniques.

---

career path

A succession of jobs that employees hold as they move upward through an organization to positions of increasing responsibility and pay.

job rotation

The practice of moving employees through a series of jobs for set periods of time to give them an understanding of a variety of business functions.

succession planning

A formal evaluation to determine which individuals within an organization are capable of future moves into key positions.

At General Electric Co., where a highly developed system of management development and evaluation is in place, succession planning is serious business. Members of the company's board of directors review extensive files on up to 15 key executives twice a year. Based on these reviews, the directors make recommendations for each executive's continued development and progress in the organization. At the same time, the board of directors becomes familiar with the best and the brightest within the corporation—the men and women who may one day succeed GE's CEO, John Welch. The practice was tested recently when Welch underwent triple-bypass heart surgery. Although rumors about who would lead the company in Welch's place were rampant in the media, investor confidence in GE's system of succession planning was reflected in the price of its stock, which actually increased in value the day after Wall Street learned of Welch's heart ailment.[41]

Mentoring

Mentoring is an informal relationship in which a more experienced employee guides and sponsors a less experienced employee in a similar work role. Although mentoring relationships may develop spontaneously between employees on the job, many companies set up formal mentoring programs.

Networking

Many employees agree with the director of human resources at Nabisco that an individual has to take charge of his or her own career. These employees often manage their own career paths in part through *networking*, the informal process in which people linked by a common interest provide advice, information, and resources to one another. The networking process for individual employees is similar to the networking process described for entrepreneurs in Chapter 6. Possible network contacts includes co-workers, managers, relatives, family friends, and acquaintances. Networking ranges from telephone conversations to chats during informal get-togethers after work or during training sessions or professional conferences. Letters are a very common and effective form of networking communications. Networking is an excellent way to learn about the availability of other types of jobs and the qualifications necessary to be considered for such opportunities.

Compensation and Benefits

You may recall from Chapter 11 that money is not always the main reason people work. Without fair payment, however, most employees would have little reason to work. **Compensation** is the payment employees receive for their work. Compensation takes two forms:

- **Pay**—cash compensation in the form of wages, salary, or incentive bonuses
- **Benefits**—noncash compensation, such as health insurance, paid vacations, or retirement plans, which employees select or receive by virtue of being members of the organization

The sum of the pay and benefits of all the organization's employees is the total labor cost of the employer. For example, a 23-person organization that each year averages $20,000 per employee in pay and $6,000 per employee in benefits will have a total annual labor cost of $598,000. With this kind of money at stake, it is small wonder that determining how much employees will be paid is such an important process.

Career Development

Face it: You are responsible for your career. Take advantage of every opportunity for training, networking, and mentoring. Don't hesitate to ask more experienced workers for help. Most people are flattered, and will be more than willing to share their knowledge with you.

7. Identify the two forms of compensation available to employees today and describe the types of cash compensation.

Wages and Salary

Wages are pay provided to hourly employees. **Salary** is pay provided to professional employees in weekly, monthly, or yearly amounts.

How does an employer calculate the value of an employee's work? Training and experience play a large part in determining compensation, as do a number of other factors. At the organization level, experts in human resources look at economic and employment trends for similar employees in the geographic area in which the business operates. These specialists try to determine the availability of similarly trained workers as well as the state of the national and local job markets and the economy. The condition of the company's own business also plays a role.

At the individual level, each employee's qualifications and experience help determine the value of his or her work. One trend is to pay for newly acquired skills. For example, at Johnsonville Foods, employees can earn an hourly increase when they learn a new job skill such as accounting, regardless of whether they need the skill in their current job. A similar pay-for-skills plan is in place at Corning Inc., where, according to a senior vice president and corporate director for quality, "If you went to work for some of our high-performance factories, you'd find your pay level depends on what skill level you reach. We're paying for what you know, not what you do."[42] By rewarding employees who learn new skills, Corning is investing in its future growth by enhancing the potential of its employees. And, as we have seen, companies review employee performance records regularly to determine whether past performance deserves to be rewarded and, if so, to what extent.

Sometimes companies try to avoid the appearance of unfairness by giving everyone wage increases or cuts of the same percentage amount. Although this may sound fair, in reality it often is not. If everyone receives a 3 percent raise, for example, a top manager making $100,000 will receive only $3,000 extra, which he or she may find demoralizing after a full year of high-stress performance. Meanwhile, the lowest-paid employee will receive only $450 on an annual wage of $15,000, which may not even cover the year's increase in basic living expenses. Neither will be satisfied, and both may feel punished rather than rewarded for their year's work.

A fairer, although more difficult, means of allocating compensation is through **pay for performance**, linking pay increases directly to an employee's level of performance. At the Yoplait Yogurt unit of General Mills, Inc., a team of managers on a pay-for-performance plan set its own goals, which were even higher than those set by the parent company. The group surpassed its goal of increasing operating earnings by 100 percent and collected bonuses of $30,000 to $50,000 each, about 50 percent of their salaries.[43]

Even with pay for performance, however, stresses can develop, especially if wage increases are limited and high rewards are given only to upper management. Andrew Romegialli, an executive with the International Association of Machinists, the union that represents employees at Pratt & Whitney in East Hartford, Connecticut, expressed these sentiments: "Pratt is making profits. They are giving big raises to top executives. If there is money for that, there is money for us, too."[44] The situation at Pratt & Whitney is not unique. In 1994, earnings of Standard & Poor's top 500 firms rose 40 percent. However, during the same period, wages increased by an average of only 2.9 percent.[45] Although most workers have resigned themselves to this state of affairs, few like it.

Another compensation issue is **comparable worth**, the payment of equal compensation to women and men in different positions that require similar levels of education, training, and skill. According to recent statistics, women still earn only 70 cents for every dollar earned by men in comparable jobs.[46] A different but related compensation issue is *equal pay*, which addresses the differ-

mentoring
An informal relationship in which a more experienced employee guides and sponsors a less experienced employee in a similar work role.

compensation
The payment—pay and benefits—that employees receive for their work.

pay
Cash compensation in the form of wages, salary, or incentive bonuses.

benefits
Noncash compensation, such as health insurance, paid vacations, or retirement plans, which employees select or receive by virtue of being members of the organization.

wages
Pay provided to hourly employees.

salary
Pay provided to professional employees in weekly, monthly, or yearly amounts.

pay for performance
Linking pay increases directly to an employee's level of performance.

comparable worth
The payment of equal compensation to women and men in different positions that require similar levels of education, training, and skill.

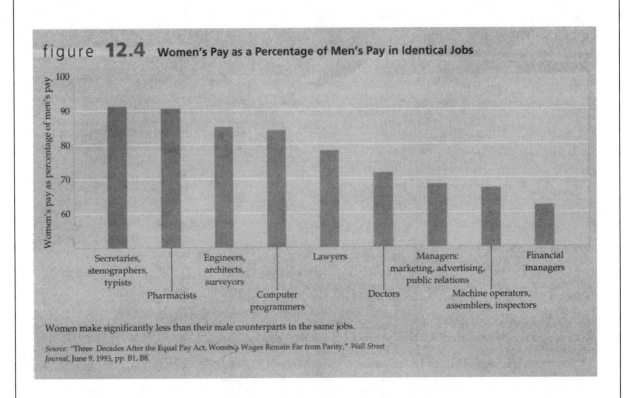

figure **12.4**   **Women's Pay as a Percentage of Men's Pay in Identical Jobs**

Women make significantly less than their male counterparts in the same jobs.

Source: "Three Decades After the Equal Pay Act, Women's Wages Remain Far from Parity," *Wall Street Journal,* June 9, 1993, pp. B1, B8.

ence in pay between men and women doing the same work. Figure 12.4 shows women's pay as a percentage of men's pay in identical positions.

Commissions, Bonuses, and Profit Sharing

commission

Pay based on a percentage of the money an employee brings into a business.

bonus

A cash payment that rewards employees for achieving an organizational goal.

gain sharing

The granting of periodic (quarterly, semiannual, or annual) bonuses to employees based on organizational performance, not individual performance.

profit sharing

An incentive system that gives some or all employees a percentage of the profits earned by a business.

A **commission** is pay based on a percentage of the money an employee brings into a business. Salespeople are typically paid in whole or in part by commission. A salesperson who works on straight commission receives a commission on each sale—perhaps 4 percent of the selling price of a television, for example—but no base pay. The more typical arrangement is for an employee to receive a draw—a small base salary as well as commissions, which still form the largest part of the salesperson's compensation.

A **bonus** is a cash payment that rewards employees for achieving an organizational goal—exceeding a sales quota, achieving a quality improvement target, or developing a new product. At Cooper Tire & Rubber Co., all employees can receive bonuses. Executive bonuses are tied to financial performance benchmarks and contribute up to 30 percent of these employees' total compensation. Hourly workers get paid extra for producing over their goal, and salaried employees can earn bonuses of up to 7.5 percent of their base pay.[47]

Gain sharing is the granting of periodic (quarterly, semiannual, or annual) bonuses to employees based on organizational performance, not individual performance. Gain sharing plans are usually based on either cost savings or profit sharing. **Profit sharing** is an incentive system that gives some or all employees a percentage of the profits earned by a business. This gives employees a stake in the financial success of the company, motivating them to keep costs low and increase productivity. A similar program that attempts to motivate employees to maintain high levels of performance is the **employee stock option plan**, which allows employees to buy company stock at discounted prices.

Benefits

In the 35-year period from 1955 through 1990, the cost of employee benefits rose from 17 percent of payroll to approximately 38 percent of payroll.[48] As large as this number is, it continues to increase. Many organizations see the high cost of employee benefits as an incentive to downsize, outsource, or use temporary workers. Many employees, however, would willingly change jobs for better health coverage, retirement benefits, or family-care provisions. Benefits can be either fixed or flexible, as we are about to see.

Fixed Benefits

Fixed benefits are benefits that all employees receive by virtue of being a member of the organization. Some fixed benefits are required by law, while others are provided to employees at the sole discretion of the employer. Although many employers have cut back on the fixed benefits they provide to employees in an effort to reduce costs, some companies—like San Francisco's Business Wire—offer quite extensive fixed benefit packages.

At Business Wire, employees receive fixed benefits equal to 37 percent of their salary. This figure climbs to 60 percent for employees who stay with the company for six years. Why are some companies so generous? It's just good business. According to Lorry Lokey, Business Wire's president and founder, "If you use benefits to build a cadre of talented people who stay with you for

employee stock option plan

Program that attempts to motivate employees to maintain high levels of performance by allowing them to buy company stock at discounted prices.

fixed benefits

Benefits that all employees receive by virtue of being a member of the organization.

8. Differentiate between fixed and flexible benefits.

"Before I forget, Detrick, here's the dental plan."

Drawing by Leo Cullum; © 1995 The New Yorker Magazine, Inc.

years, you'll hold on to your power. Your company's future will just get stronger and stronger."[49]

Fixed employee benefits can be categorized into six groups, although not all companies offer all of them:

1. Benefits required by law.

2. Payment for time not worked. This is by far the most expensive type of benefit to the employer, and one of the most prized by employees. At Business Wire, all new employees receive seven paid holidays, two weeks of paid vacation, and five days of paid sick leave.

3. Health and accident insurance. Business Wire pays 90 percent of each employee's medical insurance. While 98 percent of firms with 100 to 499 employees offer health insurance, only 60 percent of businesses with 25 or fewer employees do.[50]

4. Insurance and security benefits. These benefits, which include life insurance, long-term disability, and supplemental unemployment benefits, have also increased in cost in recent years.

5. Employee services. This is the newest and most rapidly expanding group of benefits, limited only by the imagination. For example, Business Wire pays its veteran employees $480 a year toward membership in a health club. And PepsiCo Inc. has hired a concierge at its Purchase, New York, headquarters to run personal errands for employees, including making restaurant reservations, purchasing theater tickets, arranging events for children, and arranging for household repairs. The company started providing this service after a recent company survey showed that employees experienced stress over having no free time to take care of such matters themselves.[51]

6. Family benefits. At General Electric Co., managers in the aerospace division were startled to learn that many employees would consider changing jobs for better family benefits.[52] They obviously were unaware of the growing importance to employees of family and quality of life issues, one of the trends discussed at the beginning of this chapter.

Flexible Benefits

In fixed plans, employees receive identical benefits whether they want them, need them, or use them. Such plans have markedly decreased recently as their cost has escalated.

In their place, many businesses are offering **flexible benefits**, also known as *cafeteria benefits*, which employees choose according to their wants and needs. This option produces a customized benefit package for each employee, and it reduces costs for employers.

Most flexible benefit plans grant employees a specific number of "flex dollars," or flexible benefit credits, to spend on company benefits each year. Employees can use these flex dollars to buy any combination of benefits, or they can apply them to an employee savings plan, a stock purchase plan, or some other financial investment. For example, an employee who is 33 years old, single, and in good health may not need the wide range of benefits that the company's fixed plan offers employees with families. Instead, this employee could select a less costly medical plan, which would allow him or her to save 135 flex dollars to buy company stock or invest in a savings plan. This sort of option appeals to young employees in today's workplace. In a recent poll conducted by Roper Starch Worldwide Inc., almost 60 percent of workers in their twenties said they or their spouse participated in some retirement-focused plan offered by their employers. About 75 percent said retirement saving is a priority in their financial planning.[53]

 flexible benefits
Benefits that employees choose according to their wants and needs; also called *cafeteria benefits*.

doing
business

AT&T's Flexible Workplace

At AT&T, employees can take advantage of many innovative programs designed to increase flexibility and productivity. Telecommuting, job sharing, flextime, and alternative work schedules cater to employees who want to spend less time at the office and more time at home. Liz Cabarle and Kathy Knight share a job in the human resource department at AT&T. Their working hours are arranged so that each works three days a week, with overlapping schedules on Wednesdays.

Why do Liz Cabarle and Kathy Knight share a job? Wouldn't it be easier—and much more lucrative—to work a full-time schedule? Perhaps, but by sharing a job, Cabarle and Knight get the best of both worlds—time to spend with friends and family, plus a career with pay and benefits. According to Cabarle, "Even though being at home is fulfilling, sometimes you need to do something else." Knight says, "It's something we put a lot of ourselves into even before we had our kids. It would be hard to give up."

Why does AT&T allow employees to share jobs? Wouldn't it be easier to have fewer employees to keep track of? People in favor of job sharing point out that the company benefits by having the unique skills and knowledge of two employees while paying for only one. Also, when one employee calls in sick, the other is available as backup. A trained, fully functional backup is much more efficient and productive than a temporary employee—someone who has to learn the ropes before being fully competent at all job tasks.

Researchers have seen measurable improvement in worker productivity as a result of flexible work programs such as those at AT&T. Kathleen Christensen, director of the Work Environments Research Group at City University of New York Graduate School, says companies "will see a bottom-line pay off. You have better, more creative, and more productive management." Companies such as AT&T are leading the way to the workplace of the future, when flexible work arrangements like the one Liz Cabarle and Kathy Knight participate in may be the norm and not the exception.

Source: Based on Sallie Han, "We Can Work It Out," (New York) *Daily News,* Jan. 6, 1995.

Scheduling and Leaves

More and more workers now define success in terms of their personal life, not their work life. In a recent Roper poll, for example, approximately 80 percent of respondents said success was having a happy family life or relationship. In last place came money, career, and power.[54] But at the same time, Americans are working longer hours than ever. According to a poll of 10,000 professionals and managers conducted by Work/Family Directions, working men average 47 hours per week on the job, and working women 44 hours per week.[55] Ronald LeMay, president of Sprint Corp.,[55] in Westwood, Kansas, believes "forty-hour workweeks are a relic of the past."[56] Benefits that grant employees free time— flexible scheduling, paid and unpaid leaves, job sharing, and work-at-home programs—carry a high value because they allow employees to balance their priorities.

9. Discuss the use of flexible work schedules and leaves to increase employee satisfaction.

Flexible Work Schedules

One of the most common ways for employees to gain flexibility in their work schedules is through **flextime**, which allows them to work during hours of their choice as long as they work their required number of hours and are present during prescribed core periods. During core hours, all employees must be present for meetings, interaction with co-workers, and so forth.

Another progressive scheduling arrangement is **job sharing**, in which two employees share a full-time job, each working part time. It takes a special relationship for such an arrangement to work well, but if it does it can provide the company with savings in equipment, space, and other resources. For a glimpse at how two employees share a job at AT&T, see the doing business box "AT&T's Flexible Workplace."

flextime

Program that allows employees to work during hours of their choice as long as they work their required number of hours and are present during prescribed core periods.

job sharing

Arrangement in which two employees share a full-time job, each working part time.

work-at-home programs

Benefit that allows employees to work all or some of their scheduled hours at home.

telecommuting

A form of work-at-home program in which employees communicate with the office by computer or fax machine.

leave

Time away from the job, with or without pay.

Family and Medical Leave Act

Federal law requiring firms with 50 or more employees to grant up to 12 weeks of unpaid leave following the birth or adoption of a child or the placement of a foster child, or during the serious illness of the employee or a member of his or her family.

A final, relatively new benefit is **work-at-home programs**, in which employees are allowed to work all or some of their scheduled hours at home. Employees who **telecommute** work at home and communicate with the office by computer or fax machine. Many employees report that working at home allows them to focus on a project for longer, uninterrupted periods of time. It also eliminates time wasted in commuting or socializing with co-workers. The number of people in the United States who work at home at least part time has grown by about 15 percent annually in recent years, for a total of approximately 8 million. A recent study that tracked 280 at-home workers for one year found that two-thirds of them liked it but the other third gave it up. The most common reasons for quitting were a lack of equipment and support, and problems back at the office.[57]

Leaves

Time away from the job, with or without pay, is known as **leave**. Leaves can be either short term or long term. Short-term leaves are paid periods, often of up to eight weeks at full pay. Jury leave and disability leave are examples of short-term leaves. In 1993, President Clinton signed the **Family and Medical Leave Act**, which requires firms with 50 or more employees to grant up to 12 weeks of unpaid leave following the birth or adoption of a child or the placement of a foster child in their home, or during the serious illness of the employee or members of the employee's immediate family. Although company policies vary, many disability policies include a number of weeks at full pay and some additional weeks at a portion of full pay.

Long-term leaves for periods exceeding six months are usually unpaid but may still carry continuing benefits and the guarantee of a job when the employee returns to work. Reasons for such leaves include public service activities, such as running for or holding political office or serving in the military during wartime. Some firms have even granted long-term leaves to employees who join the Peace Corps or work with a United Way agency. More common, however, are leaves to pursue additional education or training. Some employers encourage their employees to obtain advanced degrees, and they may even offer funding, in whole or in part.

While benefits cost employers a great deal of money, a well-administered benefits plan can pay for itself through increased employee productivity. One Boston University report concluded that benefits increase workers' job satisfaction and morale and also reduce carelessness, absenteeism, turnover, and tardiness.[58]

Changes in Employment Status

10. Outline the various ways in which employees can change status in an organization.

The human resource manager's work does not end with the hiring, training, periodic evaluation, and compensation of employees. Much of the human resource manager's time is also spent on maintaining appropriate staffing levels. In this section we'll look first at the many ways in which people move within an organization through reassignment and then we'll address the ways in which they separate from an organization through layoffs, terminations, and retirement.

Reassignment

During the course of their employment, employees may be reassigned to other jobs within the organization through promotion, transfer, or demotion. Although most promotions and many transfers are good news for the employee, some transfers and all demotions are bad news.

Promotion

Promotion is advancement to a position of greater responsibility and higher compensation. How does a firm decide whom to promote? Some business owners, managers, and human resource departments maintain a "promotables" list as part of their planning. Typically, such a list indicates the people who are in line for each position in the firm and an estimate of their readiness for promotion.

Many firms rely on the recommendations of managers to determine who will be promoted. For example, let's say a firm's senior accountant resigns to accept a position with another firm. Rather than recruit outside the firm, the accounting manager may select one of the company's staff accountants as a replacement. The accounting manager's hiring recommendation would be made on the basis of his or her personal knowledge of the employee's performance and personality, other managers' experience with the employee, and perhaps a series of interviews with other eligible candidates.

There are several ways for employees to prepare themselves for promotion. One is to master the skills required for a current job. Another is to seek training in skills necessary to perform higher-level tasks. Employees can also show an interest in promotion by expressing a desire to move up the career ladder. Given the option of promoting two employees, one who seems excited by the prospect of more authority and responsibility and another who seems to have little interest, most employers will choose the former.

Transfer

A **transfer** is a lateral, or sideways, move from one job to another with a similar level of authority and compensation. Some transfers are required by the organization. Ford Motor Company and many other firms now require managers and other employees to increase their flexibility by serving stints in various parts of the organization, where they can gain a larger view of the company and learn a variety of jobs and processes. Organizations also sometimes transfer troublesome employees, reassigning them to a different manager or work team where they may fit in better or be more productive.

Other transfers are initiated by employees. An employee who tires of a particular position may request a transfer into another area. Employees may also choose to transfer rather than lose their job when an organization downsizes.

Transfers that require a physical relocation to another work site can be costly to the organization and disruptive to the employee and his or her family. As a result, several companies are experimenting with alternatives to moving their employees. Ford and others use task forces or special projects instead of transfers to broaden workers' experience; Mobil Corp. moves managers within each of its three U.S. "hub" locations, where a wide range of functions and operations are clustered. And General Motors Corp. offers some managers overseas "professional development" stints lasting not more than six months, rather than the two- to three-year relocations of the past.[59]

Demotions

A **demotion** is the movement of an employee to a position of lesser responsibility, usually as a result of poor performance in a higher-level position. Demotion assumes that the person will be able to perform satisfactorily in the new position. If this does not happen, separation from the company may be required.

promotion

Advancement to a position of greater responsibility and higher compensation.

transfer

A lateral, or sideways, move from one job to another with a similar level of authority and compensation.

demotion

Movement of an employee to a position of lesser responsibility, usually as a result of poor performance in a higher-level position.

Should Fifty-Somethings Step Down?
Toyota Thinks So

How would you like it if you were removed or dismissed from a job because your employer decided that you were too young—or too old? If you are like most members of the American public, you probably would consider such an act patently unfair. In the United States, federal law prohibits job discrimination based on age, such as forced retirement. Other countries may view this issue from a different perspective.

In Tokyo, Japan, the Toyota Motor Corp. recently decided to enact a new policy that sets strict age limits for certain management positions: 50 years for section chiefs and 53 years for deputy general managers. Upon reaching these age limits, managers are removed from their management positions and given nonsupervisory duties at the same salary.

Why is Toyota relieving its most experienced managers of their management duties? For two reasons, according to a company spokesperson. First, Toyota believes that its management team has become stale and that the best way to pump new energy into it is to remove older employees and replace them with younger ones. Second, there are large numbers of junior managers at Toyota looking forward to promotions and career development, and older managers must make room at the top for these up-and-comers.

If a U.S. corporation like General Motors enacted make-way-for-up-and-comers policy like this, it would probably be greeted with a barrage of lawsuits alleging age discrimination. Isn't Toyota concerned about the possibility of legal action? According to a company spokesperson, management does not have to worry about such opposition because Toyota's employees accept what is best for the company.

As the American work force continues to gray and large numbers of baby-boomers continue to march upward through the organization, many U.S. companies will devote the largest percentage of their compensation costs to these older workers—increasing the pressure to cut compensation costs elsewhere in the company. Given these conditions, what options do you see for junior managers in the United States? Would you want to see Toyota's solution applied to your co-workers so that you could advance? Would you want it applied to you when you reach 50 years of age?

Source: Andrew Pollack, "Toyota Has Decided to Set Age Limits on Its Managers," *New York Times,* Oct. 25, 1994, p. 16.

Demotions usually occur because an employee has failed to perform satisfactorily in some other position, or as punishment for a serious ethical violation or infraction of company rules. In some cases, however, demotions are based on unproved assumptions about a worker's capacity. For a discussion of one company's policy of age-based demotion, see the ethics check "Should Fifty-Somethings Step Down? Toyota Thinks So."

Separation

Eventually, all employees leave their job. **Separation** is the severing of an employee's relationship with an employer. Employees may leave an organization for several reasons, including layoffs, terminations, or retirement.

Layoffs

Over the past several years, many of America's biggest businesses have laid off a large number of their employees. A **layoff** is the dismissal of an employee because of financial constraints on the firm. For example, between 1991 and 1994, IBM laid off 85,000 workers, AT&T laid off 83,500, and General Motors laid off 74,000.[60] Such large-scale layoffs are known as *downsizing,* the elimination of jobs to cut costs and make a business smaller, and they have sent shock waves throughout the country. Since the passage of the Worker Adjustment and Retraining Notification Act in 1988, employers must give at least 60 days notice of a large-scale layoff or plant closing. Many companies also extend to employees

 separation

The severing of an employee's relationship with an employer through layoff, termination, or retirement.

 layoff

Dismissal of an employee because of financial constraints on the firm.

the chance of returning to work if economic conditions improve. In the United States, most permanent employees who are laid off are covered by **unemployment insurance**, which pays workers who have lost their jobs a basic level of compensation for a limited time while they look for new work.

Layoffs are traumatic—not only for the workers who are laid off but also for those who are left behind, who often worry that they will be next to join the line at the unemployment office. Alternatives to layoffs include the policy of **attrition**, reducing an organization's work force through normal turnover and voluntary terminations. When employers anticipate a labor surplus, they may be able to stop hiring in time for voluntary resignations, retirements, and firings to reduce the work force to an acceptable level.

Another alternative to layoffs is to reduce the hours of all employees. About one-third of the states in the United States have "shared work" programs that allow employers to reduce workers' hours (and hence their wages) by 20 to 60 percent; the employees collect unemployment insurance for the unworked hours.[61] Shared work programs reduce layoffs and downsizings and help save employees' jobs.

A final alternative to layoffs is a voluntary early retirement program, which is part of the topic we turn to next.

Termination

Termination is a voluntary or involuntary permanent departure from a job. Most employer-employee relationships are **employment at will**, which means that either party may, in the absence of a contract, terminate the arrangement at any time and for any reason. One form of termination, **retirement**, is an employee's voluntary departure on reaching a certain age, often in combination with a requirement of having served some length of time with the company. As the average age of employees increases from year to year, retirement issues concern more and more employees. Federal legislation forbids mandatory retirement before age 70 in most private-sector jobs, but it does not prevent an organization from offering incentives to all employees who are near retirement age in return for their taking early retirement. These incentives may include a lump-sum payment, continuation of a portion of the employee's regular salary, and continued health and other retirement benefits. In some cases, the package offers greater benefits than the employee would receive by staying with the firm through normal retirement age.

Voluntary termination also occurs when employees move away, find new jobs, start their own businesses, join the military, return to school, or for a number of other reasons. In all these cases, the common factor is that the employee initiates the action, without any dismissal action on the part of the employer.

Involuntary terminations occur when employees are asked to leave the organization. As we saw earlier in the discussion of layoffs, some involuntary terminations occur through no fault of the employee. In recent years, many of the largest U.S. businesses have terminated whole work groups, departments, and even divisions in the course of mergers, reorganizations, or downsizings. Automation also frequently results in cuts in the work force.

In other cases, however, involuntary terminations happen because of an unfortunate fact of organizational life: Some people just don't work out as employers thought they would. Although there are few enforceable regulations for dealing with such employees, most organizations accept the principle of "just cause" as a basis for involuntary termination. This means that to terminate an employee, an organization must have a good reason that is related to his or her performance and behavior on the job. Generally accepted reasons include fighting or injuring others; stealing; lying (in the form of padding sales figures with dummy order forms to make a sales quota, for example); misrepre-

---

✓ **unemployment insurance**

Program that pays workers who have lost their jobs a basic level of compensation for a limited time while they look for new work.

✓ **attrition**

Policy of reducing an organization's work force through normal turnover and voluntary terminations.

✓ **termination**

A voluntary or involuntary permanent departure from a job.

✓ **employment at will**

An employer-employee relationship in which either party may, in the absence of a contract, terminate the arrangement at any time and for any reason.

✓ **retirement**

An employee's voluntary departure from a job on reaching a certain age.

sentation (such as saying one has an M.B.A. when that is not true); and insubordination. Doing a poor job and failing to perform to the standards set for a job is, of course, a valid reason for dismissal.

An employee may be able to appeal an involuntary termination to an individual, to an appeals board within the firm, or, as you will see in Chapter 13, to a union grievance committee. If it is determined that the employee was dismissed unfairly, the decision may be reversed. The law requires businesses to have a rational and nondiscriminatory basis for terminating employees.

Companies are very careful with dismissals, since employees who feel they were wrongfully terminated may sue their former employers, either for a cash settlement or for restoration of their job. To guard against such lawsuits, businesses must have in place a formal, defensible program for evaluation and accurate and up-to-date documentation of employee performance, as discussed earlier in this chapter.

Preparing to Be a Flexible Employee

Flexibility has been forced on employee and employer alike. Most American workers—60 percent of the work force—have held their jobs for fewer than five years. Only 1 of every 4 has held his or her current job for more than four years, and 3 of every 10 have been in the same job for less than one year.[62] This means that even so-called permanent employees are not very permanent anymore. You can expect to hold many jobs in your career and to change your occupation—the work you specialize in—several times as well.

The human resource manager of the future will help employees learn new skills in order to follow flexible career paths. But at the same time, you as an employee will have to take advantage of every opportunity to build your experience and skills. Job rotation, temporary jobs and internships, training, networking, and mentoring are some of the ways in which workers can keep learning and expanding their business contacts. It is very difficult for businesses to balance their need for both flexibility and expertise in their work force. But it will be even harder for employees unless they become fast, flexible learners themselves.

Electronic Management
At St. Louis-based Edward D. Jones & Company, a financial services firm, sales administration, support, and training are completely electronic. Local investment representatives such as Andrew Boles of Madison, New Jersey, are linked to headquarters by a computer network and by the company's business television network, shown here. The video link provides product training, sales coaching, and access to upper management, and it keeps representatives nationwide in touch with the home office every day.

Reviewing *Human Resource Management*

Managing Human Resources in Today's Business Environment

1. **Explain the functions of human resource management in relation to the changing work force.** Human resource managers are charged with supplying, training, and motivating employees. Their task is becoming increasingly complicated by several trends in the composition of the work force. For example, by 2000, more skilled workers will be needed, but most available workers will be unskilled. Furthermore, the work force, with its declining growth rate, will include older adults, as well as more women and minority and immigrant workers. More important from the human resource manager's perspective is the increased use of the contingent work force. Companies must determine how to increase productivity with fewer employees and reduced costs, perhaps through part-time or leased workers.

Human Resource Planning

2. **Identify and describe the components of human resource planning.** Like all management, human resource management begins with planning, a process consisting of research, forecasting, and job analysis. Based on research regarding internal and external factors affecting the company's operations and growth, the human resource manager determines job needs and sources of labor. He or she prepares a job analysis of every position within the company, noting necessary skills and responsibilities for each. From this analysis a job description and job specification are developed in order to locate appropriate candidates and judge performance.

The Hiring Process

3. **Identify the various sources of job applicants.** When a job requisition is submitted, the human resource manager undertakes a search for applicants. The first and preferred source of applicants is the company's own employees. Other sources are employee referrals, as well as advertising in local newspapers, contacting employment agencies, and recruiting on college campuses. Many of the decisions made throughout the hiring process are strongly influenced by government regulations.

4. **Describe methods of screening and testing potential employees and identify two alternative hiring procedures.** The screening of applicants involves review of their resumés plus personal interviews with the human resource manager, the relevant job manager, and potential co-workers. In many cases, applicants are also given skills tests and tests that provide a psychological profile. If an applicant is chosen as a likely employee and if references provide positive assessments, he or she is hired for a full-time position and placed on probation. As an alternative, a company may hire a temporary worker to see how well he or she works out before making a formal commitment.

Training and Developing Employees

5. **Describe the three forms of employee training and explain how employee performance is evaluated.** Employee training—so vital to productivity and competitiveness—begins with the basic training of new employees (employee orientation). Specific skills can be taught to new employees, as well as established employees who have been promoted or transferred, through on-the-job training or classroom training. Companies are increasingly providing diversity training to increase the flexibility of their work force. Employees needing to update their skills and knowledge undergo periodic retraining. Using evaluation forms and schedules designed by the human resource manager, individual managers are responsible for periodically preparing the performance appraisals of their employees. In some cases, employees may even have the opportunity to appraise their manager's performance.

6. **Discuss various paths in career development.** Traditionally, each employee has been responsible for his or her own career development. Today, some human resource managers are helping employees to grow. Employees may take different career paths, depending on their interests and skills. The path may be based on company-sponsored programs such as job rotation, succession planning, and mentoring or on employees' own networking. Job rotation increases the flexibility of both the company and the employee. Through succession planning, the company identifies employees best suited for key positions. Both mentoring and networking most often result from the employee's own efforts to get ahead.

Compensation and Benefits

7. **Identify the two forms of compensation available to employees today and describe the types of cash compensation.** The two forms of compensation are pay and benefits. Pay may be wages for hourly work or salaries based on qualifications and experience. A fair system for allocating pay increases is pay for performance. Two important issues are comparable worth and equal pay, which ensure that both genders are treated equally and fairly. Pay is sometimes obtained through commissions (which may be all or part of a salesperson's overall pay). Bonuses, gain sharing (which is based on either cost savings or profit sharing), and employee stock option plans also motivate employees to maintain high levels of performance.

8. **Differentiate between fixed and flexible benefits.** Fixed benefits are available to all members of the organization, although not all companies offer all possible benefits. The categories of fixed benefits include benefits required by law; paid holidays, vacation, and sick leave; health and accident insurance; life insurance, long-term disabil-

ity, and supplemental unemployment benefits; employee services; and family benefits. With flexible benefits, employees are given a number of flex dollars to spend on those benefits offered by the company that best suit their needs.

9. **Discuss the use of flexible work schedules and leaves to increase employee satisfaction.** Employees increasingly want benefits that provide free time to pursue their outside interests—in family and other relationships. To provide these benefits and thus create happier, more productive workers, employers are beginning to offer such options as flextime, job sharing, work-at-home programs (sometimes using telecommuting), and leave. In fact, the Family and Medical Leave Act requires firms with 50 or more employees to provide up to 12 weeks of unpaid leave to employees with new babies or with serious illnesses—their own or their family members'. Long-term leaves—to pursue additional education or for public-service activities—are usually without pay, although the employee will retain the job until he or she returns.

Changes in Employment Status

10. **Outline the various ways in which employees can change status in an organization.** Besides hiring and training employees, the human resource manager is responsible for moving them within the organization in order to maintain appropriate staffing levels. Employees may be reassigned through a promotion to a job with more responsibility or through transfer to a job with comparable compensation but involving different skills. Transfers may result because company or employee needs change or because an employee is causing problems in his or her current job. Employees who perform poorly may be demoted and eventually terminated. Employees may leave a company because they are temporarily laid off or permanently terminated. Termination may be voluntary—as in retirement or when the employee moves, accepts another job, or starts a new company—or involuntary—as when the employee is fired for poor performance, fighting, stealing, or lying, or when a position has been eliminated.

✔ Key Terms

human resource management 351	performance appraisal 366	gain-sharing 370	transfer 375
contingent work force 351	career development 366	profit sharing 370	demotion 375
employee leasing 353	career path 367	employee stock option plan 371	separation 376
job analysis 355	job rotation 367	fixed benefits 371	layoff 376
job description 355	succession planning 367	flexible benefits 372	unemployment insurance 377
job specification 356	mentoring 368	flextime 373	attrition 377
job requisition 357	compensation 368	job sharing 373	termination 377
job posting 358	pay 368	work-at-home programs 374	employment at will 377
employee referral 358	benefits 368	telecommuting 374	retirement 377
resumé 359	wages 369	leave 374	
probation period 361	salary 369	Family and Medical Leave Act 374	
employee orientation 363	pay for performance 369	promotion 375	
on-the-job training 364	comparable worth 369		
diversity training 365	commission 370		
	bonus 370		

● Review Questions

1. How might human resource managers compensate for the changing makeup of the work force?

2. As human resource manager for Babble Company, a manufacturer of infants' toys, how would you plan for the company's current and future job needs?

3. Marshall Company has an opening for a systems engineer. Where would the human resource manager look for applicants?

4. Why would a company hire a permanent, full-time employee instead of obtaining temporary help? Why might a company prefer hiring temporary help?

5. How does the training of new employees differ from that of seasoned employees?

6. What options are available to employees interested in advancing through a company's hierarchy to, say, vice president of sales?

7. What types of cash compensation can employees receive for their work?

8. What is the difference between fixed and flexible benefits? What are the advantages of each?

9. Why would an employee be reassigned?

10. For what reasons would an employee leave a company?

● Critical Thinking Questions

1. If you were a member of the contingent work force, what advantages would you have over a permanent employee? What would be the disadvantages?

2. How do organizations benefit from providing initial and ongoing training and retraining for employees?

3. Considering what you learned in Chapter 11 about motivation and performance, why is it important for managers to give employees feedback about how they are doing on the job?

4. Assuming the cost of employee benefits becomes excessively high, what options do employers have?

5. How could the material you learned in this chapter help you to get a job and keep it? Give some specific examples that might help you during a job search or performance appraisal.

REVIEW CASE *Xerox Evaluates Performance Evaluations*[63]

Xerox Corp. once had a performance appraisal system that was not unlike that used by thousands of other companies in the United States. Conducted annually, the system numerically rated various aspects of each employee's responsibilities and ranked the employee's overall performance on a scale from 1 to 5. Merit increases were directly tied to the overall rating, which was communicated to employees at the performance appraisal meeting.

This type of system, implementation of which can cost a huge company like Xerox millions of dollars in employee and management time, was intended to improve communication and reward and encourage good performance. Analysis of the ratings themselves revealed that more than 95 percent of employees received either a 3 ("meets and sometimes exceeds expected level of performance") or a 4 ("consistently exceeds expected level of performance"). As a result, virtually all employees received merit increases within 1 to 2 percent of the same amount. Employees who received less than a 5 (the highest rating) felt cheated, and surveys revealed that many employees were discouraged, dissatisfied, and in many cases totally surprised by how their managers rated their work performance.

Given such a large measure of discontent among so many talented, well-trained, and valuable employees, something was clearly wrong with the entire appraisal system. Management realized that company efforts to develop a supportive team atmosphere were being undermined by an evaluation process.

Based on suggestions from employees and managers, a new process, Performance Feedback and Development, was designed. For the first time, objectives were set by both manager and employee at the beginning of each year. These were documented and approved by a second-level manager, reviewed after six months, and then used as a basis for the year-end appraisal. The emphasis of the process was on performance feedback and improvement, not on numerical rankings and a corresponding salary increase (which now takes place one to two months following the appraisal discussion). Numerical ratings were eliminated and replaced by written narratives. A survey taken during the first year of the new system showed that employees and managers liked the revised process. More than 80 percent of all employees said they better understood their work group objectives, 70 percent had met the objectives that they and their managers had set for them, and almost 85 percent considered the new appraisal process to be fair.

1. Xerox's original performance appraisal system did not clearly differentiate between the performance levels of different employees. Why would this be a problem for high-performing employees? What message does such a system send to marginal or low-performing employees?

2. How important is it for employees to perceive that they are being fairly evaluated? What should be the major objectives of any appraisal process?

3. The personal and professional development objectives set each year by managers and employees in the Performance Feedback and Development process related both to skills important in all professions—such as communication, planning, time management, and human relations—and to specialized skills and knowledge relevant to each employee's individual job. How valuable are such skills for individuals? For the organization?

CRITICAL THINKING CASE *Digital Votes for Redeployment, Not Unemployment*[64]

Like many mature companies, Digital Equipment Corp., the Massachusetts-based computer maker, was experiencing escalating costs and evaporating profits because of a glut of management employees and outdated manufacturing equipment. Although many companies in such a situation would seek to reduce costs through massive layoffs, Digital took a different approach. Management knew that the use of newer technology, combined with the same work force, could virtually double the company's output. Thus, says Frank Lanza, manager of manufacturing training, Digital in effect had an additional "5,000 people we could do something with."

Digital conducted a thorough analysis of the skills the company's employees already had and the skills they would need to install and work with an updated manufacturing system. It found that there was an excess of assemblers, product technicians, materials planners, hardware technicians, line supervisors, and managers, but that there was a clear need for more process controllers and designers, programmers, computer operators, network analysts, and multi-product specialist.

The company set out to retrain the "excess" employees to meet the future needs of the company. For example, materials planners, who tend to be detail oriented, were trained as programmers. Supervisors who had overseen certain processes in the old system were trained to design new manufacturing processes for future products. About one hundred production supervisors were trained as salespeople. Finally, middle managers had to develop skills in project management, which Digital considered an important characteristic for managers of the future organization. All told, the company spent 9 to 12 months retraining more than 3,800 workers out of its manufacturing population of 33,500.

1. Digital's executives believe their company saved money by retraining employees instead of laying them off and hiring other people who already had the required skills. A study by the Work in America Institute, a research organization in New York, supports this conclusion. Why, then, do you think so many companies rely on downsizing and massive layoffs when times are lean?

2. Digital offered its retraining program on a voluntary basis to its manufacturing employees. An estimated 600 employees left the organization rather than learn new skills. If you had been a manager at Digital, what steps would you have taken to retain high performers who wanted to leave? Would you have tried to convince them to retrain and remain with the company? Why or why not?

3. Given the steps to effective training discussed in this chapter, describe how you might design a program to retrain the group of materials planners to become computer programmers.

CHAPTER **12** Human Resource Management **383**

Critical Thinking with the ONE MINUTE MANAGER

"There seem to be so many changes going on in business today that it must be hard to be either a manager or a person being managed," Joanna observed.

"That's true to some degree," the One Minute Manager responded. "Management can get so caught up in making changes that it forgets to consider the impact those changes have on the people in the organization. Even good changes can be stressful, and one change after another is bound to take a toll on employees."

"What can management do to make change less stressful?" asked Carlos.

"Provide lots of information and communication. Announce plans far in advance. Involve employees, especially in decisions that affect them. Those are a few of the tactics that we know can help," explained the One Minute Manager.

"But the most important thing organizations can do is to realize that management is what you do *with* people, not *to* them. We all have to remember that we're in the same boat and that if we cooperate, that boat can carry us all to our destination."

1. As a new entry in the labor market, how do you think the changes in the work force, as discussed in this chapter, will affect you?

2. The goal of many businesses today seems to be to do more with less. What assumptions must employees and managers make to turn this goal into reality?

3. Do increased outsourcing, part-time employment, and flexible working hours increase or decrease opportunities for students entering the labor market? Support your answer by discussing issues raised in this chapter.

NOTES

1   Jacklyn Fierman, "The Contingency Work Force," *Fortune,* Jan. 24, 1994, p. 31.

2   Fierman, "The Contingency Work Force," p. 3.

3   Vicki Elliot and Anna Orgera, "Competing for and with Workforce 2000," *HR Focus,* June 1993, p. 3.

4   Data from the National Association of Manufacturers and the Hudson Institute; William B. Johnston and Arnold E. Packer, *Workforce 2000: Work and Workers for the Twenty-First Century* (Indianapolis, Ind.: Hudson Institute, 1987), pp. xiii–xxvii.

5   1992 AMA Survey on Basic Skills Testing and Training (New York: American Management Association), p. 3.

6   Lynn Franey, "Failure Stalks the Halls in L.A.," *San Diego Union-Tribune,* Dec. 12, 1993, pp. A33, 42.

7   Sharon Nelton, "Nurturing Diversity," *Nation's Business,* June 1995, p. 25.

8   Perri Capell, "'Young Turks' at Work," *National Business Employment Weekly,* Nov. 26–Dec. 2, 1993, p. 15.

9   "Automatic Data Processing, Inc." *Hoover's Handbook Database* (Austin, Texas: The Reference Press, 1995), on-line.

10 Personal communication with authors, Blanchard Training and Development, Inc., 1995.

11 Albert R. Karr, "Labor Letter: Lease, Don't Hire," *Wall Street Journal,* March 16, 1993, p. A1.

12 Charles Stein, "The Stingy Boss Syndrome," *Boston Sunday Globe,* May 21, 1995, p. 106.

13 Laura M. Litvan, "Casting a Wider Employment Net," *Nation's Business,* Dec. 1994, p. 49.

14 William B. Johnston, "Global Work Force 2000: The New World Labor Market," *Harvard Business Review,* March–April 1991, p. 115.

15 *The 1994 Information Please Almanac* (New York: McGraw-Hill, 1993).

16 Litvan, "Casting a Wider Employment Net."

17 Nelton, "Nurturing Diversity," p. 25.

18 James P. Womack, Daniel T. Jones, and Daniel Ross, *The Machine That Changed the World: The Story of Lean Production* (New York: HarperPerennial, 1990), pp. 198–99.

19 Litvan, "Casting a Wider Employment Net."

20 Litvan, "Casting a Wider Employment Net."

21 Kathy Rebello and Evan I. Schwartz, "How Microsoft Makes Offers People Can't Refuse," *Business Week,* Feb. 24, 1992, p. 65.

22 Litvan, "Casting a Wider Employment Net."

23 Hal Rosenbluth and Diane McFerrin Peters, "The Customer Comes Second," *Audio-Tech Business Book Summaries, Inc.,* July 1993, p. 5.

24 Paul Burnham Finney, "A Temp(t)ing Solution," *Newsweek,* Dec. 20, 1993, p. 4.

25 Finney, "A Temp(t)ing Solution," p. 1.

26 Linda Grant, "A School for Success; Motorola's Ambitious Job-Training Program Generates Smart Profits," *U.S. News & World Report,* May 22, 1995, p. 53.

27 Ronald Henkoff, "Companies That Train Best," *Fortune,* March 22, 1993, pp. 62, 64.

28 Michael L. Dertouzos, Richard K. Lester, and Robert M. Solow, *Made in America: Regaining the Productive Edge* (New York: HarperPerennial, 1989), pp. 82, 88.

29 Grant, "A School for Success; Motorola's Ambitious Job-Training Program Generates Smart Profits."

30 William Wiggenhorn, "Motorola U: When Training Becomes an Education," *Harvard Business Review,* July–Aug. 1990, p. 71.

31 Cherrington, *Personnel Management,* 3rd ed., 1990, p. 239; George T. Milkovich and William F. Glueck, *Personnel and Human Resource Management,* 4th ed. (Plano, Texas: Business Publications, 1985), p. 348.

32 "Kelly Services, Inc.," *Hoover's Handbook Database* (Austin, Texas: The Reference Press, 1995), on-line.

33 Grant, "A School For Success: Motorola's Ambitious Job-Training Program Generates Smart Profits."

34 Robert Levering and Milton Moskowitz, *The 100 Best Companies to Work for in America,* rev. ed. (New York: Currency Doubleday, 1993), p. 164.

35 Catherine Romano, "Fear of Feedback," *Management Review,* Dec. 1993, p. 38.

36 Federal Express leadership survey, 1993, quoted by Federal Express executive in interview with author.

37 Joan E. Rigdon, "Sideways Moves Grow Increasingly Common," *Wall Street Journal,* Jan. 27, 1992, p. B1.

38 "Iacocca, Lee," *Microsoft Encarta,* 1993, on-line.

39 Dertouzos, Lester, and Solow, *Made in America: Regaining the Productive Edge.*

40 Womack, Jones, and Roos, *The Machine That Changed the World: The Story of Lean Production;* S.L. Mintz, "Redesigning Finance at Ford," *CFO,* March 1995, pp. 26–34.

41 Linda Grant, "GE: The Envelope, Please," *Fortune,* June 26, 1995, p. 89.

42 Alexander Hiam, *Closing the Quality Gap: Lessons from America's Leading Companies* (Englewood Cliffs, N.J.: Prentice Hall, 1992), p. 237.

43 Shawn Tully, "Your Paycheck Gets Exciting," *Fortune,* Nov. 1, 1993, p. 95.

44 Tully, "Your Paycheck Gets Exciting."

45 Charles Stein, "The Stingy Boss Syndrome," *Boston Sunday Globe,* May 21, 1995, pp. 105–106.

46 Joan E. Rigdon, "Three Decades After the Equal Pay Act, Women's Wages Remain Far from Parity," *Wall Street Journal,* June 9, 1993, pp. B1, 8.

47 Alex Taylor III, "Now Hear This, Jack Welch!" *Fortune,* April 6, 1992, p. 94.

48 W. Keith McLeod, "Survey Shows What Benefits Banks Offer," *ABA Banking Journal,* Oct. 1993, p. 47.

49 Jill Andresky Fraser, "'Tis Better to Give and Receive," *Inc.,* Feb. 1995, p. 84.

50 Christine Woolsey, "Not All Firms Want to Offer a Health Plan, Study Finds," *Business Insurance,* July 4, 1994, p. 58.

51 Julie Amparano Lopez, "Undivided Attention: How Pepsi-Co Gets Work Out of People," *Wall Street Journal,* April 1, 1993, pp. A1, 9.

52 Sue Shellenbarger, "GE Unit Sees Advantage in More Family Benefits," *Wall Street Journal,* Feb. 12, 1992, p. B1.

53 "Active Savers," *Boston Globe,* Business Section, June 25, 1995, p. 1.

54 Jaclyn Fierman, "Are Companies Less Family-Friendly?" *Fortune,* March 21, 1994, p. 65.

55 Fierman, "Are Companies Less Family-Friendly?"

56 Fierman, "Are Companies Less Family-Friendly?"

57 Sue Shellenbarger, "Some Thrive, but Many Wilt Working at Home," *Wall Street Journal,* Dec. 14, 1993, p. B1.

58 Sue Shellenbarger, "Work-Family Plans Cut Absenteeism, Stress," *Wall Street Journal,* Jan. 20, 1992, p. B1.

59 Sue Shellenbarger, "Allowing Fast Trackers to Stay in One Place," *Wall Street Journal,* Jan. 7, 1992, p. B1.

60 John A. Byrne, "The Pain of Downsizing," *Business Week,* May 9, 1994, p. 61.

61 Ellyn E. Spragins, "Eliminating Layoffs," *Inc.,* Sept. 1992, p. 31.

62 "Musical Chairs," *The Economist,* July 17, 1993, p. 67.

63 Norman R. Deets and Timothy D. Tyler, "How Xerox Improved Its Performance Appraisals," *Personnel Journal,* April 1986, pp. 50–52.

64 Womack, Jones, and Roos, *The Machine That Changed the World: The Story of Lean Production.*

Practicing Your Textbook Reading Skills

1. Where in the chapter can you find information to help you achieve Learning Goal 8: "Differentiate between fixed and flexible benefits"?

   a. under "Strategies of Flexibility" on page 353

   b. under "Benefits" on pages 371–72

   c. in the boxed feature called "Doing Business" on page 373

   d. under "Flexible Work Schedules" on pages 373–74

2. Evaluate the chapter's headings to identify which of the following is a subtopic of "Compensation and Benefits."

   a. "Career Development"

   b. "Pay-for-Performance"

   c. "Scheduling and Leaves"

   d. "Changes in Employment Status"

3. According to Figure 12.3, what is the second step of the hiring process?

   a. locating candidates   c. job requisition

   b. screening candidates   d. hiring

4. What is the meaning of *pool* as it is used in the section titled "Screening Candidates"?

   a. a place for swimming   c. a game

   b. a puddle of liquid   d. a group

5. The "Skills Check" boxed feature on page 360

   a. summarizes the discussion in the chapter so far.

   b. suggests how the material covered in the text can be applied to real life.

   c. presents statistical data to back up the claims made in the book.

   d. explains how employee screening works.

6. What is the topic of the highlighted "Doing Business" discussion on page 365?

   a. doing business

   b. the Washington State Ferry System

   c. diversity training

   d. sexual harassment

7. Which of the following sentences best expresses the main idea of the highlighted "Doing Business" discussion on page 365?

   a. "According to some predictions, white males, formerly the majority workers in the American work force, will soon make up less than 40 percent of all U.S. workers."

b. "Workers were trained to call African Americans 'people of color' and to refrain from calling women 'ladies' or 'gals'."

c. "In addition, African-American workers reported that they were treated with increased respect and female workers said male co-workers were less likely to tell them jokes with sexual content."

d. "The workplace is changing, and companies have to keep up with that change."

8. What topic does the cartoon on page 371 relate to?
   a. commissions
   b. employee stock option plans
   c. benefits
   d. salary

9. What concept is illustrated by the photograph on page 378?
   a. work-from-home programs
   b. electronic management
   c. sales training
   d. none of the above

10. Use the "Key Terms" section at the end of the chapter to determine where in the chapter you can find a discussion of career development.
    a. page 351
    b. page 366
    c. page 367
    d. page 375

Testing Your Understanding

Identify the following statements as true or false.

1. Laying off employees to cut costs requires that the remaining employees become more skilled and productive.

   T __X__   F _____

2. Most job openings can be found through advertisements, employment agencies, federal and state job services, job lines, or college recruitment fairs.

   T __X__   F _____

3. Most employees need to be retrained every year or two.

   T __X__   F _____

4. Americans are working longer hours than ever.

   T __X__   F _____

5. Job discrimination based on age is illegal in the United States and Japan.

   T __X__   F _____

Select the best answer to each of the following questions.

6. In *Workforce 2000,* the Hudson Institute predicted all of the following *except* that
   a. half of all jobs will require college degrees.
   b. most available workers will be unskilled.
   c. many more women will work from home.
   d. the percentage of minority and immigrant workers will increase.

7. Employee referrals are an example of
   a. job postings.
   b. job requisition.
   c. external sources of job applicants.
   d. internal sources of job applicants.

8. Ideally, a resumé should be
   a. chronological.
   b. one to two pages long.
   c. printed on light blue paper.
   d. anonymous.

9. The Immigration Reform and Control Act of 1986
   a. prohibits the hiring of illegal aliens and requires employers to verify that employees can legally work in the United States.
   b. prohibits employment discrimination against qualified people who have disabilities.
   c. requires companies that sell goods and services to the federal government to make special efforts to employ Vietnam War veterans.
   d. prohibits discrimination in employment on the basis of national origin, race, color, sex, pregnancy, and religion.

10. Employee training programs benefit
    a. new employees.
    b. experienced employees.
    c. companies.
    d. all of the above.

11. Which of the following elements of career development is not sponsored by employers?
    a. job rotation   c. mentoring
    b. succession planning   d. networking

12. Types of fixed benefits include
    a. wages.
    (b.) paid holidays, vacation, and sick days.
    c. bonuses.
    d. job sharing.

13. Flexible benefits are also known as
    (a.) cafeteria benefits.   c. flextime.
    b. subsidized lunch.   d. telecommuting.

14. The Family and Medical Leave Act of 1993 requires companies with fifty or more employees to offer unpaid leave to an employee
    a. after the birth or adoption of a child.
    b. after a foster child is placed in his or her home.
    c. during a family member's serious illness.
    (d.) for any of the above reasons.

15. Which of the following changes in employment status is most likely to result from poor work performance?
    a. transfer   c. short-term leave
    (b.) demotion   d. promotion

In your own words, define the following terms as they are used in the chapter.

16. *employee leasing* – 9

_____

_____

17. *contingent work force* – 8

_____

_____

18. *performance appraisal* – 22

_____

_____

19. *telecommuting* – 30

_____

_____

_____

20. *layoff*

Answer each of the following questions using the space provided.

21. Identify and briefly explain the three stages of human resource planning.

_____

_____

_____

_____

22. Identify the various sources of job applicants (Learning Goal 3).

_____

_____

_____

_____

_____

_____

23. Why is employment testing controversial?

_____

_____

_____

24. How does employee training benefit employers?

_____

_____

_____

25. List and explain three types of compensation other than salary or wages.

_____

_____

_____

_____

_____

Making Thematic Connections

Some people find their jobs to be a major source of stress, while others in the same positions might not be bothered by workplace demands at all. The next chapter, "Stress, Health, and Coping," from *Psychology,* Third Edition, examines what causes stress, how people respond to it, and what strategies can help people deal with it effectively. The authors, Don H. Hockenbury and Sandra E. Hockenbury, define *stress* as "a negative emotional state occurring in response to events that are perceived as taxing or exceeding a person's resources or ability to cope." (Read or reread pages 540–45 of the psychology chapter in Unit 2 for more information.) They also explain that stress can make a person ill, resulting in sick days or poor job performance. What can human resources professionals do to reduce employees' stress levels without lightening their workloads or spending more money on health benefits? Explain your answer. (You might want to review the "Human Resource Management" chapter headings or the key terms listed on p. 380 of that chapter to get some ideas.)

Psychology

"Stress, Health, and Coping"

Introduction

If you've ever wondered why somebody behaved a certain way, how your brain works, or where emotions come from, you've asked yourself a question about psychology. A very popular subject for undergraduate study, psychology is the science of the human mind. And as the authors of the following textbook chapter see it, psychology is "the most fascinating and personally relevant science that exists." It's easy to see why: The topics explored by psychologists include memory, sexuality, personality, dreams, and therapy. You can apply just about anything you learn in a psychology class to yourself, to your friends and acquaintances, and to your family. Psychologists might work with patients in a clinical or school setting, but more often they focus on research and teaching. Their findings are applied by people in many other fields, including business, advertising and marketing, history, literature, education, medicine, and urban planning.

Psychology, Third Edition, by Don H. Hockenbury and Sandra E. Hockenbury, is a best-selling introduction to the science and has taught more than a hundred thousand students. The authors actively seek feedback from their students and have been careful to respond to what those new learners suggest. The chapter you're about to read, as a result, is easy to follow and relevant to your own experiences. Many of its elements will help you identify what is important and understand psychological concepts. These include a narrative—or storytelling—style that begins with examples and then explains how those stories illustrate what psychologists have learned. Examining the "Chapter Outline" before you read will give you a sense of the chapter's main ideas and the supporting details. Each section begins with what the authors call an "Advance Organizer": a "Key Theme" to consider and "Key Questions" that identify the section's most important points (see, for example, "What Is Stress?" on page 540). Key terms and the names of important psychologists are highlighted in bold and reviewed at the end of the chapter. The "Concept Reviews" that end each section help

---

This unit's textbook reading comes from *Psychology,* Third Edition, by Don H. Hockenbury and Sandra E. Hockenbury, Worth Publishers, 2003, Chapter 13, pages 536–69.

you think carefully about and answer those key questions. (You can even find the authors' answers to the questions at the end of the chapter.) Boxes in the text—"In Focus," "Critical Thinking," "Culture and Human Behavior," and "Focus on Neuroscience"—home in on particularly interesting topics. (As you learned in the previous unit, you can read these boxes either before or after you read the discussion in the text; don't feel you have to interrupt your reading because of where they appear on the page.) Finally, an "Application" at the end of the chapter suggests how you can use what you've learned in your own life.

The chapter that follows will help you understand how people (yourself included) respond—and why they respond in certain ways—to difficult situations in the workplace, in school, and in life in general. If you read the chapter attentively, you will come away from it armed with new and useful ideas about how to cope with stress.

Preparing to Read the Textbook Chapter

1. What makes you feel stressed? What do you do when you start to feel overwhelmed? Is there anything you can do to deal with pressure and conflict more effectively?

2. Flip through the chapter and note the various headings within it. Before you read, convert those headings into questions. What do you think the answers might be?

3. Some kinds of work are naturally more stressful than others. Air traffic controllers, doctors, and firefighters, for example, take other people's lives into their hands. But even in jobs where lives are not at stake, many people suffer from the emotional and physical effects of stress. Why? What can people and their employers do to minimize or control stress?

Buy One Get One Free

chapter 13

Stress, Health, and Coping

Prologue
Katie's Story

In her high-rise apartment at 1 West Street, our 20-year-old niece Katie was fixing herself some eggs for breakfast on a beautiful, crystal-clear New York morning. In the background, Katie could hear the muted sound of sirens down on the streets below, but she thought nothing of it. The phone rang. It was Lydia, her roommate, calling from her job in mid-Manhattan. "Katie, you're not going to believe this. A plane hit the World Trade Center. Go up on the roof and take a look!"

Katie hung up the phone and scurried up the fire escape stairwell, joining other residents already gathered on the roof. Down below, sirens were blaring and she could see emergency vehicles, fire engines, and people racing from all directions toward the World Trade Center, just a few blocks away. There was a gaping hole in the north tower. Black, billowing smoke was gushing out, drifting upward, and filling the sky. She thought she could see the flames. *What a freaky accident.*

After watching and talking with some of the other residents for a few minutes, Katie was ready to go back downstairs and get ready for her dance lesson. "Look at that plane!" one of the people suddenly yelled. Just as Katie turned to look, a massive jet roared overhead and slammed into the World Trade Center's south tower, exploding into a huge fireball.

People screaming. Panic. Pushing and shoving at the stairwell door. *Get back to the apartment.* The television. Live views of the burning towers. Newscaster shouting: "Terrorist attack! New York is being attacked!" The TV went dead. *Don't panic. What am I going to do? Are we being bombed?*

Two thousand miles away. A sunny Colorado morning. Phone ringing. Judy was sound asleep. Ringing. Answer the phone. "Katie? What's wrong? Is someone in your apartment? Calm down, I can't understand . . ."

"Mom, New York is being attacked! I don't know what to do! What should I do?" Katie sobbed uncontrollably.

As Katie tried to explain to Judy what was happening, Judy held the portable phone to her ear as she stood up and fumbled for the remote control, flipping on the bedroom television. Pandemonium. Bizarre scenes of chaos in New York. *Oh my God, New York is being attacked . . . Katie's only a couple of blocks from the World Trade Center . . .*

"Katie, breathe. Calm down. It's chaos out on the street, Katie, it's horrible. Don't go out there! Just stay in your apartment. Don't leave, Katie! You'll be safe in your apartment. Katie, I want you to . . ." The phone connection went dead. Desperately, Judy dialed and redialed Katie's number, only to hear a busy signal. She tried Katie's cell phone. Nothing. *Katie has to get out of there . . .*

Katie dropped the phone. *Worthless.* Lights flickered off, then on. Pounding on the door. "Evacuate the building! Get out!" a man's voice shouted. "Get out now! Use the stairwell!" *Gotta get out of here. Get out.*

Putting on her shoes and pulling a T-shirt over her pajamas, Katie grabbed her cell phone and raced out of her apartment toward the crowded stairwell. As she emerged on the street, it was mass confusion. *Cross the street.* She joined a throng of people gathering in Battery Park. *Stay calm.* As the crowd watched the burning towers, people shouted out more news. *Pentagon has been hit. White House is on fire. More planes in the air. President on Air Force One.*

Shaking, she couldn't take her eyes off the burning towers. *What's falling?* Figures falling from the windows of the Trade Center, a hundred stories high. *On fire. That person was on fire. Oh my God, they're jumping out of the building! Don't look!* Watching the firefighters, EMT workers, media people swarming at the base of the site. *This is not real. It's a movie. It's not real.*

Suddenly, unbelievably, the south tower crumbled. Screaming. *It's collapsing! It's coming down.* A vast ball of smoke formed, like an atomic mushroom cloud. Like everyone else in the park, Katie turned and started running blindly. Behind her, a huge cloud of black smoke, ash, and debris followed, howling down West Street like a tornado.

Running. Cops shouting. "Go north! Don't go back! Get out of here!" *Don't go north. The ferry.* Choking on the smoke and dust, Katie covered her face with her T-shirt and stumbled down the street, moving toward the river. *I'm going to*

choke . . . can't breathe. She saw a group of people near the Staten Island ferry. *Get on the ferry, get out of Manhattan.* Another explosion. Panic. More people running.

Dazed and disoriented, Katie is still not certain how she ended up on a boat—a commuter ferry taking people to Atlantic Highlands, New Jersey. *On the boat at last. I'm safe.* Covered with soot. Filthy. Standing in her pajamas amid stunned Wall Street workers in their suits and ties. Call anyone. Trying to call people. *Cell phone dead.* "Here, Miss, use mine, it's working." Call anyone. Crying. *They're dead. Those firemen, the EMT workers at the base of the towers. Dead. They're all dead.* From the boat, she got a call through to her dance teacher, Pam, who lived in New Jersey. Pam would come and get her. She could stay with Pam.

In Colorado, Judy was crying, frantic. What had happened to Katie? She tried to help the boys, Jordon and Zak, get ready for school. She called her ex-husband, who told her not to worry. Katie would be fine, he said. She called your author Sandy and left a frantic phone message. *Where was Katie? Was she dead?* It was not for many hours—later that Tuesday afternoon—that Judy finally heard Katie's voice and knew that she was alive.

Katie survived, but the next few weeks were difficult ones. She had no money, no clothes, none of her possessions. When she got off the ferry in Atlantic Highlands, government workers wearing masks and special yellow protective clothing made her throw her shoes away. "They're filled with asbestos," one worker said. "I don't care if they're new."

Like the other residents in her area near the World Trade Center, Katie wasn't allowed back into her apartment for many days. Her dance teacher, Pam, lent her money to buy new clothes. Late on Tuesday afternoon, she called her workplace, an upscale retail store. The manager wanted her back at work the next day. "Show up or lose your job," the manager said. When Katie did show up, the manager chewed her out because her blouse was wrinkled. Taking the train every day from New Jersey, she saw the same cars parked in the lot, day after day. It suddenly dawned on her. The owners of the cars were commuters. *They're dead. Dead.*

For the first few weeks, Katie was fine, almost lighthearted. Everyone was pulling together. "It was really beautiful," she said. "New Yorkers were helping each other." But there were constant reminders, new fears. In the week following the attack, there were more than 70 bomb scares in the area where she worked. She went out with some friends one night, downtown, everyone wearing face masks because of the dust. It was like living in the twilight zone.

Two weeks after the attacks, the nightmares started. Katie felt panicky on buses, trains, subways. She had to will herself to stay in her seat. On one crowded bus, her fear became overwhelming. Shaking uncontrollably, she got off the bus. "I couldn't help it. I was afraid I would start screaming."

The reminders were everywhere—the fire station shrines, signs for the subway stop that didn't exist anymore. Photographs and notes and flowers on fences, walls. People still missing. And then there were the mental images . . . the images of people jumping, falling, the faces of the rescue workers, the plane ripping through the building. Then it was the men in the white coats and masks at NBC, anthrax right next door to the store where she worked.

Judy kept calling her every day, telling her, "Katie, come home. I want you to get out of New York, it's not safe." Her older brother, Josh, called repeatedly from Miami and said the same thing. "Kate, you can dance in Los Angeles. Or Denver. Or Miami. Please, Katie, get out of there."

But like millions of other New Yorkers, Katie regained her equilibrium. After pleading with the National Guardsmen patrolling the area, Katie and Lydia were allowed to get their belongings out of their apartment. They loaded as much as they could into a shopping cart, dragging and pushing the cart some 30 blocks north to a friend's home. They found a new apartment.

The best thing that Katie did, she said, was go back to her daily dance class. In that two hours a day, Katie began to feel right again, doing what she loved, surrounded by the people she loved. The nightmares slowly receded, although the memories never will.

"Are things back to normal?" Katie said. "No, things will never be normal again, not in a hundred years. But it's okay. I'm fine. And I'm not going to leave New York. This is where I am, this is where I live, this is where I can dance."

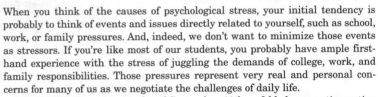

540 CHAPTER 13 *Stress, Health, and Coping*

Introduction

What Is Stress?

Key Theme
■ When events are perceived as exceeding your ability to cope with them, you experience an unpleasant emotional and physical state—stress.

Key Questions
■ What is health psychology, and what is the biopsychosocial model?
■ How do life events, daily hassles, and conflict contribute to stress?
■ What are some social and cultural sources of stress?

How Do You Define Stress? From a ripped grocery bag to the threat of unemployment, stressors come in all sizes. Any event can produce stress—if you think you don't have the resources to cope with it.

stress
A negative emotional state occurring in response to events that are perceived as taxing or exceeding a person's resources or ability to cope.

health psychology
The branch of psychology that studies how biological, behavioral, and social factors influence health, illness, medical treatment, and health-related behaviors.

biopsychosocial model
The belief that physical health and illness are determined by the complex interaction of biological, psychological, and social factors.

stressors
Events or situations that are perceived as harmful, threatening, or challenging.

When you think of the causes of psychological stress, your initial tendency is probably to think of events and issues directly related to yourself, such as school, work, or family pressures. And, indeed, we don't want to minimize those events as stressors. If you're like most of our students, you probably have ample first-hand experience with the stress of juggling the demands of college, work, and family responsibilities. Those pressures represent very real and personal concerns for many of us as we negotiate the challenges of daily life.

But as the terrorist attacks of September 11th unfolded, our entire nation was thrown into an extraordinary state of shared psychological stress as we watched, minute by minute, reeling in disbelief. It is impossible, of course, to convey the sense of agony, grief, and despair experienced by the thousands of people who lost loved ones as a result of the terrorist attacks on September 11th. It is equally impossible to convey the sense of relief that thousands of other people felt when they eventually learned that their loved ones—like our niece Katie—had survived the attack.

Both the extraordinary events of September 11th and the ordinary events of daily life can provide us with insights about how stress affects us and, equally important, how we cope with stress. What exactly is *stress?* It's one of those words that is frequently used but is hard to define precisely. Early stress researchers, who mostly studied animals, defined stress in terms of the physiological response to harmful or threatening events (e.g., Selye, 1956). However, people are far more complex than animals in their response to potentially stressful events. Two people may respond very differently to the same potentially stressful event.

Since the 1960s, psychologists have been actively studying the human response to stress, including the effects of stress on health and how people cope with stressful events. As research findings have accumulated, it has become clear that psychological and social factors, as well as biological factors, are involved in the stress experience and its effects.

Today, **stress** is widely defined as a negative emotional state occurring in response to events that are perceived as taxing or exceeding a person's resources or ability to cope. This definition emphasizes the important role played by a person's perception or appraisal of events in the experience of stress. Whether we experience stress depends largely on our *cognitive appraisal* of an event and the resources we have to deal with the event (Lazarus & Folkman, 1984; Tomaka & others, 1993).

If we think that we have adequate resources to deal with a situation, it will probably create little or no stress in our lives. But if we perceive our resources as being inadequate to deal with a situation we see as threatening, challenging, or even harmful, we'll experience the effects of stress. If our coping efforts are effective, stress will decrease. If they are ineffective, stress will increase.

The study of stress is a key topic in **health psychology,** one of the most rapidly growing specialty areas in psychology. Health psychology is also sometimes referred to as *behavioral medicine* or *medical psychology*. Health psychogists are interested in how biological, psychological, and social factors influence health, illness, and treatment. Along with developing strategies to foster emotional and physical well-being, they investigate issues such as the following:

- How to promote health-enhancing behaviors
- How people respond to being ill
- How people respond in the patient–health practitioner relationship
- Why some people don't follow medical advice

Health psychologists work with many different health care professionals, including physicians, dentists, nurses, social workers, and occupational and physical therapists. In their research and clinical practice, health psychologists are guided by the **biopsychosocial model.** According to this model, health and illness are determined by the complex interaction of biological factors (e.g., genetic predispositions), psychological and behavioral factors (e.g., health beliefs and attitudes, lifestyle, stress), and social conditions (e.g., family relationships, social support, cultural influences). Throughout this chapter, we'll look closely at the roles that different biological, psychological, and social factors play in our experience of stress.

Sources of Stress

Life is filled with potential **stressors**—events or situations that produce stress. Virtually any event or situation can be a source of stress if you question your ability or resources to deal effectively with it (Lazarus & Folkman, 1984). In this section, we'll survey some of the most important and common sources of stress.

Life Events and Change: Is *Any* Change Stressful?

Early stress researchers Thomas Holmes and Richard Rahe (1967) believed that any change that required you to adjust your behavior and lifestyle would cause stress. In an attempt to measure the amount of stress people experienced, they developed the *Social Readjustment Rating Scale.* The scale included 43 life events that are likely to require some level of adaptation. Each life event was assigned a numerical rating that estimates its relative impact in terms of *life change units.* Sample items from the original Social Readjustment Rating Scale are shown in Table 13.1.

Life event ratings range from 100 life change units for the most stress-producing to 11 life change units for the least stress-producing events. Cross-cultural studies have shown that people in many different cultures tend to rank the magnitude of stressful events in a similar way (McAndrew & others, 1998). Notice that some of the life events are generally considered to be positive events, such as a vacation. According to the life events approach, *any* change, whether positive or negative, is inherently stress-producing.

To measure their level of stress, people simply check off the life events they have experienced in the past year and total the life change units. Holmes and Rahe found that people who had accumulated more than 150 life change units within a year had an increased rate of physical or psychological illness (Holmes & Masuda, 1974; Rahe, 1972).

Despite its initial popularity, several problems with the life events approach have been noted. First, the link between scores on the Social Readjustment Rating Scale and the development of physical and psychological problems is relatively weak. In general, scores on the Social Readjustment Rating Scale are *not* very good predictors of poor physical or mental health. Instead, researchers have found that most people weather major life events without developing serious physical or psychological problems (Coyne & Downey, 1991; Kessler & others, 1985).

Table 13.1

The Social Readjustment Rating Scale: Sample Items

Life Event	Life Change Units
Death of spouse	100
Divorce	73
Marital separation	65
Death of close family member	63
Major personal injury or illness	53
Marriage	50
Fired at work	47
Retirement	45
Pregnancy	40
Change in financial state	38
Death of close friend	37
Change to different line of work	36
Mortgage or loan for major purchase	31
Foreclosure on mortgage or loan	30
Change in work responsibilities	29
Outstanding personal achievement	28
Begin or end school	26
Trouble with boss	23
Change in work hours or conditions	20
Change in residence	20
Change in social activities	18
Change in sleeping habits	16
Vacation	13
Christmas	12
Minor violations of the law	11

SOURCE: Holmes & Rahe (1967).

The Social Readjustment Rating Scale, developed by Thomas Holmes and Richard Rahe (1967), was an early attempt to quantify the amount of stress experienced by people in a wide range of situations. Holmes and Rahe reasoned that any life event that required some sort of adaptation or change would create stress, whether the life event was pleasant or unpleasant.

Major Life Events and Stress Would a welcome pregnancy or losing your home in a fire both produce damaging levels of stress? According to the life events approach, any event that required you to change or adjust your lifestyle would produce significant stress—whether the event was positive or negative, planned or unexpected. How was the life events approach modified by later research?

Second, the Social Readjustment Rating Scale does not take into account a person's subjective appraisal of an event, response to that event, or ability to cope with the event (Lazarus, 1999). Instead, the number of life change units on the scale is preassigned, reflecting the assumption that a given life event will have the same impact on virtually everyone. But clearly, the stress-producing potential of an event might vary widely from one person to another. For instance, if you are in a marriage that is filled with conflict, tension, and unhappiness, getting divorced (73 life change units) might be significantly less stressful than remaining married.

Third, the life events approach assumes that change in itself, whether good or bad, produces stress. However, researchers have found that negative life events have the greatest adverse effects on health, especially when they're unexpected and uncontrollable (Dohrenwend & others, 1993). In contrast, positive or desirable events are much *less* likely to affect your health adversely. Today, most researchers agree that undesirable events are significant sources of stress but that change in itself is not necessarily stressful.

Nonetheless, the Social Readjustment Rating Scale is still often used in stress research (e.g., Toews & others, 1997; York & others, 1998). And efforts have recently been made to revise and update the scale so that it more fully takes into account the influences of gender, age, marital status, and other characteristics (C. Hobson & others, 1998; M. Miller & Rahe, 1997).

Daily Hassles: That's *Not* What I Ordered!

What made you feel "stressed out" in the last week? Chances are it was not a major life event. Instead, it was probably some unexpected but minor annoyance, such as splotching ketchup on your new white T-shirt, misplacing your keys, or discovering that you've been standing in the wrong line.

Stress researcher **Richard Lazarus** and his colleagues suspected that such ordinary irritations in daily life might be an important source of stress. To explore this idea, they developed a scale measuring **daily hassles**—everyday occurrences that annoy and upset people (DeLongis & others, 1982; Kanner & others, 1981). The *Daily Hassles Scale* measures the occurrence of everyday annoyances, such as losing something, getting stuck in traffic, and even being inconvenienced by lousy weather.

Are there gender differences in the frequency of daily hassles? One study measured the daily hassles experienced by married couples (Almeida & Kessler, 1998). The women experienced both more daily hassles and higher levels of psychological stress than their husbands did. For men, the most common sources of daily stress were financial and job-related problems. For women, family demands and interpersonal conflict were the most frequent causes of stress.

What about the hassle of bad hair days? Are only women affected by them? Although it is commonly believed that men are not affected by their appearance, Yale psychologist Marianne LaFrance (2000) found that bad hair days intensify feelings of social insecurity, self-consciousness, and self-criticism for both women and men. According to LaFrance, "Individuals perceive their capabilities to be significantly lower than others when experiencing bad hair." In response to unruly hair or, worse yet, a horrible haircut, women tend to feel embarrassed or

Richard Lazarus Psychologist Richard Lazarus (b. 1922) has made several influential contributions to the study of stress and coping. His definition of stress emphasizes the importance of cognitive appraisal in the stress response. He also demonstrated the significance of everyday hassles in producing stress.

daily hassles
Everyday minor events that annoy and upset people.

self-conscious. In contrast, men tend to feel less confident and more unsociable.

How important are daily hassles in producing stress? The frequency of daily hassles is linked to both psychological distress and physical symptoms, such as headaches and backaches (DeLongis & others, 1988). In fact, the number of daily hassles people experience is a better predictor of physical illness and symptoms than is the number of major life events experienced (Burks & Martin, 1985).

Why do daily hassles take such a toll? One explanation is that such minor stressors are *cumulative* (Repetti, 1993). Each hassle may be relatively unimportant in itself, but after a day filled with minor hassles, the effects add up. People feel drained, grumpy, and stressed out. Daily hassles also contribute to the stress produced by major life events. Any major life change, whether positive or negative, can create a ripple effect, generating a host of new daily hassles (Pillow & others, 1996).

Daily Hassles Life's little hassles and irritants can be a significant source of stress—especially when they pile up. Traffic jams, slow-moving lines when you're in a hurry, and computer crashes are just a few examples of daily hassles. What daily hassles have you experienced in the past week?

For example, like many other New Yorkers, Katie had to contend with a host of daily hassles after the terrorist attacks. She had no place to live, could not get access to her clothing or other possessions, and was unable to get money from the Red Cross because her roommate's father's name was on the lease. Transportation to and around New York was frequently de-

Major Life Events, Daily Hassles, and Stress After the collapse of the two World Trade Center towers, people who lived in nearby apartments were evacuated. More than a week after the disaster, these lower Manhattan residents are waiting to be escorted by members of the National Guard to retrieve some of their possessions. Even after people were allowed to return to their homes, they had to deal with damaged apartments, air filled with smoke and dust, and a lack of basic services, like telephone service. The daily hassles created by major disasters add to the level of stress felt by those affected.

layed, and she had a persistent cough from all of the soot and fumes she had inhaled. She hated her job in the upscale clothing store, because selling overpriced leather jackets to "Fifth Avenue matrons," as she called them, seemed so inconsequential after the tragedies she had witnessed. Eventually, she quit working at the store and took on two waitressing jobs to help finance her dance lessons, pay for her new apartment, and save for college.

Conflict: Torn Between Two Choices

Another common source of stress is **conflict**—feeling pulled between two opposing desires, motives, or goals (Mellers, 2000). There are three basic types of conflict, each with a different potential to produce stress. These conflicts are described in terms of *approach* and *avoidance*. An individual is motivated to *approach* desirable or pleasant outcomes and to *avoid* undesirable or unpleasant outcomes.

An *approach–approach conflict* represents a win–win situation—you're faced with a choice between two equally appealing outcomes. As a rule, approach–approach conflicts are usually easy to resolve and don't produce much stress. More stressful are *avoidance–avoidance conflicts*—choosing between two unappealing

conflict
A situation in which a person feels pulled between two or more opposing desires, motives, or goals.

or undesirable outcomes. A common response is to avoid both outcomes by delaying the decision (Tversky & Shafir, 1992).

Most stressful are *approach–avoidance conflicts.* Here, a goal has both desirable and undesirable aspects. When faced with an approach–avoidance conflict, people often *vacillate,* unable to decide whether to approach or avoid the goal. From a distance, the desirable aspects of the goal can exert a strong pull. But as you move toward or approach the goal, the negative aspects loom more vividly in your mind, and you pull back (Epstein, 1982). Not surprisingly, people facing approach–avoidance conflicts often find themselves "stuck"—unable to resolve the conflict but unable to stop thinking about it, either (Emmons & King, 1988). The result is a significant increase in feelings of stress and anxiety.

How can you get "unstuck"? There are several things you can do to resolve an approach–avoidance conflict. First, accept the reality that very few of life's major decisions are likely to be simple, with one alternative standing head and shoulders above the others. Second, see if you can adopt a *partial approach strategy,* in which you test the waters but leave yourself an "out" before making a final decision or commitment.

Third, get as much information as you can about each option. Try to analyze objectively the pros and cons of every option. (We described this strategy of decision making in Chapter 7.) Finally, discuss the issue with a friend or someone outside the conflict. Doing so may help you see other possible rewards or pitfalls that your own analysis might have missed.

Social and Cultural Sources of Stress

Social conditions can also be an important source of stress. Racism and discrimination, whether real or suspected, can create stress (Contrada & others, 2000). Crowding, crime, unemployment, poverty, inadequate health care, and substandard housing are all associated with increased stress (Graig, 1993; Pearlin, 1993). When people live in an environment that is inherently stressful, they often experience ongoing, or *chronic,* stress (Krantz & McCeney, 2002).

People in the lowest socioeconomic levels of society tend to have the highest levels of psychological distress, illness, and death (Cohen & Williamson, 1988). In a poverty-stricken neighborhood, people are likely to be exposed to more negative life events and to have fewer resources available to cope with those events. Daily hassles are also more common.

Stress can also result when cultures clash (Berry, 1994). For refugees, immigrants, and their children, adapting to a new culture can be extremely stress producing (Shuval, 1993). In Culture and Human Behavior Box 13.1, we describe the stress that can result from adapting to a different culture.

acculturative stress
(ah-KUL-chur-uh-tiv) The stress that results from the pressure of adapting to a new culture.

CULTURE AND HUMAN BEHAVIOR 13.1

The Stress of Adapting to a New Culture

Refugees and immigrants are often unprepared for the dramatically different values, language, food, customs, and climate that await them in their new land. Coping with a new culture can be extremely stress-producing (Johnson & others, 1995). The process of changing one's values and customs as a result of contact with another culture is referred to as *acculturation.* Thus, the term **acculturative stress** describes the stress that results from the pressure of adapting to a new culture (Williams & Berry, 1991).

Many factors can influence the degree of acculturative stress that a person experiences. For example, when the new society is one that accepts ethnic and cultural diversity, acculturative stress is reduced (Shuval, 1993). The ease of transition is also enhanced when the person has some familiarity with the new language and customs, advanced education, and social support from friends, family members, and cultural associations (Berry, 1994).

Cross-cultural psychologist John Berry has found that a person's attitudes are important in determining how much acculturative stress is experienced. When people encounter a new cultural environment, they are faced with two fundamental questions: (1) Should I seek positive relations with the dominant society? (2) Is my original cultural identity of value to me, and should I try to maintain it?

The answers to these questions result in one of four possible patterns of acculturation: integration, assimilation, separation, or marginalization (see the diagram). Each pattern represents a different way of coping with the stress of

		Question 1: Should I seek positive relations with the dominant society?	
		Yes	**No**
Question 2: Is my original cultural identity of value to me, and should I try to maintain it?	**Yes**	Integration	Separation
	No	Assimilation	Marginalization

Patterns of Adapting to a New Culture According to cross-cultural psychologist John Berry (1994), there are four basic patterns of adapting to a new culture. Which pattern is followed depends on how the person responds to the two key questions shown.

adapting to a new culture (Berry, 1994, 1997). Let's briefly describe each pattern.

Integrated individuals continue to value their original cultural customs but also seek to become part of the dominant society. Ideally, the integrated individual feels comfortable in both her culture of origin and the culture of the dominant society, moving easily from one to the other (LaFromboise & others, 1993). The successfully integrated individual's level of acculturative stress will be low (Ward & Rana-Deuba, 1999).

Assimilated individuals give up their old cultural identity and try to become part of the new society. They may adopt the new clothing, religion, and social values of the new environment and abandon their old customs and language.

Assimilation usually involves a moderate level of stress, partly because it involves a psychological loss—one's previous cultural identity. People who follow this pattern also face the possibility of being

rejected either by members of the majority culture or by members of their original culture (LaFromboise & others, 1993). The process of learning new behaviors and suppressing old behaviors can also be moderately stressful.

Individuals who follow the pattern of *separation* maintain their cultural identity and avoid contact with the new culture. They may refuse to learn the new language, live in a neighborhood that is primarily populated by others of the same ethnic background, and socialize only with members of their own ethnic group.

In some instances, such withdrawal from the larger society is self-imposed. However, separation can also be the result of discrimination by the dominant society, as when people of a particular ethnic group are discouraged from fully participating in the dominant society. Not surprisingly, the level of acculturative stress associated with separation is likely to be very high.

Finally, the *marginalized* person lacks cultural and psychological contact with *both* his traditional cultural group and the culture of his new society. By taking the path of marginalization, he has lost the important features of his traditional culture, but has not replaced them with a new cultural identity.

Marginalized individuals are likely to experience the greatest degree of acculturative stress, feeling as if they don't really belong anywhere. Essentially, they are stuck in an unresolved conflict between the traditional culture and the new social environment. They are also likely to experience feelings of alienation and a loss of identity (Berry & Kim, 1988).

Acculturative Stress As this Sikh family crossing a busy street in Chicago has discovered, adapting to a new culture can be a stressful process. What factors can make the transition less stressful? How can the acculturation process be eased?

546   **CHAPTER 13** *Stress, Health, and Coping*

fight-or-flight response
A rapidly occurring chain of internal physical reactions that prepare people either to fight or take flight from an immediate threat.

FIGURE 13.1 Disrupted Sleep: One Indicator of Stress In the weeks immediately following the September 11th terrorist attacks, the psychological stress of those events was evident in the increased sleep disruptions experienced by millions of Americans. Almost a year after the attack, hundreds of the firefighters and emergency medical workers who responded to the situation continued to experience sleep disruptions as the psychological stress lingered.

SOURCE: National Sleep Foundation (2002).

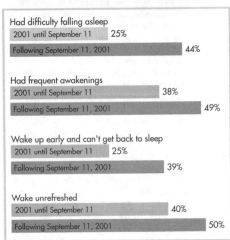

Had difficulty falling asleep
| 2001 until September 11 | 25% |
| Following September 11, 2001 | 44% |

Had frequent awakenings
| 2001 until September 11 | 38% |
| Following September 11, 2001 | 49% |

Wake up early and can't get back to sleep
| 2001 until September 11 | 25% |
| Following September 11, 2001 | 39% |

Wake unrefreshed
| 2001 until September 11 | 40% |
| Following September 11, 2001 | 50% |

Percent of American Adults Who Have Had Sleep Problems Prior to and Following September 11

Physical Effects of Stress
The Mind–Body Connection

Key Theme
■ The effects of stress on physical health were demonstrated in research by Walter Cannon and Hans Selye.

Key Questions
■ What endocrine pathways are involved in the fight-or-flight response and the general adaptation syndrome?
■ What is psychoneuroimmunology, and how does the immune system interact with the nervous system?
■ What kinds of stressors affect immune system functioning?

From headaches to heart attacks, stress contributes to a wide range of disorders, especially when it is long-term or chronic (Krantz & McCeney, 2002). Basically, stress appears to undermine physical well-being in two ways: indirectly and directly.

First, stress can *indirectly* affect a person's health by prompting behaviors that jeopardize physical well-being, such as not eating or sleeping properly (see Figure 13.1). Many studies have shown that people under chronic stress are more likely to use alcohol, coffee, and cigarettes than are people under less stress (Baer & others, 1987; Cohen & Williamson, 1988). High levels of stress can also interfere with cognitive abilities, such as attention, concentration, and memory (Mandler, 1993). In turn, such cognitive disruptions can increase the likelihood of accidents and injuries (Holt, 1993).

Second, stress can *directly* affect physical health by altering body functions, leading to symptoms, illness, or disease (Kiecolt-Glaser & others, 2002). Here's a very common example: When people are under a great deal of stress, their neck and head muscles can contract and tighten, resulting in stress-induced tension headaches. But exactly how do stressful events influence bodily processes, such as muscle contractions?

Stress and the Endocrine System

To explain the connection between stress and health, researchers have focused on how the nervous system, including the brain, interacts with two other important body systems: the endocrine and immune systems. We'll first consider the role of the endocrine system in our response to stressful events and then look at the connections between stress and the immune system.

Walter Cannon: Stress and the Fight-or-Flight Response

Any kind of immediate threat to your well-being is a stress-producing experience that triggers a cascade of changes in your body. As we've noted in previous chapters, this rapidly occurring chain of internal physical reactions is called the **fight-or-flight response.** Collectively, these changes prepare us either to fight or to take flight from an immediate threat.

The fight-or-flight response was first described by American physiologist **Walter Cannon,** one of the earliest contributors to stress research. Cannon (1932) found that the fight-or-flight response involved both the sympathetic nervous system and the endocrine system (see Chapter 2).

With the perception of a threat, the hypothalamus and lower brain structures activate the sympathetic nervous system (see left side of Figure 13.2). The sympathetic nervous system stimulates the adrenal medulla to secrete hormones called **catecholamines,** including *adrenaline* and *noradrenaline.* Circulating through the blood, catecholamines trigger the rapid and intense bodily changes associated with the fight-or-flight response. Once the threat is removed, the high level of bodily arousal subsides gradually, usually within about 20 to 60 minutes.

As a short-term reaction, the fight-or-flight response helps ensure survival by swiftly mobilizing internal physical resources to defensively attack or flee an immediate threat. Without question, the fight-or-flight response is very useful if you're suddenly faced with a life-threatening situation, such as a guy pointing a gun at you in a deserted parking lot. However, when exposure to an unavoidable threat is prolonged, the intense arousal of the fight-or-flight response can also become prolonged. Under these conditions, Cannon believed, the fight-or-flight response could prove harmful to physical health.

Walter B. Cannon (1875–1945) Cannon made many lasting contributions to psychology, including an influential theory of emotion, which we discussed in Chapter 8. During World War I, Cannon's research on the effects of stress and trauma led him to recognize the central role of the adrenal glands in mobilizing the body's resources in response to threatening circumstances—the essence of the *fight-or-flight response.* Cannon also coined the term *homeostasis,* which is the tendency of the body to maintain a steady internal state.

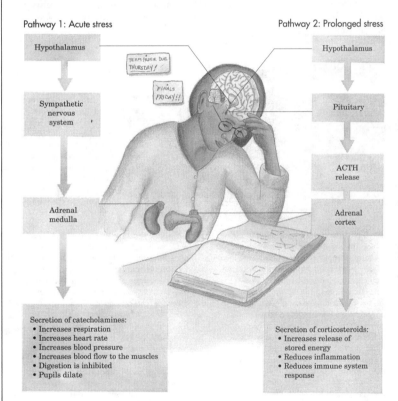

Pathway 1: Acute stress

Hypothalamus

Sympathetic nervous system

Adrenal medulla

Secretion of catecholamines:
• Increases respiration
• Increases heart rate
• Increases blood pressure
• Increases blood flow to the muscles
• Digestion is inhibited
• Pupils dilate

Pathway 2: Prolonged stress

Hypothalamus

Pituitary

ACTH release

Adrenal cortex

Secretion of corticosteroids:
• Increases release of stored energy
• Reduces inflammation
• Reduces immune system response

FIGURE 13.2 Endocrine System Pathways in Stress Two different endocrine system pathways are involved in the response to stress. Walter Cannon identified the endocrine pathway shown on the left side of this diagram. This is the pathway involved in the fight-or-flight response to immediate threats. Hans Selye identified the endocrine pathway shown on the right. This second endocrine pathway plays an important role in dealing with prolonged or chronic stressors.

Hans Selye: Stress and the General Adaptation Syndrome

Does the man in the photograph on the next page look like someone who had met and conquered stress? **Hans Selye** was the Canadian endocrinologist whose pioneering scientific investigations confirmed Cannon's suggestion that prolonged stress could be physically harmful. Most of Selye's pioneering research was done with rats that were exposed to prolonged stressors, such as electric shock, extreme heat or cold, or forced exercise. Regardless of the condition that Selye used to produce prolonged stress, he found the same pattern of physical changes in the rats.

catecholamines
(*cat*-eh-COLE-uh-meens) Hormones secreted by the adrenal medulla that cause rapid physiological arousal; include adrenaline and noradrenaline.

548   CHAPTER 13 *Stress, Health, and Coping*

A Pioneer in Stress Research With his tie off and his feet up, Canadian endocrinologist Hans Selye (1907–1982) looks the very picture of relaxation. Selye's research at the University of Montreal documented the physical effects of exposure to prolonged stress. His popular book *The Stress of Life* (1956) helped make stress a household word.

First, the adrenal glands became enlarged. Second, stomach ulcers and loss of weight occurred. And third, there was shrinkage of the thymus gland and lymph glands, two key components of the immune system. Selye believed that these distinct physical changes represented the essential effects of stress—the body's response to any demand placed on it.

Selye discovered that if the bodily "wear and tear" of the stress-producing event continued, the effects became evident in three progressive stages. He called these stages the **general adaptation syndrome.** During the initial *alarm stage,* intense arousal occurs as the body mobilizes internal physical resources to meet the demands of the stress-producing event. Selye (1976) found that the rapidly occurring changes during the alarm stage result from the release of catecholamines by the adrenal medulla, as Cannon had previously described.

In the *resistance stage,* the body actively tries to resist or adjust to the continuing stressful situation. The intense arousal of the alarm stage diminishes, but physiological arousal remains above normal and resistance to new stressors is impaired.

focus on **Neuroscience**

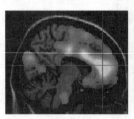
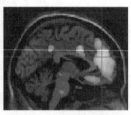

Received opiate painkiller   **Received placebo**

Mind, Body, and the Mysterious Placebo Effect The *placebo effect* is perhaps one of the most dramatic examples of how the mind influences the body. A *placebo* is an inactive substance with no known effects, like a sugar pill or an injection of sterile water. Placebos are often used in biomedical research to help gauge the effectiveness of an actual medication or treatment. But after being given a placebo, many research participants, including those suffering from pain or diseases, experience benefits from the placebo treatment. How can this be explained?

In Chapter 2 we noted that one possible way that placebos might reduce pain is by activating the brain's own natural painkillers—the *endorphins.* The endorphins are structurally similar to opiate painkillers, like morphine. One reason for believing this is that a drug called *naloxone,* which blocks the brain's endorphin response, also blocks the painkilling effects of placebos (Fields & Levine, 1984). Might placebos reduce pain by activating the brain's natural opioid network?

A brain-imaging study by Swedish neuroscientist Predrag Petrovic and his colleagues (2002) tackled this question. In the study, painfully hot metal was placed on the back of each volunteer's hand. Each volunteer was then given an injection of either an actual opioid painkiller or a saline solution placebo. About 30 seconds later, positron emission tomography (PET) was used to scan the participants' brain activity.

Both the volunteers who received the painkilling drug *and* the volunteers who received the placebo treatment reported that the injection provided pain relief. In the two PET scans shown here, you can see that the genuine painkilling drug (left) and the placebo (right) activated the same brain area, called the *anterior cingulate cortex* (marked by the cross). The anterior cingulate cortex is known to contain many opioid receptors. Interestingly, the level of brain activity was directly correlated with the participants' subjective perception of pain relief. The right PET scan shows the brain activity of those participants who had strong placebo responses.

Although questions remain about exactly how placebos can produce their effects, the PET scan study by Petrovic and his colleagues (2002) vividly substantiates the mind–body interaction. Clearly, "higher" mental processes—such as cognitive expectations, learned associations, and emotional responses—can have a profound effect on the perception of pain. Other studies have shown that placebos produce measurable effects on other types of brain processes, including those of people experiencing Parkinson's disease or major depression (Fuente-Fernandez & others, 2001; Leuchter & others, 2002).

general adaptation syndrome
Selye's term for the three-stage progression of physical changes that occur when an organism is exposed to intense and prolonged stress. The three stages are alarm, resistance, and exhaustion.

corticosteroids
Hormones released by the adrenal cortex that play a key role in the body's response to long-term stressors.

immune system
Body system that produces specialized white blood cells that protect the body from viruses, bacteria, and tumor cells.

lymphocytes
Specialized white blood cells that are responsible for immune defenses.

If the stress-producing event persists, the *exhaustion stage* may occur. In this third stage, the symptoms of the alarm stage reappear, only now irreversibly. As the body's energy reserves become depleted, adaptation begins to break down, leading to exhaustion, physical disorders, and, potentially, death.

Selye (1956, 1976) found that prolonged stress activates a second endocrine pathway (see Figure 13.2) that involves the hypothalamus, the pituitary gland, and the adrenal cortex. In response to a stressor, the hypothalamus signals the pituitary gland to secrete a hormone called *adrenocorticotropic hormone,* abbreviated *ACTH.* In turn, ACTH stimulates the adrenal cortex to release stress-related hormones called **corticosteroids,** the most important of which is *cortisol.*

In the short run, the corticosteroids provide several benefits, helping protect the body against the harm caused by stressors. For example, corticosteroids reduce inflammation of body tissues and enhance muscle tone in the heart and blood vessels. However, unlike the effects of catecholamines, which tend to diminish rather quickly, corticosteroids have long-lasting effects. If a stressor is prolonged, continued high levels of corticosteroids can weaken important body systems, lowering immunity and increasing susceptibility to physical symptoms and illness. Chronic stress can also lead to depression and other psychological problems (Nemeroff, 1998).

Selye's pioneering studies are widely regarded as the cornerstone of modern stress research. His description of the general adaptation syndrome firmly established some of the critical biological links between stress-producing events and their potential impact on physical health. But as you'll see in the next section, the endocrine system is only part of the equation in the mind–body connection between stress and health.

Stress and the Immune System

Stress can diminish the effectiveness of the immune system. The **immune system** is your body's surveillance system. It detects and battles foreign invaders, such as bacteria, viruses, and tumor cells. Your immune system comprises several organs, including bone marrow, the spleen, the thymus, and lymph nodes (see Figure 13.3). The most important elements of the immune system are **lymphocytes**—the specialized white blood cells that fight bacteria, viruses, and other foreign invaders. Lymphocytes are initially manufactured in the bone marrow. From the bone marrow, they migrate to other immune system organs, such as the thymus and spleen, where they develop more fully and are stored until needed.

Until the 1970s, the immune system was thought to be completely independent of other body systems. Many scientists believed that the nervous system, the endocrine system, and psychological processes had no impact on immune system functioning. As you'll see in this section, the scientific view of the immune system has changed dramatically in the last few decades.

FIGURE 13.3 The Immune System Your immune system battles bacteria, viruses, and other foreign invaders that try to set up housekeeping in your body. The specialized white blood cells that fight infection are manufactured in the bone marrow and are stored in the thymus, spleen, and lymph nodes until needed.

Thymus — Lymph nodes
— Spleen
Lymph nodes
Lymphatic vessels
Bone marrow — Lymph nodes

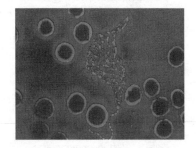

Lymphocytes in Action In this color-enhanced photo, you can see white blood cells, or lymphocytes, attacking and ingesting the beadlike chain of streptococcus bacteria, which can cause diseases such as pneumonia and scarlet fever.

Ader and Cohen: Conditioning the Immune System

The notion that the immune system operated independently was challenged in the mid-1970s, when psychologist **Robert Ader** teamed up with immunologist Nicholas Cohen. As Ader (1993) recalled, "You have to understand that as a

Conditioning the Immune System
Psychologist Robert Ader (*left*) teamed with immunologist Nicholas Cohen (*right*) and demonstrated that immune system responses could be classically conditioned. Ader and Cohen's groundbreaking research helped lead to the new field of psychoneuroimmunology—the study of the connections among psychological processes, the nervous system, and the immune system.

psychoneuroimmunology
An interdisciplinary field that studies the interconnections among psychological processes, nervous and endocrine system functions, and the immune system.

psychologist, I was not aware of the general position of immunology that there were no connections between the brain and the immune system." In their landmark study, Ader and Cohen (1975) demonstrated that immune system functions could be influenced by the brain. They did so by showing that the immune system response in rats could be classically conditioned.

Using the same basic procedure that Pavlov used to condition dogs to salivate in response to the sound of a bell (see Chapter 5), Ader and Cohen (1975) paired saccharin-flavored water with a drug (cyclophosphamide) that suppressed immune system functioning. After being paired with the drug, the saccharin-flavored water *alone* suppressed the rat's immune system. As Ader (1993) explained, "In effect, we had demonstrated that learning processes could influence immune responses. The experiment was a direct and rather dramatic demonstration of a relationship between nervous system function and immune function."

Ader and Cohen's study was important for two reasons. First, it challenged the prevailing scientific view that the immune system operated independently of the brain and psychological processes. Since the publication of Ader and Cohen's research, hundreds of other studies have demonstrated that immune system responses can be conditioned to various stimuli (see Ader & Cohen, 1991, 1993).

Second, Ader and Cohen's study triggered interest in other possible influences on the immune system, including the effects of stress and emotional states. By stimulating diverse lines of research, Ader and Cohen's study helped establish a new interdisciplinary field, called psychoneuroimmunology (Ader, 2001). **Psychoneuroimmunology** is the scientific study of the interconnections among psychological processes (*psycho-*), the nervous and endocrine systems (*-neuro-*), and the immune system (*-immunology*).

In the last decade, researchers in psychoneuroimmunology have made many important discoveries (see Vitkovic, 1995). First, they discovered that the central nervous system and the immune system are *directly* linked. Sympathetic nervous system fibers go into virtually every organ of the immune system, where they directly influence the production and functioning of lymphocytes.

Second, the surfaces of lymphocytes contain receptor sites for neurotransmitters and hormones, including catecholamines and cortisol. Thus, rather than operating independently, the activities of lymphocytes and the immune system are directly influenced by neurotransmitters, hormones, and other chemical messengers from the nervous and endocrine systems.

Third, psychoneuroimmunologists have discovered that lymphocytes themselves *produce* neurotransmitters and hormones. These neurotransmitters and hormones, in turn, influence the nervous and endocrine systems. In other words, there is ongoing interaction and communication among the nervous system, the endocrine system, and the immune system. Each system influences *and* is influenced by the other systems (Ader, 2001).

Stressors That Can Influence the Immune System

When researchers began studying how stress affects the immune system, they initially focused on extremely stressful events (see Kiecolt-Glaser & Glaser, 1993). For example, researchers looked at how the immune system was affected by such intense stressors as the reentry and splashdown of returning *Skylab* astronauts, being forced to stay awake for days, and fasting for a week (Kimzey, 1975; Leach & Rambaut, 1974; Palmblad & others, 1979). Each of these highly stressful events, it turned out, was associated with reduced immune system functioning.

Could immune system functioning also be affected by more common negative life events, such as the death of a spouse, divorce, or marital separation? In a word, yes. Researchers consistently found that the stress caused by the end or disruption of important interpersonal relationships impairs immune function, putting people at greater risk for health problems (Kiecolt-Glaser, 1999; Kiecolt-Glaser & Newton, 2001). And perhaps not surprisingly, chronic stressors that continue for years, such as caring for a family member with Alzheimer's disease, also diminish immune system functioning (see Kiecolt-Glaser & others, 2002).

What about the ordinary stressors of life, such as the pressure of exams? Do they affect immune system functioning? Since 1982, psychologist **Janice Kiecolt-Glaser** and her husband, immunologist Ronald Glaser, have collected immunological and psychological data from medical students. Several times each academic year, the medical students face three-day examination periods. Kiecolt-Glaser and Glaser (1991, 1993) have consistently found that even the rather commonplace stress of exams adversely affects the immune system.

What are the practical implications of reduced immune system functioning? One consistent finding is that psychological stress can increase the length of time it takes for a wound to heal. In one study, dental students volunteered to receive two small puncture wounds on the roof of their mouths (Marucha & others, 1998). To compare the impact of stress on wound healing, the students received the first wound when they were on summer vacation and the second wound three days before their first major exam during the fall term. The results? The wounds inflicted before the major test healed an average of 40 percent more slowly—an extra three days—than the wounds inflicted on the same volunteers during summer vacation. Other studies have shown similar findings (see Kiecolt-Glaser & Glaser, 2001).

Taken together, the research evidence suggests that a wide variety of stressors are associated with diminished immune system functioning, putting us at greater risk for health problems and slower recovery times (Kiecolt-Glaser & others, 1998, 2002). In Focus Box 13.2 on the next page describes another compelling study demonstrating the relationship between stress and a health risk to which we are all frequently exposed: the common cold virus.

While stress-related decreases in immune system functioning may heighten our susceptibility to health problems, exposure to stressors does not automatically translate into poorer health. Your physical health is affected by the interaction of many factors, such as your unique genetic makeup, nutrition, exercise, personal habits, and access to medical care. Also required, of course, is exposure to bacteria, viruses, and other disease-causing agents.

It's also important to keep in mind that the stress-induced decreases in immune system functioning that have been demonstrated experimentally are often small. As psychoneuroimmunology researchers are careful to note, these small decreases in immune function may not translate into an added health risk for most people. As Kiecolt-Glaser and Glaser (1993) have explained:

> Our best understanding at this point is that the people most likely to become ill in response to stress are probably those whose immune systems are already compromised to some extent, either by a disease like AIDS or by a natural process like aging. These people start out with poorer immunological defenses, so that small changes associated with stress could have more important consequences. But even young, generally healthy people may find themselves getting sick more often if they are subject to severe or ongoing, long-term stress.

Finally, the simple fact is that some people are more vulnerable to the negative effects of stress than others (Adler & Matthews, 1994). Why? As you'll see in the next section, researchers have found that a wide variety of psychological factors can influence people's reactions to stressors.

Ron Glaser and Janice Kiecolt-Glaser Two of the leading researchers in psychoneuroimmunology are psychologist Janice Kiecolt-Glaser and her husband, immunologist Ron Glaser. Their research has shown that the effectiveness of the immune system can be lowered by many common stressors—from marital arguments to caring for sick relatives.

Can Exams Be Hazardous to Your Health? From studies of medical students, Kiecolt-Glaser and Glaser have shown that the common student stressor of taking exams can lower the effectiveness of the immune system.

552   **CHAPTER 13** *Stress, Health, and Coping*

IN FOCUS 13.2

Stress and the Common Cold

Does stress increase your susceptibility to the common cold? That's certainly what many people believe. But if you think critically about the matter, other explanations are possible. For example, it may be that high-stressed people interact with more people than low-stressed people. In turn, this would mean that high-stressed people have more opportunities for exposure to cold viruses. Or it could be that stressed-out people engage in more health-compromising behaviors, such as smoking, eating poorly, not exercising, and not getting enough sleep.

Psychologist Sheldon Cohen and his colleagues (1991, 1993) tackled such issues in a carefully controlled experiment. More than 400 healthy volunteers underwent a thorough medical examination and completed questionnaires assessing their stress levels and health behaviors. The participants were then given nasal drops containing either a cold virus or salt water. For two days before and seven days after receiving the drops, the participants were quarantined together in apartments. Each day during the study, the participants were medically examined for any signs or symptoms of a cold. Blood samples were also monitored for evidence of infection.

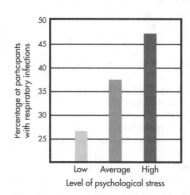

The results? Of the people exposed to cold virus, one factor stood out in determining the rate of infection: the level of stress. The researchers found an almost perfect relationship between the level of stress and the rate of respiratory infection and colds. Put simply, the higher the psychological stress score, the higher the rate of respiratory infection and colds.

Could it be that other factors, such as health-compromising behaviors, were underlying the stress–illness connection? Not at all. The stress–illness effect held even when the researchers took into ac-count the number of participants housed together, whether roommates were also infectious, and the participants' age, sex, smoking, alcohol consumption, exercise, diet, and quality of sleep. In other words, *none* of these factors could account for the relationship between stress and increased susceptibility to infection (Cohen & others, 1991, 1993).

In a later study, Cohen and his colleagues (1998) found that particular kinds of life stresses seemed to be most highly associated with susceptibility to infection. People who experienced *chronic* stressors that lasted more than a month were more than twice as likely to develop colds than people who were not under chronic stress. The longer the duration of the stressor, the greater was the risk for colds. Unemployment, problems at work, and interpersonal conflict were among the chronic stressors that were associated with increased susceptibility to disease.

So how does stress increase our susceptibility to colds and infections? Basically, stress reduces the effectiveness of the immune system and its ability to fight off viruses, bacteria, and other foreign invaders (see Kiecolt-Glaser & Glaser, 1991, 1993).

13.1 R·E·V·I·E·W

C·O·N·C·E·P·T

Sources and Effects of Stress

Indicate whether each of the following items is true or false. Rewrite each false statement to correct it.

_____ *1.* According to the biopsychosocial model, physical well-being is wholly determined by stress and social adjustment.

_____ *2.* In the past year, Andrea has gotten divorced, changed jobs, moved three times, and lost her closest friend in an auto accident. Because of the number of stress-producing life events Andrea has experienced, she is certain to develop a major illness in the next six months.

_____ *3.* The level of stress due to daily hassles is measured by the Social Readjustment Rating Scale.

_____ *4.* During periods of prolonged stress, the adrenal medulla secretes stress-related hormones called catecholamines.

_____ *5.* Shelley's manager has just unexpectedly informed her that she is being laid off, effective immediately. Shelley is probably experiencing the "exhaustion" stage of the general adaptation syndrome.

_____ *6.* The study of interconnections among the nervous system, immune system, endocrine system, and psychological factors is called *psychoneuroimmunology.*

Individual Factors That Influence the Response to Stress

Key Theme
- ∎ Psychologists have identified several psychological factors that can modify an individual's response to stress and affect physical health.

Key Questions
- ∎ How do feelings of control, explanatory style, and negative emotions influence stress and health?
- ∎ What is Type A behavior, and what role does hostility play in the relationship between Type A behavior and health?

People vary a great deal in the way they respond to a distressing event, whether it's a parking ticket or a pink slip. In part, individual differences in reacting to stressors result from how people appraise an event and their resources for coping with the event. However, psychologists and other researchers have identified several different factors that influence an individual's response to stressful events. In this section, we'll take a look at some of the most important psychological and social factors that seem to affect an individual's response to stress.

Psychological Factors

It's easy to demonstrate the importance of psychological factors in the response to stressors. Sit in any airport waiting room during a busy holiday travel season and observe how differently people react to news of flight cancellations or delays. Some people take the news calmly, while others become enraged and indignant. Psychologists have confirmed what common sense suggests: Psychological processes play a key role in determining the level of stress experienced.

Personal Control

Who is more likely to experience more stress, a person who has some control over a stressful experience or a person who has no control? Psychological research has consistently shown that having a sense of control over a stressful situation reduces the impact of stressors and decreases feelings of anxiety and depression (Taylor & others, 1991; Thompson & Spacapan, 1991). Those who can control a stress-producing event often show no more psychological distress or physical arousal than people who are not exposed to the stressor.

Psychologists Judith Rodin and Ellen Langer (1977) demonstrated the importance of a sense of control in a classic series of studies with nursing home residents. One group of residents—the "high-control" group—was given the opportunity to make choices about their daily activities and to exercise control over their environment. For example, the residents were allowed to determine where they would receive visitors and when they would attend a movie screening. In contrast, the "low-control" group had little control over their daily activities. Decisions were made for them by the nursing home staff.

Rodin and Langer found that having a sense of control over their environment had powerful effects on the nursing home residents. Eighteen months later, the high-control residents were more active, alert, sociable,

Uncontrollable Stressors There was nothing this man could do to protect his apartment, which faced the World Trade Center towers. A month after the terrorist attacks, he surveys his damaged possessions and sorts through the wreckage that was once his home. Psychological research has shown that stressors that are experienced as beyond your control can be especially damaging to physical and mental health.

and healthier than the low-control residents. Members of the high-control group were also more likely to be alive: twice as many of the low-control residents had died (Langer & Rodin, 1976; Rodin & Langer, 1977).

How does a sense of control affect health? If you feel that you can control a stressor by taking steps to minimize or avoid it, you will experience less stress, both subjectively and physiologically (Thompson & Spacapan, 1991). Having a sense of personal control also works to our benefit by enhancing positive emotions, such as self-confidence and feelings of self-efficacy, autonomy, and self-reliance (Burger, 1992). In contrast, feeling a lack of control over events produces all the hallmarks of the stress response. Levels of catecholamines and corticosteroids increase, and the effectiveness of immune system functioning decreases (see Maier & Watkins, 2000; Rodin, 1986).

However, the perception of personal control in a stressful situation must be *realistic* to be adaptive (Helgeson, 1992; Taylor & others, 1991). Studies of people with chronic diseases, like heart disease and arthritis, have shown that unrealistic perceptions of personal control contribute to stress and poor adjustment (Affleck & others, 1987a, 1987b). But, even in low-control situations, there is often some aspect of the overall situation that people can realistically influence.

For example, Suzanne Thompson and her colleagues (1993) found that the best-adjusted cancer patients accepted the fact that they could not actually control the course of their disease. Rather, they focused on what they realistically could do to control the *consequences* of the disease. They exercised control by managing their emotions, seeking medical information, improving their personal relationships, and changing their diet. In this way, they lowered their subjective level of stress and increased their sense of personal well-being.

Explanatory Style: Optimism Versus Pessimism

We all experience defeat, rejection, or failure at some point in our lives. Yet despite repeated failures, rejections, or defeats, some people persist in their efforts. In contrast, some people give up in the face of failure and setbacks—the essence of *learned helplessness,* which we discussed in chapter 5. What distinguishes between those who persist and those who give up?

According to psychologist **Martin Seligman** (1990, 1992), how people characteristically explain their failures and defeats makes the difference. People who have an **optimistic explanatory style** tend to use *external, unstable,* and *specific* explanations for negative events. In contrast, people who have a **pessimistic explanatory style** use *internal, stable,* and *global* explanations for negative events. Pessimists are also inclined to believe that no amount of personal effort will improve their situation. Not surprisingly, pessimists tend to experience more stress than optimists.

Let's look at these two explanatory styles in action. Optimistic Olive sees an attractive guy at a party and starts across the room to introduce herself and strike up a conversation. As she approaches him, the guy glances at her, then abruptly turns away. Hurt by the obvious snub, Optimistic Olive retreats to the buffet table. Munching on some fried zucchini, she mulls the matter over in her mind. At the same party, Pessimistic Pete sees an attractive female across the room and approaches her. He, too, gets a cold shoulder and retreats to the chips and clam dip. Standing at opposite ends of the buffet table, here is what each of them is thinking:

OPTIMISTIC OLIVE: *What's* his *problem? (External explanation: The optimist blames other people or external circumstances.)*

PESSIMISTIC PETE: *I must have said the wrong thing. She probably saw me stick my elbow in the clam dip before I walked over. (Internal explanation: The pessimist blames self.)*

How Do You Explain Your Setbacks and Failures? Everyone experiences setbacks, rejection, and failure at some point. The way you explain your setbacks has a significant impact on motivation and on mental and physical health. If the owner of this store blames his business failure on temporary and external factors, such as a short-lived downturn in the economy, he might be more likely to try opening a new store in the future.

OPTIMISTIC OLIVE: *I'm really not looking my best tonight. I've just got to get more sleep.* (Unstable, temporary *explanation*)

PESSIMISTIC PETE: *Let's face it, I'm a pretty boring guy and really not very good-looking.* (Stable, permanent *explanation*)

OPTIMISTIC OLIVE: *He looks pretty preoccupied. Maybe he's waiting for his girlfriend to arrive. Or his boyfriend! Ha!* (Specific *explanations*)

PESSIMISTIC PETE: *Women never give me a second look, probably because I dress like a nerd and I never know what to say to them.* (Global, pervasive *explanation*)

OPTIMISTIC OLIVE: *Whoa! Who's that hunk over there?! Okay, Olive, turn on the charm! Here goes!* (Perseverance *after a rejection*)

PESSIMISTIC PETE: *Maybe I'll just hold down this corner of the buffet table . . . or go home and soak up some TV.* (Passivity *and* withdrawal *after a rejection*)

> **optimistic explanatory style**
> Accounting for negative events or situations with external, unstable, and specific explanations.
>
> **pessimistic explanatory style**
> Accounting for negative events or situations with internal, stable, and global explanations.

Most people, of course, are neither as completely optimistic as Olive nor as totally pessimistic as Pete. Instead, they fall somewhere along the spectrum of optimism and pessimism, and their explanatory style may vary somewhat in different situations (Peterson & Bossio, 1993). Even so, a person's characteristic explanatory style, particularly for negative events, is relatively stable across the lifespan (Burns & Seligman, 1989).

Like personal control, explanatory style is related to health consequences (Gilham & others, 2001). One study showed that explanatory style in early adulthood predicted physical health status decades later. On the basis of interviews conducted at age 25, explanatory style was evaluated for a large group of Harvard graduates. At the time of the interviews, all the young men were in excellent physical and mental health. Thirty-five years later, however, those who had an optimistic explanatory style were significantly healthier than those with a pessimistic explanatory style. They also were more likely to be alive (Peterson & others, 1988).

Other studies have shown that a pessimistic explanatory style is associated with poorer physical health, including increased occurrences of infectious disease (Peterson & Bossio, 2001). A recent study of first-year law school students confirmed the benefits of optimism (Segerstrom & others, 1998). Students who had an optimistic, confident, and generally positive outlook experienced fewer negative moods than students who were more pessimistic. And, in terms of their immune system measures, the optimistic students had significantly higher levels of lymphocytes, T cells, and helper T cells than the pessimistic students.

Chronic Negative Emotions: The Hazards of Being Grouchy

Everyone experiences an occasional bad mood. However, some people almost always seem to be unhappy campers—they frequently experience bad moods and negative emotions (Marshall & others, 1992; Watson & Pennebaker, 1989). Are people who are prone to chronic negative emotions more likely to suffer health problems?

Howard S. Friedman and Stephanie Booth-Kewley (1987) set out to answer this question. After systematically analyzing more than 100 studies investigating the potential links between personality factors and disease, they concluded that people who are habitually anxious, depressed, angry, or hostile *are* more likely to develop a chronic disease such as arthritis or heart disease.

Calvin and Hobbes   by Bill Watterson

Type A behavior pattern
A behavioral and emotional style characterized by a sense of time urgency, hostility, and competitiveness.

How might chronic negative emotions predispose people to develop disease? Not surprisingly, tense, angry, and unhappy people experience more stress than do happier people. They also report more frequent and more intense daily hassles than people who are generally in a positive mood (Bolger & Schilling, 1991; Bolger & Zuckerman, 1995). And they react much more intensely, and with far greater distress, to stressful events (Marco & Suls, 1993).

Of course, everyone occasionally experiences bad moods. Are transient negative moods also associated with health risks? One series of studies investigated the relationship between daily mood and immune system functioning (Stone & others, 1987, 1994). For three months, participants recorded their mood every day. On the days on which they experienced negative events and moods, the effectiveness of their immune system dipped. But their immune system improved on the days on which they experienced positive events and good moods.

Type A Behavior and Hostility

The concept of Type A behavior originated about 30 years ago, when two cardiologists, Meyer Friedman and Ray Rosenman, noticed that many of their patients shared certain traits. The original formulation of the **Type A behavior pattern** included a cluster of three characteristics: (1) an exaggerated sense of time urgency, often trying to do more and more in less and less time; (2) a general sense of hostility, frequently displaying anger and irritation; and (3) intense ambition and competitiveness. In contrast, people who were more relaxed and laid back were classified as displaying the *Type B behavior pattern* (Janisse & Dyck, 1988; Rosenman & Chesney, 1982).

Friedman and Rosenman (1974) interviewed and classified more than 3,000 middle-aged, healthy men as either Type A or Type B. They tracked the health of these men for eight years and found that Type A men were twice as likely to develop heart disease as Type B men. This held true even when the Type A men did not display other known risk factors for heart disease, such as smoking, high blood pressure, and elevated levels of cholesterol in their blood. The conclusion seemed clear: The Type A behavior pattern was a significant risk factor for heart disease.

Although early results linking the Type A behavior pattern to heart disease were impressive, studies soon began to appear in which Type A behavior did *not* reliably predict the development of heart disease (see Krantz & McCeney, 2002). These findings led researchers to question whether the different components of the Type A behavior pattern were equally hazardous to health. After all, many people thrive on hard work, especially when they enjoy their jobs. And high achievers don't necessarily suffer from health problems (Robbins & others, 1991).

The Type A Behavior Pattern The original formulation of the Type A behavior pattern included hostility, ambition, and a sense of time urgency. Type A people always seem to be in a hurry, hate wasting time, and often try to do two or more things at once. Do you think any of the people in this photograph might qualify as Type A?

When researchers focused on the association between heart disease and each separate component of the Type A behavior pattern—time urgency, achievement striving, and hostility—an important distinction began to emerge. Feeling a sense of time urgency and being competitive or achievement-oriented did *not* seem to be associated with the development of heart disease. Instead, the critical component that emerged as the strongest predictor of cardiac disease was hostility (Miller & others, 1996). *Hostility* refers to the tendency to feel anger, annoyance, resentment, and contempt and to hold negative beliefs about human nature in general. Hostile people are also prone to believing that the disagreeable behavior of others is intentionally directed against them. Thus, hostile people tend to be suspicious, mistrustful, cynical, and pessimistic (Barefoot, 1992).

Hostile men and women are much more likely than other people to develop heart disease. In one study that covered a 25-year span, hostile men were five times as likely to develop heart disease and nearly seven times as likely to die as nonhostile men (Barefoot & others, 1983). The results of this prospective study are shown in Figure 13.4. Subsequent research has found that high hostility levels increase the likelihood of dying from *all* natural causes, including cancer (Miller & others, 1996).

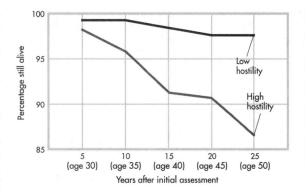

FIGURE 13.4 Hostility and Mortality Beginning when they were in medical school, more than 250 doctors were monitored for their health status for 25 years. In this prospective study, those who had scored high in hostility in medical school were seven times more likely to die by age 50 than were those who had scored low in hostility.

SOURCE: Based on Barefoot & others (1983), p. 61.

How does hostility predispose people to heart disease and other health problems? First, hostile Type A's tend to react more intensely to a stressor than other people do (Lyness, 1993). They experience greater increases in blood pressure, heart rate, and the production of stress-related hormones. Because of their attitudes and behavior, hostile men and women also tend to *create* more stress in their own lives. They experience more frequent, and more severe, negative life events and daily hassles than other people (Smith, 1992).

In general, the research evidence demonstrating the role of personality factors in the development of stress-related diseases is impressive. However, it's important to keep in mind that personality characteristics are just some of the risk factors involved in the overall picture of health and disease (Adler & Matthews, 1994; Cohen & Herbert, 1996). We look at this issue in more detail in Critical Thinking Box 13.3.

13.2 R·E·V·I·E·W

C·O·N·C·E·P·T

Psychological Factors and Stress

Identify the psychological characteristic that is best illustrated by each of the examples below. Choose from the following:

  a. high level of personal control
  b. optimistic explanatory style
  c. Type A behavior pattern
  d. Type B behavior pattern
  e. pessimistic explanatory style
  f. chronic negative emotions

_____ *1.* No matter what happens to her, Lucy is dissatisfied and grumpy. She constantly complains about her health, her job, and how awful her life is. She dislikes most of the people she meets.

_____ *2.* Cheryl was despondent when she received a low grade on her algebra test. She said, "I never do well on exams because I'm not very smart. I might as well drop out of school now before I flunk out."

_____ *3.* In order to deal with the high levels of stress associated with returning to college full-time, Pat selected her courses carefully, arranged her work and study schedules to make the best use of her time, and scheduled time for daily exercise and social activities.

_____ *4.* Richard is a very competitive, ambitious stockbroker who is easily irritated by small inconveniences. If he thinks that someone or something is wasting his time, he blows up and becomes completely enraged.

_____ *5.* Max flubbed an easy free throw in the big basketball game but told his coach, "My game was off today because I'm still getting over the flu and I pulled a muscle in practice yesterday. I'll do better in next week's game."

558 CHAPTER 13 *Stress, Health, and Coping*

CRITICAL THINKING 13.3

Do Personality Factors Cause Disease?

■ You overhear a co-worker saying, "I'm not surprised he had a heart attack—the guy is a workaholic!"

■ An acquaintance casually remarks, "She's been so depressed since her divorce. No wonder she got cancer."

■ A tabloid headline hails, "New Scientific Findings: Use Your Mind to Cure Cancer!"

Statements like these make health psychologists, physicians, and psychoneuro-immunologists extremely uneasy. Why? Throughout this chapter, we've presented scientific evidence that emotional states can affect the functioning of the endocrine system and the immune system. Both systems play a significant role in the development of various physical disorders. We've also shown that personality factors, such as hostility and pessimism, are associated with an increased likelihood of developing poor health. But saying that "emotions affect the immune system" is a far cry from making such claims as "a positive attitude can cure cancer."

Psychologists and other scientists are cautious in the statements they make about the connections between personality and health for several reasons. First, many studies investigating the role of psychological factors in disease are *correlational*. That is, researchers have statistical evidence that two factors happen together so often that the presence of one factor reliably predicts the occurrence of the other. However, correlation does not necessarily indicate causality—it indi-

"What do you mean, I have an ulcer? I give ulcers, I don't get them!"

cates only that two factors occur together. It's completely possible that some third, unidentified factor may have caused the other two factors to occur.

Second, personality factors might indirectly lead to disease via poor health habits. Low control, pessimism, chronic negative emotions, and hostility are each associated with poor health habits (Herbert & Cohen, 1993; Peterson, 2000). In turn, poor health habits are associated with higher rates of illness. That's why psychologists who study the role of personality factors in disease are typically careful to measure and consider the possible influence of the participants' health practices.

Third, it may be that the disease influences a person's emotions, rather than the other way around. After being diag-

nosed with advanced cancer or heart disease, most people would probably find it difficult to feel cheerful, optimistic, or in control of their lives.

One way researchers try to disentangle the relationship between personality and health is to conduct carefully controlled prospective studies. A *prospective study* starts by assessing an initially healthy group of participants on variables thought to be risk factors, such as certain personality traits. Then the researchers track the health, personal habits, health habits, and other important dimensions of the participants' lives over a period of months, years, or decades. In analyzing the results, researchers can determine the extent to which each risk factor contributed to the health or illness of the participants. Thus, prospective studies provide more compelling evidence than do correlational studies that are based on people who are already in poor health.

Critical Thinking Questions

■ Given that health professionals frequently advise people to change their health-related behaviors to improve physical health, should they also advise people to change their psychological attitudes, traits, and emotions? Why or why not?

■ What are the advantages and disadvantages of prospective studies?

Social Factors: A Little Help from Your Friends

Key Theme
■ Social support refers to the resources provided by other people.

Key Questions
■ How has social support been shown to benefit health?
■ How can relationships and social connections sometimes increase stress?
■ What gender differences have been found in social support and its effects?

Psychologists have become increasingly aware of the importance that close relationships play in our ability to deal with stressors and, ultimately, in our physical health. Consider the following research evidence:

■ Patients with advanced breast cancer who attended weekly support group sessions survived twice as long as a matched group of patients with equally advanced cancer who did not attend support groups. Both groups of women received comparable medical treatment. The added survival time for those who attended support group sessions was longer than that which could have been provided by any known medical treatment (Spiegel, 1993b; Spiegel & others, 1989).

■ After monitoring the health of 2,800 people for seven years, researchers found that people who had no one to talk to about their problems were three times as likely to die after being hospitalized for a heart attack than were those who had at least one person to provide such support (Berkman & others, 1992).

■ The health of nearly 7,000 adults was tracked for nine years. Those who had few social connections were twice as likely to die from all causes than were those who had numerous social contacts, even when risk factors such as cigarette smoking, obesity, and elevated cholesterol levels were taken into account (Berkman, 1995; Berkman & Syme, 1979).

■ In a study begun in the 1950s, college students rated their parents' level of love and caring. More than 40 years later, 87 percent of those who had rated their parents as being "low" in love and caring had been diagnosed with a serious physical disease. In contrast, only 25 percent of those who had rated their parents as being "high" in love and caring had been diagnosed with a serious physical disease (Russek & Schwartz, 1997).

The Health Benefits of Companionship This married couple in their seventies are enjoying an afternoon of cross-country skiing. Numerous research studies have shown that married people and couples live longer than people who are single, divorced, or widowed (Burman & Margolin, 1992). How do close relationships benefit health?

These are just a few of the hundreds of studies conducted in the last few years exploring how interpersonal relationships influence our health and ability to tolerate stress. To investigate the role played by personal relationships in stress and health, psychologists measure the level of **social support**—the resources provided by other people in times of need (Hobfoll & Stephens, 1990). Repeatedly, researchers have found that socially isolated people have poorer health and higher death rates than people who have many social contacts or relationships (Uchino & others, 1996). In fact, social isolation seems to be just as potent a health risk as smoking, high blood cholesterol, obesity, and physical inactivity (Cohen & others, 2000).

How Social Support Benefits Health

Social support may benefit our health and improve our ability to cope with stressors in several ways (Cohen & others, 2000). First, the social support of friends and relatives can modify our appraisal of a stressor's significance, including the degree to which we perceive it as threatening or harmful. Simply knowing that support and assistance are readily available may make the situation seem less threatening.

Second, the presence of supportive others seems to decrease the intensity of physical reactions to a stressor. Thus, when faced with a painful medical procedure or some other stressful situation, many people find the presence of a supportive friend to be calming.

Third, social support can influence our health by making us less likely to experience negative emotions (Cohen & Herbert, 1996). Given the well-established link between chronic negative emotions and poor health, a strong social support network can promote positive moods and emotions, enhance self-esteem, and increase feelings of personal control. In contrast, loneliness and depression are unpleasant emotional states that increase levels of stress hormones and adversely affect immune system functioning (Weisse, 1992).

The flip side of the coin is that relationships with others can also be a significant *source* of stress. In fact, negative interactions with other people are often more effective at creating psychological distress than positive interactions are at improving well-being (Lepore, 1993; Rook, 1992). And, although married people tend

social support
The resources provided by other people in times of need.

560 **CHAPTER 13** *Stress, Health, and Coping*

The Social Support of Friends Hundreds of studies have documented the beneficial effects of social support, whether it is emotional support or tangible support. By listening to us when we're upset, helping us move, or simply being there when we need them, friends help us handle problems and cope with stress.

Pets and Social Support Pets can be an important source of companionship, especially for people with limited social contacts. Can the social support of pets help buffer the negative effects of stress? In a study of elderly individuals, pet owners reported feeling less stress and were less likely to go to the doctor than were people without pets (Siegel, 1990). Another study showed that a companion pet helped reduce the effects of stress in caregivers to people with Alzheimer's disease (Fritz & others, 1996).

to be healthier than unmarried people overall, marital conflict has been shown to have adverse effects on physical health, especially for women (Kiecolt-Glaser & Newton, 2001).

Clearly, the quality of interpersonal relationships is an important determinant of whether those relationships help or hinder our ability to cope with stressful events (Feeney & Kirkpatrick, 1996). When other people are perceived as being judgmental, their presence may increase the individual's physical reaction to a stressor. In a clever study, psychologist Karen Allen and her colleagues (1991) demonstrated that the presence of a favorite dog was more effective than the presence of a friend in lowering reactivity to a stressor. Why? Perhaps because the dog was perceived as being nonjudgmental, nonevaluative, and unconditionally supportive. Unfortunately, the same is not always true of friends, family members, and spouses.

Stress may also increase when well-meaning friends or family members offer unwanted or inappropriate social support. The chapter Application offers some suggestions on how to provide helpful social support and avoid inappropriate support behaviors.

Gender Differences in the Effects of Social Support

Women may be particularly vulnerable to some of the problematic aspects of social support, for a couple of reasons. First, women are more likely than men to serve as providers of support, which can be a very stressful role (Hobfoll & Vaux, 1993; Shumaker & Hill, 1991). Consider the differences found in one study. When middle-aged male patients were discharged from the hospital after a heart attack, they went home and their wives took care of them. But when middle-aged female heart attack patients were discharged from the hospital, they went home and fell back into the routine of caring for their husbands (Coyne & others, 1990).

Second, women may be more likely to suffer from the *stress contagion effect,* becoming upset about negative life events that happen to other people whom they care about (Belle, 1991). Since women tend to have larger and more intimate social networks than men, they have more opportunities to become distressed by what happens to people who are close to them. And women are more likely than men to be upset about negative events that happen to their relatives and friends. For example, when your author's sister Judy was unable to reach Katie by phone on the morning of September 11th, she quickly called two family members for advice and comfort: your author Sandy in Tulsa and her mother, Fern, in Chicago. Like Judy, there was nothing Sandy or Fern could do to help Katie escape the maelstrom of lower Manhattan. And, like Judy, they became increasingly upset and worried as they watched the events of the day unfold from hundreds of miles away. Nevertheless, when stressful events strike, women tend to reach out to one another (Taylor & others, 2000).

In contrast, men are more likely to be distressed only by negative events that happen to their immediate family—their wives and children (Wethington & others, 1987). Men tend to rely heavily on a close relationship with their spouse, placing less importance on relationships with other people. Women, in contrast, are more likely to list close friends along with their spouse as confidants (Shumaker & Hill, 1991). Because men tend to have a much smaller network of intimate others, they may be particularly vulnerable to social isolation, especially if their spouse dies. Thus, it's not surprising that the health benefits of being married are more pronounced for men than for women (Kiecolt-Glaser & Newton, 2001).

In summary, it should be clear that having a strong network of social support is generally advantageous to your ability to cope with stressors and to maintain health. This is especially true when you are fundamentally satisfied with both the quality and the quantity of your relationships.

Coping
How People Deal with Stress

coping
Behavioral and cognitive responses used to deal with stressors; involves efforts to change circumstances, or your interpretation of circumstances, to make them more favorable and less threatening.

Key Theme
■ Coping refers to the ways in which we try to change circumstances, or our interpretation of circumstances, to make them less threatening.

Key Questions
■ What are the two basic forms of coping, and when is each form typically used?
■ What are some of the most common coping strategies?
■ How does culture affect coping style?

Think about some of the stressful periods that have occurred in your life. What kinds of strategies did you use to deal with those distressing events? Which strategies seemed to work best? Did any of the strategies end up working against your ability to reduce the stressor? If you had to deal with the same events again today, would you do anything differently?

Katie survived a terrorist attack on her neighborhood by being resourceful, and, as she would be the first to admit, through sheer good luck. But how did she survive the months following? Along with having a good support system—friends, relatives, and a dance teacher who could offer her help—she used a number of different strategies to help her to cope with the stress that she continued to experience.

Two Ways of Coping
Problem-Focused and Emotion-Focused Coping

The strategies that you use to deal with distressing events are examples of coping. **Coping** refers to the ways in which we try to change circumstances, or our interpretation of circumstances, to make them more favorable and less threatening (Folkman & Lazarus, 1991; Lazarus, 1999, 2000).

Coping tends to be a dynamic, ongoing process. We may switch our coping strategies as we appraise the changing demands of a stressful situation and our available resources at any given moment. We also evaluate whether our efforts have made a stressful situation better or worse, and adjust our coping strategies accordingly.

Ways of Coping Like the stress response itself, adaptive coping is a dynamic and complex process. Imagine that you had lost your home and most of your possessions in a fire. What kinds of coping strategies might prove most helpful?

IN FOCUS 13.4

Gender Differences in Responding to Stress: "Tend-and-Befriend" or "Fight-or-Flight"?

It was in 1932 that Walter Cannon detailed the physiological chain of events called the "fight-or-flight" response, which we described earlier in this chapter. Faced with a threat or other stressor, our body automatically gears up to defensively fight or flee the situation. Ever since Cannon's landmark description, the fight-or-flight response has been regarded as the central mechanism in the stress response. *Physiologically,* both sexes show the same hormonal and sympathetic nervous system activation that Walter Cannon detailed. Yet *behaviorally,* men and women react very differently.

To illustrate, consider this finding: When fathers come home after a stressful day at work, they tend to withdraw from their families, wanting to be left alone—an example of the "flight" response. If their workday was filled with a lot of interpersonal conflicts, they tend to initiate conflicts with family members—evidence of the "fight" response. In contrast, when mothers experience high levels of stress at work, they come home and are *more* nurturing toward their children (Repetti, 1989; Repetti & Wood, 1997).

As we have noted in this chapter, women tend to be much more involved in their social networks than men. And, as compared to men, women are much more likely to seek out and use social support when they are under stress (Belle, 1991; Glynn & others, 1999). Throughout their lives, women tend to mobilize social support—especially from other women—in times of stress (Taylor & others, 2000). We saw this pattern in our chapter Prologue. Just as Katie called her mother, Judy, when her neighborhood came under attack, Judy called her sister and her *own* mother when she feared that her daughter's life was in danger.

Why the gender difference in coping with stress? Health psychologists Shelley Taylor, Laura Klein, and their colleagues (2000) believe that evolutionary theory offers some insight. According to the evolu-

"I'm somewhere between O. and K."

tionary perspective, the most adaptive response in virtually any situation is one that promotes the survival of both the individual *and* the individual's offspring. Given that premise, neither fighting nor fleeing is likely to have been an adaptive response for females, especially females who were pregnant, nursing, or caring for their offspring. According to Taylor and her colleagues (2000), "Stress responses that enabled the female to simultaneously protect herself and her offspring are likely to have resulted in more surviving offspring." Rather than fighting or fleeing, they argue, women developed a *tend-and-befriend* behavioral response to stress.

What is the "tend-and-befriend" pattern of responding? *Tending* refers to "quieting and caring for offspring and blending into the environment," Taylor and her colleagues (2000) write. That is, rather than confronting or running from the threat, females take cover and protect their young. Evidence supporting this behavior pattern includes studies of nonhuman animals showing that many female animals adopt a "tending" strategy when faced by a threat (Francis & others, 1999; Liu & others, 1997).

The "befriending" side of the equation refers to the fact that, as compared to men, women seek out and use social support in all types of stressful situations,

including conflicts at work, relationship and health problems, and concern about the well-being of family members. Taylor and her colleagues (2000) describe *befriending* as "the creation of networks of associations that provide resources and protection for the female and her offspring under conditions of stress."

But that still leaves us with the question of why females respond with "tend-and-befriend" rather than "fight-or-flight." Remember, both males and females show the same neuroendocrine responses to an acute stressor—the sympathetic nervous system activates, stress hormones pour into the bloodstream, and, as those hormones reach different organs, the body kicks into high gear. So why do women tend and befriend, rather than fight or flee, as men do? Taylor (2000) points to the effects of another hormone, *oxytocin.* Higher in females than in males, oxytocin is associated with maternal behaviors in all female mammals, including humans. It also tends to have a calming effect on male and female animals.

Taylor speculates that oxytocin might simultaneously help calm stressed females and promote affiliative behavior. Supporting this speculation is research showing that oxytocin increases affiliative behaviors and reduces stress in many mammals (Carter & DeVries, 1999; Light & others, 2000).

In humans, oxytocin is highest in nursing mothers. Pleasant physical contact, such as hugging, cuddling, and touching, stimulates the release of oxytocin. In the laboratory, higher oxytocin levels in female research volunteers were associated with reduced cortisol responses to stress and faster recovery following an acute stressor (Taylor & others, 2000). In combination, all of these oxytocin-related changes seem to help turn down the physiological intensity of the fight-or-flight response for women. And perhaps, Taylor and her colleagues suggest, they also promote the tend-and-befriend response.

When coping is effective, we adapt to the situation and stress is reduced. Unfortunately, coping efforts do not always help us adapt. Maladaptive coping can involve thoughts and behaviors that intensify or prolong distress or that produce self-defeating outcomes (Bolger & Zuckerman, 1995). The rejected lover who continually dwells on her former companion, passing up opportunities to form new relationships and letting her studies slide, is demonstrating maladaptive coping.

Adaptive coping responses serve many functions. Most important, adaptive coping involves realistically evaluating the situation and determining what can be done to minimize the impact of the stressor. But adaptive coping also involves dealing with the emotional aspects of the situation. In other words, adaptive coping often includes developing emotional tolerance for negative life events, maintaining self-esteem, and keeping emotions in balance. Finally, adaptive coping efforts are directed toward preserving important relationships during stressful experiences (Lazarus, 1993; R. Lazarus & Folkman, 1984).

Psychologists Richard Lazarus and Susan Folkman (1984) have described two basic types of coping, each of which serves a different purpose. **Problem-focused coping** is aimed at managing or changing a threatening or harmful stressor. If we think there's nothing that can be done to alter a situation, we tend to rely on **emotion-focused coping:** We direct our efforts toward relieving or regulating the emotional impact of the stressful situation. Although emotion-focused coping doesn't change the problem, it can help you feel better about the situation.

People are flexible in the coping styles they adopt, often relying on different coping strategies for different stressors. Table 13.2 shows some of the coping behaviors of people in the United States immediately after the September 11th terrorist attacks.

problem-focused coping
Coping efforts primarily aimed at directly changing or managing a threatening or harmful stressor.

emotion-focused coping
Coping efforts primarily aimed at relieving or regulating the emotional impact of a stressful situation.

Problem-Focused Coping Strategies: Changing the Stressor

Problem-focused coping strategies represent actions that have the goal of changing or eliminating the stressor. When people use aggressive or risky efforts to change the situation, they are engaging in *confrontive coping*. Ideally, confrontive coping is direct and assertive without being hostile. When it is hostile or aggressive, confrontive coping may well generate negative emotions in the people being confronted, damaging future relations with them (Folkman & Lazarus, 1991).

In contrast, *planful problem solving* involves efforts to rationally analyze the situation, identify potential solutions, and then implement them. In effect, you take the attitude that the stressor represents a problem to be solved. Once you assume that mental stance, you follow the basic steps of problem solving (see Chapter 7).

Problem-Focused Coping People rely on different coping strategies at different times in dealing with the same stressor. After dealing with the emotional impact of losing their home to a wildfire, this California family is engaged in problem-focused coping as they help clear the site before rebuilding.

Table 13.2

Coping Behaviors the Week After September 11, 2001

How much have you:	A lot	A medium amount	A little bit	Not at all
Talked with someone about your thoughts and feelings about what happened?	57%	30%	12%	1%
Turned to prayer, religion, or spiritual feelings?	44	31	15	10
Participated in a public or group activity in recognition of what happened?	11	23	26	40
Avoided activities such as watching TV because they remind you of what happened?	5	14	20	61

SOURCE: Schuster & others (2001).

Interviews with randomly selected Americans in the days immediately following the September 11, 2001, terrorist attacks revealed some of the strategies that people used to cope with the horrifying events. As you can see, seeking social support was an important coping strategy. The same survey also found that 36% of the respondents had given blood, donated money, or performed volunteer services to aid those directly affected by the attacks.

Emotion-Focused Coping Strategies: Changing Your Reaction to the Stressor

When the stressor is one over which we can exert little or no control, we often focus on dimensions of the situation that we *can* control—the emotional impact of the stressor on us (Thompson & others, 1994). All the different forms of emotion-focused coping share the goal of reducing or regulating the emotional impact of a stressor. For ways of reducing the physical effects of stress, look at In Focus Box 13.5.

When you shift your attention away from the stressor and toward other activities, you're engaging in the emotion-focused coping strategy called *escape–avoidance*. As the name implies, the basic goal is to escape or avoid the stressor and neutralize distressing emotions. Examples of using escape–avoidance to deal with a stressful situation might include escaping into fantasy (also called wishful thinking), exercising, or immersing yourself in your work, studies, or hobbies. Katie, for example, found that her daily dance classes were a way of forgetting the anxieties of life in New York after September 11th. Maladaptive forms of escape–avoidance include excessive sleeping and the use of drugs or alcohol (Grunberg & others, 1999).

By focusing your attention on something other than the stressor, escape–avoidance tactics provide emotional relief in the short run. Thus, avoidance strategies can be helpful when facing a stressor that is brief and has limited consequences. But avoidance strategies such as wishful thinking tend to be counter-

---

IN FOCUS 13.5

Minimizing the Physical Effects of Stress

Sometimes stressful situations persist despite our best efforts to resolve them. Knowing that chronic stress can jeopardize your health, what can you do to minimize the adverse impact of stress on your physical well-being? Here are three simple suggestions that you should find helpful.

Suggestion 1: Exercise Regularly

Regular exercise, particularly aerobic exercise like walking, swimming, or running, is one of the best ways to reduce the impact of stress. Simply walking briskly for 20 minutes four or five times a week will improve your physical health and help you cope with stress. Compared to sofa slugs, physically fit people are less physiologically reactive to stressors and produce lower levels of stress hormones (Rejeski & others, 1991, 1992). Psychologically, regular exercise reduces anxiety and depressed feelings and increases self-confidence and self-esteem (Sacks, 1993).

Suggestion 2: Avoid or Minimize the Use of Stimulants

In dealing with a stressful situation, people often turn to stimulants such as coffee or tea to keep them going. And most smokers react to stress by increasing their smoking (Epstein & Jennings, 1985). However, common stimulants like

Managing Stress We all experience stressful periods in our lives. How does exercise help people cope with stress?

caffeine and nicotine actually increase the physiological effects of stress by raising heart rate and blood pressure (Lovallo & others, 1996). In effect, users of stimulant drugs are already primed to respond with greater reactivity, exaggerating the physiological consequences of stress.

The best advice? Avoid stimulant drugs altogether. The next best advice? Make a conscious effort to monitor your use of

stimulants, especially when you're under stress. You'll find it easier to deal with stressors when your nervous system is not already in high gear because of caffeine, nicotine, or other stimulants.

Suggestion 3: Regularly Practice a Relaxation Technique

You can significantly reduce stress-related symptoms by regularly using any one of a variety of relaxation techniques (Benson, 1993). One effective relaxation technique is *meditation,* which involves focusing your attention on an object, word, or phrase. We provided you with instructions for a simple meditation technique in Chapter 4.

Another effective technique is *progressive muscle relaxation.* This technique involves systematically tensing and then relaxing the major muscle groups of your body while lying down or sitting in a comfortable chair. You begin by tensing your facial and jaw muscles, paying careful attention to the feeling of muscle tightness. Then, take a deep breath, hold it for a few seconds, and exhale slowly as you relax your facial and jaw muscles as completely as possible. Notice the difference between the sensations of tension and the warm feelings of relaxation. Progressively work your way down your body, tensing and then relaxing muscle groups.

productive when the stressor is severe or long-lasting, like a serious or chronic disease (Stanton & Snider, 1993). Escape–avoidance strategies are also associated with increased psychological distress in facing other types of stressors, such as adjusting to college (Aspinwall & Taylor, 1992).

In the long run, escape–avoidance tactics are associated with poor adjustment and symptoms of depression and anxiety (Stanton & Snider, 1993). That's not surprising if you think about it. After all, the problem *is* still there. And if the problem is one that needs to be dealt with promptly, such as a pressing medical concern, the delays caused by escape–avoidance strategies can make the stressful situation worse.

Seeking social support is the coping strategy that involves turning to friends, relatives, or other people for emotional, tangible, or informational support. As we discussed earlier in the chapter, having a strong network of social support can help buffer the impact of stressors. Confiding in a trusted friend gives you an opportunity to vent your emotions and better understand the stressful situation (Lepore & others, 1996).

When you acknowledge the stressor but attempt to minimize or eliminate its emotional impact, you're engaging in the coping strategy called *distancing*. A relatively common example of distancing occurs when people try to change the meaning of the stressor by claiming that it's "no big deal" or "not that important." Making jokes about the stressful situation is another form of distancing. Sometimes people emotionally distance themselves from a stressor by discussing it in a detached, depersonalized, or intellectual way. Among Katie's circle of young friends, distancing was common. They joked about the soot, the dust, the National Guard troops guarding the subway stations. They made light of the face masks they wore when they went downtown and generally tried to play down the magnitude of the events that they had all experienced.

In certain high-stress occupations, distancing can help workers cope with painful human problems. Clinical psychologists, social workers, rescue workers, police officers, and medical personnel often use distancing to some degree to help them deal with distressing situations without falling apart emotionally themselves.

In contrast to distancing, *denial* is a refusal to acknowledge that the problem even exists. Like escape–avoidance strategies, denial can compound problems in situations that require immediate attention.

Perhaps the most constructive emotion-focused coping strategy is *positive reappraisal*. When we use positive reappraisal, we not only try to minimize the negative emotional aspects of the situation, but we also try to create positive meaning by focusing on personal growth. People sometimes use positive reappraisal to help them make sense of a stressful experience, especially when they have experienced a tragedy, disaster, or catastrophic loss. People who can find some sense of personal meaning in the stressful event—sometimes through their religious faith—tend to cope better with loss than those who see it as senseless (Meichenbaum & Fitzpatrick, 1993; Wortman & others, 1992).

Katie, too, was able to creatively transform the meaning of her experience. She is applying to a competitive college dance program, and, as part of her application, she needs to choreograph and perform an original dance in an audition. She's using her experiences on that September morning as the inspiration, and the centerpiece, of her dance. There is sadness, fear, hope, and renewal in her dance—all of the elements that she experienced on that fateful day. Her ability to express her feelings artistically has helped her come to terms with her experience.

Most people use multiple coping strategies in stressful situations, often combining problem-focused and emotion-focused forms of coping (Dunkel-Schetter & others, 1992; Lazarus, 1993). Different coping strategies may be used at different stages of dealing with a stressor. In the initial stages of a stressful experience, we often rely on emotion-focused strategies to help us step back emotionally from a problem. Once we've regained our emotional equilibrium, we may use problem-focused coping strategies to identify potential solutions.

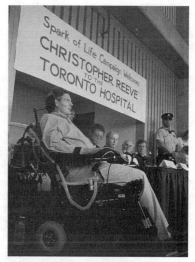

Transcending Personal Tragedy Some people cope with tragedy by channeling their energies into helping others with similar problems. Actor Christopher Reeve has been paralyzed from the neck down since he suffered a spinal cord injury in a horseback-riding accident. Reeve has become an active advocate for those with spinal cord injuries.

Katie's Dance

13.3 R·E·V·I·E·W

C·O·N·C·E·P·T

Coping Strategies

Identify the coping strategy that is being illustrated in each of the scenarios below. Choose from:

a. confrontive coping
b. planful problem solving
c. escape–avoidance
d. seeking social support
e. distancing
f. denial
g. positive reappraisal

_____ 1. In trying to contend with her stormy marriage, Bailey often seeks the advice of her best friend, Paula.

_____ 2. Lionel was disappointed that he did not get the job, but he concluded that the knowledge he gained from the application and interview process was very beneficial.

_____ 3. Whenever Dr. Mathau has a particularly hectic and stressful shift in the emergency room, she finds herself making jokes and facetious remarks to the other staff members.

_____ 4. Phil's job as a public defender is filled with long days and little thanks. To take his mind off his job, Phil jogs every day.

_____ 5. Faced with low productivity and mounting financial losses, the factory manager bluntly told all his workers, "You people had better start getting more work done in less time, or you will be looking for jobs elsewhere."

_____ 6. Because of unavoidable personal problems, Martin did very poorly on his last two tests and was very concerned about his GPA. Martin decided to talk with his professor about the possibility of writing an extra paper or taking a makeup exam.

_____ 7. Although she failed her midterm exam and got a D on her term paper, Sheila insists that she is going to get a B in her economics course.

Culture and Coping Strategies

Culture seems to play an important role in the choice of coping strategies. Americans and other members of individualistic cultures tend to emphasize personal autonomy and personal responsibility in dealing with problems. Thus, they are *less* likely to seek social support in stressful situations than are members of collectivistic cultures, such as Asian cultures (Marsella & Dash-Scheuer, 1988). Members of collectivistic cultures tend to be more oriented toward their social group, family, or community and toward seeking help with their problems.

Individualists also tend to emphasize the importance and value of exerting control over their circumstances, especially circumstances that are threatening or stressful. Thus, they favor problem-focused strategies, such as confrontive coping and planful problem solving. These strategies involve directly changing the situation to achieve a better fit with their wishes or goals (Markus & Kitayama, 1991).

In collectivistic cultures, however, a greater emphasis is placed on controlling your personal reactions to a stressful situation rather than trying to control the situation itself. This emotion-focused coping style emphasizes gaining control over inner feelings by accepting and accommodating yourself to existing realities (Thompson & others, 1994).

For example, the Japanese emphasize accepting difficult situations with maturity, serenity, and flexibility (Weisz & others, 1984). Common sayings in Japan are "The true tolerance is to tolerate the intolerable" and "Flexibility can control rigidity" (Azuma, 1984). Along with controlling inner feelings, many Asian cultures also stress the goal of controlling the outward expression of emotions, however distressing the situation (Johnson & others, 1995).

These cultural differences in coping underscore the point that there is no formula for effective coping in all situations. That we use multiple coping strategies throughout almost every stressful situation reflects our efforts to identify what will work best at a given moment in time. To the extent that any coping strategy helps us identify realistic alternatives, manage our emotions, and maintain important relationships, it is adaptive and effective.

Summing Up
Stress, Health, and Coping

From national tragedies and major life events to the minor hassles and annoyances of daily life, stressors come in all sizes and shapes. Any way you look at it, stress is an unavoidable part of life. Stress that is prolonged or intense can adversely affect both our physical and psychological well-being. Fortunately, most of the time people deal effectively with the stresses in their lives. And as Katie's story demonstrates, the effects of even the most intense stressors can be minimized if we cope with them effectively.

Ultimately, the level of stress that we experience is due to a complex interaction of psychological, biological, and social factors. We hope that reading this chapter has given you a better understanding of how stress affects your life and of how you can reduce its impact on your physical and psychological well-being. In the chapter Application, we'll suggest some ways that you can help other people cope with stressful circumstances.

APPLICATION | Providing Effective Social Support

A close friend turns to you for help in a time of crisis or personal tragedy. What should you do or say? As we've noted in this chapter, appropriate social support can help people weather crises and can significantly reduce the amount of distress that they feel. Inappropriate support, in contrast, may only make matters worse.

Researchers generally agree that there are three broad categories of social support: emotional, tangible, and informational. Each provides different beneficial functions (Peirce & others, 1996; Taylor & Aspinwall, 1993).

Emotional support includes expressions of concern, empathy, and positive regard. *Tangible support* involves direct assistance, such as providing transportation, lending money, or helping with meals, child care, or household tasks. When people offer helpful suggestions, advice, or possible resources, they are providing *informational support*.

It's possible that all three kinds of social support might be provided by the same person, such as a relative, spouse, or very close friend. More commonly, we turn to different people for different kinds of support.

Research by psychologist Stevan Hobfoll and his colleagues (1992) has identified several support behaviors that are typically perceived as helpful by people under stress. In a nutshell, you're most likely to be perceived as helpful if you:

- Are a good listener and show concern and interest.

- Ask questions that encourage the person under stress to express his or her feelings and emotions.

- Express understanding about why the person is upset.

- Express affection for the person, whether with a warm hug or simply a pat on the arm.

- Are willing to invest time and attention in helping.

- Can help the person with practical tasks, such as housework, transportation, or responsibilities at work or school.

Just as important is knowing what *not* to do or say. Here are several behaviors that, however well intentioned, are often perceived as unhelpful:

- Giving advice that the person under stress has not requested.

- Telling the person, "I know exactly how you feel"—it's a mistake to think that you have experienced distress identical to what the other person is experiencing.

- Talking about yourself or your own problems.

- Minimizing the importance of the person's problem by saying things like, "Hey, don't make such a big deal out of it; it could be a lot worse" or "Don't worry, everything will turn out okay."

- Pretending to be cheerful.

- Offering your philosophical or religious interpretation of the stressful event by saying things like, "It's just fate," "It's God's will," or "It's your karma."

Finally, remember that although social support is helpful, it is *not* a substitute for counseling or psychotherapy. If a friend seems overwhelmed by problems or emotions, or is having serious difficulty handling the demands of everyday life, you should encourage him or her to seek professional help. Most college campuses have a counseling center or a health clinic that can provide referrals to qualified mental health workers. Sliding fee schedules, based on ability to pay, are usually available. Thus, you can assure the person that cost need not be an obstacle to getting help—or an additional source of stress!

Chapter Review

Stress, Health, and Coping

Key Points

Introduction: What Is Stress?

■ **Stress** can be defined as a negative emotional state that occurs in response to events that are appraised as taxing or exceeding a person's resources.

■ **Health psychologists** study stress and other psychological factors that influence health, illness, and treatment. Health psychologists are guided by the **biopsychosocial model.**

■ **Stressors** are events or situations that produce stress. According to the life events approach, any event that requires adaptation produces stress. The Social Readjustment Rating Scale is one way to measure the impact of life events. The life events approach does not take into account a person's subjective appraisal of an event. It also assumes that any change, whether good or bad, produces stress.

■ **Daily hassles** are a significant source of stress and also contribute to the stress produced by major life events.

■ Stress can also be caused by approach–approach, avoidance–avoidance, or approach–avoidance **conflicts.** Approach–avoidance conflicts tend to create the most stress.

■ Social factors, such as unemployment, crime, and racism, can be significant sources of stress, often producing chronic stress. Stress can also result when people encounter different cultural values.

Physical Effects of Stress: *The Mind–Body Connection*

■ Stress can affect health indirectly, by influencing health-related behaviors, and directly, by influencing the body's functioning.

■ Walter Cannon identified the endocrine pathway involved in the **fight-or-flight response.** This endocrine pathway includes the sympathetic nervous system, the adrenal medulla, and the release of **catecholamines.**

■ In studying the physical effects of prolonged stressors, Hans Selye identified the three-stage **general adaptation syndrome,** which includes the alarm, resistance, and exhaustion stages. Selye found that prolonged stress involves a second endocrine pathway, which includes the hypothalamus, the pituitary gland, the adrenal cortex, and the release of **corticosteroids.**

■ Stress affects **immune system** functioning. The most important elements of the immune system are **lymphocytes.** Ader and Cohen's discovery that the immune system could be classically conditioned helped launch the new field of **psychoneuroimmunology.** Subsequent research has discovered that the nervous, endocrine, and immune systems are directly linked and continually influence one another.

■ Stressors that affect immune system functioning include both unusual and common life events, along with everyday pressures. Although stress may increase susceptibility to infection and illness, many other factors are involved in physical health.

Individual Factors That Influence the Response to Stress

■ The impact of stressors is reduced when people feel a sense of control over the stressful situation. Feelings of control have both physical and psychological benefits.

■ The way people explain negative events often determines whether they will persist or give up after failure. People with an **optimistic explanatory style** use external, unstable, and specific explanations for negative events. People with a **pessimistic explanatory style** use internal, stable, and global explanations for negative events. A pessimistic explanatory style contributes to stress and undermines health.

■ Chronic negative emotions are related to the development of some chronic diseases. People who frequently experience negative emotions experience more stress than other people. Transient negative moods have also been shown to decrease immune system functioning.

■ The **Type A behavior pattern** can predict the development of heart disease. The most critical health-compromising component of Type A behavior is hostility. Hostile people react more intensely to stressors and experience stress more frequently than do nonhostile people.

■ Social isolation contributes to poor health. **Social support** improves the ability to deal with stressors by modifying the appraisal of a stressor, decreasing the physical reaction to a stressor, and making people less likely to experience negative emotions. When the quality of relationships is poor, or when social support is inappropriate or unwanted, relationships may increase stress.

■ Women are more likely than men to be the providers of social support and tend to be more vulnerable to the stress contagion effect. Men are less likely to be upset by negative events that happen to people outside their immediate family.

Coping: *How People Deal with Stress*

■ **Coping** refers to the way in which people try to change either their circumstances or their interpretations of circumstances in order to make them more favorable and less threatening. Coping may be maladaptive or adaptive.

■ When people think that something can be done to change a situation, they tend to use **problem-focused coping** strategies, which involve changing a harmful stressor.

■ When people think that a situation cannot be changed, they tend to rely on **emotion-focused coping** strategies, which involve changing their emotional reactions to the stressor.

■ Problem-focused coping strategies include confrontive coping and planful problem solving.

■ Emotion-focused coping strategies include escape–avoidance, seeking social support, distancing, denial, and positive reappraisal. People usually rely on multiple coping strategies in stressful situations.

■ Culture affects the choice of coping strategies. People in individualistic cultures tend to favor problem-focused strategies. People in collectivistic cultures are more likely to seek social support, and they emphasize emotion-focused coping strategies more.

Key Terms

stress, p. 540

health psychology, p. 540

biopsychosocial model, p. 541

stressors, p. 541

daily hassles, p. 542

conflict, p. 543

acculturative stress, (p. 545)

fight-or-flight response, p. 546

catecholamines, p. 547

general adaptation syndrome, p. 548

corticosteroids, p. 549

immune system, p. 549

lymphocytes, p. 549

psychoneuroimmunology, p. 550

optimistic explanatory style, p. 554

pessimistic explanatory style, p. 554

Type A behavior pattern, p. 556

social support, p. 559

coping, p. 561

problem-focused coping, p. 563

emotion-focused coping, p. 563

Key People

Robert Ader (b. 1932) American psychologist who, with immunologist Nicholas Cohen, first demonstrated that immune system responses could be classically conditioned; helped establish the new interdisciplinary field of psychoneuroimmunology. (p. 549)

Walter B. Cannon (1871–1945) American physiologist who made several important contributions to psychology, especially in the study of emotions. Described the fight-or-flight response, which involves the sympathetic nervous system and the endocrine system (also see Chapter 8). (p. 546)

Janice Kiecolt-Glaser (b. 1951) American psychologist who, with immunologist Ronald Glaser, has conducted extensive research on the effects of stress on the immune system. (p. 551)

Richard Lazarus (b. 1922) American psychologist who helped promote the cognitive perspective in the study of emotion and stress; developed the cognitive appraisal model of stress and coping with co-researcher Susan Folkman (also see Chapter 8). (p. 542)

Martin Seligman (b. 1942) American psychologist who conducted research on explanatory style and the role it plays in stress, health, and illness. (p. 554)

Hans Selye (1907–1982) Canadian endocrinologist who was a pioneer in stress research; defined stress as "the nonspecific response of the body to any demand placed on it" and described a three-stage response to prolonged stress that he termed the *general adaptation syndrome.* (p. 547)

Concept Review Answers

13.1   page 552

1. False. The biopsychosocial model holds that health and illness are determined by the interaction of biological, psychological, and social factors.
2. False. Exposure to life events is only one of many factors that influence health and illness.
3. False. The Social Readjustment Rating Scale measures stress due to life events.
4. False. During periods of prolonged stress, the adrenal cortex secretes corticosteroids.

5. False. Shelley is probably experiencing the "alarm" stage of the general adaptation syndrome.
6. True.

13.2   page 557

1. f   2. e   3. a   4. c   5. b

13.3   page 566

1. d   3. e   5. a   7. f
2. g   4. c   6. b

References

Ader, Robert. (2001). Psychoneuroimmunology. *Current Directions in Psychological Science, 10,* 94–98.

Ader, Robert, & Cohen, Nicholas. (1975). Behaviorally conditioned immunosuppression. *Psychosomatic Medicine, 37,* 333–340.

Ader, Robert, & Cohen, Nicholas. (1993). Psychoneuroimmunology: Conditioning and stress. *Annual Review of Psychology, 44,* 53–85.

Adler, Nancy, & Matthews, Karen. (1994). Health psychology: Why do some people get sick and some stay well? *Annual Review of Psychology, 45,* 229–259.

Affleck, Glenn; Tennen, Howard; Pfeiffer, Carol; & Fifield, Judith. (1987a). Appraisals of control and predictability in reacting to a chronic disease. *Journal of Personality and Social Psychology, 53,* 273–279.

Affleck, Glenn; Tennen, Howard; & Croog, Sydney. (1987b). Causal attribution, perceived control, and recovery from a heart attack. *Journal of Social and Clinical Psychology, 5,* 399–355.

Allen, Karen M.; Blascovich, Jim; Tomaka, Joe; & Kelsey, Robert M. (1991). Presence of human friends and pet dogs as moderators of autonomic responses to stress in women. *Journal of Personality and Social Psychology, 61,* 582–589.

Almeida, David M., & Kessler, Ronald C. (1998). Everyday stressors and gender differences in daily distress. *Journal of Personality and Social Psychology, 75,* 670–680.

Aspinwall, Lisa G., & Taylor, Shelley E. (1992). Modeling cognitive adaptation: A longitudinal investigation of the impact of individual differences and coping on college adjustment and performance. *Journal of Personality and Social Psychology, 63,* 989–1003.

Azuma, Hiroshi. (1984). Secondary control as a heterogeneous category. *American Psychologist, 39,* 970–971.

Baer, Paul E.; Garmezy, Lisa B.; McLaughlin, Robert J.; Pokorny, Alex D.; & Wernick, M. J. (1987). Stress, coping, family conflict, and adolescent alcohol use. *Journal of Behavioral Medicine, 10,* 449–466.

Barefoot, John C. (1992). Developments in the measurement of hostility. In Howard S. Friedman (Ed.), *Hostility, health, and coping.* Washington, DC: American Psychological Association.

Barefoot, John C.; Dahlstrom, W. Grant; & Williams, Redford B. (1983). Hostility, CHD incidence, and total mortality: A 25-year follow-up study of 255 physicians. *Psychosomatic Medicine, 45,* 59–63.

Belle, Deborah. (1991). Gender differences in the social moderators of stress. In Alan Monat & Richard S. Lazarus (Eds.), *Stress and coping: An anthology* (3rd ed.). New York: Columbia University Press.

Benson, Herbert. (1993). The relaxation response. In Daniel Goleman & Joel Gurin (Eds.), *Mind/body medicine: How to use your mind for better health.* Yonkers, NY: Consumer Reports Books.

Berkman, Lisa F. (1995). The role of social relations in health promotion. *Psychosomatic Medicine, 57,* 245–254.

Berkman, Lisa F.; Leo-Summers, Linda; & Horowitz, Ralph I. (1992). Emotional support and survival after myocardial infarction. *Annals of Internal Medicine, 117,* 1003–1009.

Berkman, Lisa F., & Syme, S. Leonard. (1979). Social networks, host resistance, and mortality: A nine-year follow-up study of Alameda County residents. *American Journal of Epidemiology, 109,* 186–204.

Berry, John W. (1994). Acculturative stress. In Walter J. Lonner & Roy Malpass (Eds.), *Psychology and culture.* Boston: Allyn & Bacon.

Berry, John W. (1997). Immigration, acculturation, and adaptation. *Applied Psychology: An International Journal, 46,* 5–68.

Berry, John W., & Kim, Uichol. (1988). Acculturation and mental health. In Pierre R. Dasen, John W. Berry, & Norman Sartorius (Eds.), *Health and cross-cultural psychology: Toward applications* (Cross-cultural Research and Methodology Series, Vol. 10). Newbury Park, CA: Sage.

Bolger, Niall, & Schilling, Elizabeth A. (1991). Personality and problems of everyday life: The role of neuroticism in exposure and reactivity to stress. *Journal of Personality, 59,* 355–386.

Bolger, Niall, & Zuckerman, Adam. (1995). A framework for studying personality in the stress process. *Journal of Personality and Social Psychology, 69,* 890–902.

Burger, Jerry M. (1992). *Desire for control: Personality, social, and clinical perspectives.* New York: Plenum Press.

Burks, Nancy, & Martin, Barclay. (1985). Everyday problems and life change events: Ongoing versus acute sources of stress. *Journal of Human Stress, 11,* 27–35.

Burns, Melanie, & Seligman, Martin E. P. (1989). Explanatory style across the lifespan: Evidence for stability over 52 years. *Journal of Personality and Social Psychology, 56,* 471–477.

Cannon, Walter B. (1932). *The wisdom of the body.* New York: Norton.

Carter, C. Sue, & DeVries, A. Courtney. (1999). Stress and soothing: An endocrine perspective. In Michael Lewis & Douglas Ramsay (Eds.), *Soothing and stress.* Mahwah, NJ: Erlbaum.

Cohen, Sheldon; Frank, Ellen; Doyle, William J.; Skoner, David P.; Rabin, Bruce; & Gwaltney, Jack M., Jr. (1998). Types of stressors that increase susceptibility to the common cold in healthy adults. *Health Psychology, 17,* 214–223.

Cohen, Sheldon; Gottlieb, Benjamin H.; & Underwood, Lynn G. (2000). Social relationships and health. In Sheldon Cohen, Lynn Underwood, and Benjamin H. Gottlieb (Eds.), *Social support measurement and intervention: A guide for health and social scientists.* New York: Oxford University Press.

Cohen, Sheldon, & Herbert, Tracy B. (1996). Health psychology: Psychological factors and physical disease from the perspective of human psychoneuroimmunology. *Annual Review of Psychology, 47,* 113–142.

Cohen, Sheldon; Tyrrell, David A. J.; & Smith, Andrew P. (1991). Psychological stress and susceptibility to the common cold. *New England Journal of Medicine, 325,* 606–612.

Cohen, Sheldon; Tyrrell, David A. J.; & Smith, Andrew P. (1993). Negative life events, perceived stress, negative affect, and susceptibility to the common cold. *Journal of Personality and Social Psychology, 64,* 131–140.

Cohen, Sheldon, & Williamson, Gail M. (1988). Perceived stress in a probability sample of the United States. In Shirlynn Spacapan & Stuart Oskamp (Eds.), *The social psychology of health: The Claremont Symposium on Applied Social Psychology* (4th ed.). Newbury Park, CA: Sage.

Contrada, Richard J.; Ashmore, Richard D.; Gary, Melvin L.; Coups, Elliot; Egeth, Jill D.; Sewell, Andrea; & others. (2000). Ethnicity-related sources of stress and their effects on well-being. *Current Directions of Psychological Science, 9,* 136–139.

Coyne, James C., & Downey, Geraldine. (1991). Social factors and psychopathology: Stress, social support, and coping processes. *Annual Review of Psychology, 42,* 401–425.

Coyne, James C.; Ellard, John H.; & Smith, David A. F. (1990). Social support, interdependence, and the dilemmas of helping. In Barbara R. Sarason, Irwin G. Sarason, & Gregory R. Pierce (Eds.), *Social support: An interactional view.* New York: Wiley.

DeLongis, Anita; Coyne, James C.; Dakof, C.; Folkman, Susan; & Lazarus, Richard S. (1982). Relationship of daily hassles, uplifts, and major life events to health status. *Health Psychology, 1,* 119–136.

DeLongis, Anita; Folkman, Susan; & Lazarus, Richard S. (1988). The impact of stress on health and mood: Psychological and social resources as mediators. *Journal of Personality and Social Psychology, 54,* 486–495.

Dohrenwend, Bruce P.; Raphael, Karen G.; Schwartz, Sharon; Stueve, Ann; & Skodol, Andrew. (1993). The structured event probe and narrative rating method for measuring stressful life events. In Leo Goldberger & Shlomo Breznitz (Eds.), *Handbook of stress: Theoretical and clinical aspects* (2nd ed.). New York: Free Press.

Dunkel-Schetter, Christine; Feinstein, Lawrence G.; Taylor, Shelley E.; & Falke, Roberta L. (1992). Patterns of coping with cancer. *Health Psychology, 11,* 79–87.

Epstein, Leonard H., & Jennings, J. Richard. (1985). Smoking, stress, cardiovascular reactivity, and coronary heart disease. In Karen A. Matthews & others (Eds.), *Handbook of stress, reactivity, and cardiovascular disease.* New York: Wiley.

Epstein, Seymour. (1982). Conflict and stress. In Leo Goldberger & Shlomo Breznitz (Eds.), *Handbook of stress: Theoretical and clinical aspects.* New York: Free Press.

Feeney, Brooke C., & Kirkpatrick, Lee A. (1996). Effects of adult attachment and presence of romantic partners on physiological responses to stress. *Journal of Personality and Social Psychology, 70,* 255–270.

Fields, Howard L., & Levine, Jon D. (1984). Placebo analgesia: A role for endorphins. *Trends in Neuroscience, 7,* 271–273.

Folkman, Susan, & Lazarus, Richard S. (1991). Coping and emotion. In Alan Monat & Richard S. Lazarus (Eds.), *Stress and coping: An anthology* (3rd ed.). New York: Columbia University Press.

Francais, Darlene; Diorio, Josie; Liu, Dong; & Meaney, Michael J. (1999). Nongenomic transmission across generations of maternal behavior and stress responses in the rat. *Science, 286,* 1155–1158.

Friedman, Howard S., & Booth-Kewley, Stephanie. (1987). The "disease-prone personality": A meta-analytic view of the construct. *American Psychologist, 42,* 539–555.

Friedman, Meyer, & Rosenman, Ray H. (1974). *Type A behavior and your heart.* New York: Knopf.

Fuente-Fernández, Raúl de la; Ruth, Thomas J.; Sossi, Vesna; & others. (2001, August 10). Expectation and dopamine release: Mechanism of the placebo effect in Parkinson's disease. *Science, 293,* 1164–1166.

Geen, Russell G. (1991). Social motivation. *Annual Review of Psychology, 42,* 377–399.

Gillham, Jane E.; Shatte, Andrew J.; Reivich, Karen J.; & Seligman, Martin E. P. (2001). Optimism, pessimism, and explanatory style. In Edward C. Chang (Ed.), *Optimism and pessimism: Implications for theory, research, and practice.* Washington, DC: American Psychological Association.

Glynn, Laura M.; Christenfeld, Nicholas; & Gerin, William. (1999). Gender, social support, and cardiovascular responses to stress. *Psychosomatic Medicine, 61,* 234–242.

Graig, Eric. (1993). Stress as a consequence of the urban physical environment. In Leo Goldberger & Shlomo Breznitz (Eds.), *Handbook of stress: Theoretical and clinical aspects* (2nd ed.). New York: Free Press.

Grunberg, Leon; Moore, Sarah; Anderson-Connolly, Richard; & Greenberg, Edward. (1999). Work stress and self-reported alcohol use: The moderating role of escapist reasons for drinking. *Journal of Occupational Health Psychology, 4,* 29–36.

Helgeson, Vicki S. (1992). Moderators of the relation between perceived control and adjustment to chronic illness. *Journal of Personality and Social Psychology, 63,* 656–666.

Herbert, Tracy Bennett, & Cohen, Sheldon. (1993). Depression and immunity: A meta-analytic review. *Psychological Bulletin, 113,* 472–486.

Hobfoll, Stevan E.; Lilly, Roy S.; & Jackson, Anita P. (1992). Conservation of social resources and the self. In Hans O. F. Veiel & Urs Baumann (Eds.), *The meaning and measurement of social support.* New York: Hemisphere.

Hobfoll, Stevan E., & Stephens, Mary Ann Parris. (1990). Social support during extreme stress: Consequences and intervention. In Barbara R. Sarason, Irwin G. Sarason, & Gregory R. Pierce (Eds.), *Social support: An interactional view.* New York: Wiley.

Hobfoll, Stevan E., & Vaux, Alex. (1993). Social support: Resources and context. In Leo Goldberger & Shlomo Breznitz (Eds.), *Handbook of stress: Theoretical and clinical aspects* (2nd ed.). New York: Free Press.

Hobson, Charles J.; Kamen, Joseph; Szostek, Jana; & Nethercut, Carol M. (1998). Stressful life events: A revision and update of the Social Readjustment Rating Scale. *International Journal of Stress Management, 5*(1), 1–23.

Holmes, Thomas H., & Masuda, Minoru. (1974). Life change and illness susceptibility. In Barbara Snell Dohrenwend & Bruce P. Dohrenwend (Eds.), *Stressful life events: Their nature and effects.* New York: Wiley.

Holmes, Thomas H., & Rahe, Richard H. (1967). The Social Readjustment Rating Scale. *Journal of Psychosomatic Research, 11,* 213–218.

Holt, Robert R. (1993). Occupational stress. In Leo Goldberger & Shlomo Breznitz (Eds.), *Handbook of stress: Theoretical and clinical aspects* (2nd ed.). New York: Free Press.

Janisse, Michel Pierre, & Dyck, Dennis G. (1988). The Type A behavior pattern and coronary heart disease: Physiological and psychological dimensions. In Michel Pierre Janisse (Ed.), *Individual differences, stress, and health psychology.* New York: Springer-Verlag.

Johnson, Katrina W.; Anderson, Norman B.; Bastida, Elena; Kramer, B. Josea; Williams, David; & Wong, Morrison. (1995). Panel II: Macrosocial and environmental influences on minority health. *Health Psychology, 14,* 601–612.

Kanner, Allen D.; Coyne, James C.; Schaefer, Catherine; & Lazarus, Richard S. (1981). Comparison of two modes of stress management: Daily hassles and uplifts versus major life events. *Journal of Behavioral Medicine, 4,* 1–39.

Kessler, Ronald C.; Price, Richard H.; & Wortman, Camille B. (1985). Social factors in psychopathology: Stress, social support, and coping processes. *Annual Review of Psychology, 36,* 531–572.

Kiecolt-Glaser, Janice K. (1999). Stress, personal relationships, and immune function: Health implications. *Brain, Behavior and Immunity, 13*(1), 61–72.

Kiecolt-Glaser, Janice K., & Glaser, Ronald. (1991). Stress and immune function in humans. In Robert Ader, David L. Felten, & Nicholas Cohen (Eds.), *Psychoneuroimmunology*. San Diego, CA: Academic Press.

Kiecolt-Glaser, Janice K., & Glaser, Ronald. (1993). Mind and immunity. In Daniel Goleman & Joel Gurin (Eds.), *Mind/body medicine: How to use your mind for better health*. Yonkers, NY: Consumer Reports Books.

Kiecolt-Glaser, Janice K., & Glaser, Ronald. (2001, Winter). Psychological stress and wound healing. *Advances in Mind-Body Medicine, 17,* 15–17.

Kiecolt-Glaser, Janice K.; McGuire, Lynanne; Robles, Theodore, F.; & Glaser, Ronald. (2002). Emotions, morbidity, and mortality: New perspectives from psychoneuroimmunology. *Annual Review of Psychology, 53,* 83–107.

Kiecolt-Glaser, Janice K., & Newton, Tamara L. (2001). Marriage and health: His and hers. *Psychological Bulletin, 127,* 472–503.

Kiecolt-Glaser, Janice K.; Page, Gayle G.; Marucha, Phillip T.; MacCallum, Robert C.; & Glaser, Ronald. (1998). Psychological influences on surgical recovery: Perspectives from psychoneuroimmunology. *American Psychologist, 53,* 1209–1218.

Kimzey, Stephen L. (1975). The effects of extended spaceflight on hematologic and immunologic systems. *Journal of the American Medical Women's Association, 30,* 218–232.

Krantz, David S., & McCeney, Melissa K. (2002). Effects of psychological and social factors on organic disease: A critical assessment of research on coronary heart disease. *Annual Review of Psychology, 53,* 341–369.

LaFromboise, Teresa D.; Coleman, Hardin L. K.; & Gerton, Jennifer. (1993a). Psychological impact of biculturalism: Evidence and theory. *Psychological Bulletin, 114,* 395–412.

LaFromboise, Teresa D.; Trimble, Joseph E.; & Mohatt, Gerald V. (1993b). Counseling intervention and American Indian tradition: An integrative approach. In Donald R. Atkinson, George Morten, & Derald Wing Sue (Eds.), *Counseling American minorities: A cross-cultural perspective* (4th ed.). Madison, WI: Brown & Benchmark.

Langer, Ellen, & Rodin, Judith. (1976). The effects of choice and enhanced personal responsibility for the aged: A field experiment in an institutional setting. *Journal of Personality and Social Psychology, 34,* 191–198.

Lazarus, Richard S. (1993). From psychological stress to the emotions. A history of changing outlooks. *Annual Review of Psychology, 44,* 1–21.

Lazarus, Richard S. (1999). *Stress and emotion: A new synthesis.* New York: Springer.

Lazarus, Richard S. (2000). Toward better research on stress and coping. *American Psychologist, 55,* 556–773.

Lazarus, Richard S., & Folkman, Susan. (1984). *Stress, appraisal, and coping.* New York: Springer.

Leach, Carolyn S., & Rambaut, Paul C. (1974). Biochemical responses of the *Skylab* crewmen. *Proceedings of the Skylab Life Sciences Symposium, 2,* 427–454.

Lepore, Stephen J. (1993). Social conflict, social support, and psychological distress: Evidence of cross-domain buffering effects. *Journal of Personality and Social Psychology, 63,* 857–867.

Lepore, Stephen J.; Silver, Roxane Cohen; Wortman, Camille B.; & Wayment, Heidi A. (1996). Social constraints, intrusive thoughts, and depressive symptoms among bereaved mothers. *Journal of Personality and Social Psychology, 70,* 271–282.

Leuchter, Andrew F.; Cook, Ian A.; Witte, Elise A.; & others. (2002). Changes in brain function of depressed subjects during treatment with placebo. *American Journal of Psychiatry, 159,* 122–129.

Light, Kathleen C.; Smith, Tara E.; Johns, Josephine M.; Brownley, Kimberly A.; Hofheimer, Julie A.; & Amico, Janet. (2000). Oxytocin responsivity in mothers of infants: A preliminary study of relationships with blood pressure during laboratory stress and normal ambulatory activity. *Health Psychology, 19,* 560–567.

Liu, Dong; Diorio, Josie; Tannenbaum, Beth; Caldji, Christian; Francis, Darlene; Freedman, Alison; & others. (1997). Maternal care, hippocampal glucocorticoid receptors, and hypothalamic-pituitary-adrenal responses to stress. *Science, 277,* 1659–1662.

Lovallo, William R.; al'Absi, Mustafa; Pincomb, Gwen A.; Everson, Susan A.; Sung, Bong Hee; Passey, Richard B.; & Wilson, Michael F. (1996). Caffeine and behavioral stress effects on blood pressure in borderline hypertensive Caucasian men. *Health Psychology, 15,* 11–17.

Lyness, Scott A. (1993). Predictors of differences between Type A and B individuals in heart rate and blood pressure reactivity. *Psychological Bulletin, 114,* 266–295.

Maier, Steven F., & Watkins, Linda R. (2000). The neurobiology of stressor controllability. In Jane E. Gilham (Ed.), *The science of optimism and hope: Research essays in honor of Martin E. P. Seligman.* Philadelphia: Templeton Foundation Press.

Mandler, George. (1993). Thought, memory, and learning: Effects of emotional stress. In Leo Goldberger & Shlomo Breznitz (Eds.), *Handbook of stress: Theoretical and clinical aspects* (2nd ed.). New York: Free Press.

Marco, Christine A., & Suls, Jerry. (1993). Daily stress and the trajectory of mood: Spillover, response assimilation, contrast, and chronic negative affectivity. *Journal of Personality and Social Psychology, 64,* 1053–1063.

Markus, Hazel Rose, & Kitayama, Shinobu. (1991). Culture and the self: Implications for cognition, emotion, and motivation. *Psychological Review, 98,* 224–253.

Marsella, Anthony J., & Dash-Scheuer, Alice. (1988). Coping, culture, and healthy human development: A research and conceptual overview. In Pierre R. Dasen, John W. Berry, & Norman Sartorius (Eds.), *Health and cross-cultural psychology: Toward applications* (Vol. 10, Cross-cultural Research and Methodology Series.). Newbury Park, CA: Sage.

Marshall, Grant N.; Wortman, Camille B.; Kusulas, Jeffrey W.; Hervig, Linda K.; & Vickers, Ross R., Jr. (1992). Distinguishing optimism from pessimism: Relations to fundamental dimensions of mood and personality. *Journal of Personality and Social Psychology, 62,* 1067–1074.

Marucha, Phillip T.; Kiecolt-Glaser, Janice K.; & Favagehi, Mehrdad. (1998). Mucosal wound healing is impaired by examination stress. *Psychosomatic Medicine, 60,* 362–365.

McAndrew, Francis T.; Akande, Adebowale; Turner, Saskia; & Sharma, Yadika. (1998). A cross-cultural ranking of stressful life events in Germany, India, South Africa, and the United States. *Journal of Cross-Cultural Psychology, 29,* 717–727.

Meichenbaum, Donald H., & Fitzpatrick, Deborah. (1993). A constructivist narrative perspective on stress and coping: Stress inoculation applications. In Leo Goldberger & Shlomo Breznitz (Eds.), *Handbook of stress: Theoretical and clinical aspects* (2nd ed.). New York: Free Press.

Mellers, Barbara A. (2000). Choice and the relative pleasure of consequences. *Psychological Bulletin, 126,* 910–924.

Miller, Mark A., & Rahe, Richard H. (1997). Life changes scaling for the 1990s. *Journal of Psychosomatic Research, 43*(3), 279–292.

Miller, Todd Q.; Smith, Timothy W.; Turner, Charles W.; Guijarro, Margarita L.; & Hallet, Amanda J. (1996). A meta-analytic review of research on hostility and physical health. *Psychological Bulletin, 199,* 322–348.

Nemeroff, Charles B. (1998, June). The neurobiology of depression. *Scientific American, 278,* 42–49.

Palmblad, J.; Petrini, B.; Wasserman, J.; & Akerstedt, T. (1979). Lymphocyte and granulocyte reactions during sleep deprivation. *Psychosomatic Medicine, 41,* 273–278.

Pearlin, Leonard I. (1993). The social contexts of stress. In Leo Goldberger & Shlomo Breznitz (Eds.), *Handbook of stress: Theoretical and clinical aspects* (2nd ed.). New York: Free Press.

Peirce, Robert S.; Frone; Michael R.; Russell, Marcia; & Cooper, M. Lynne. (1996). Financial stress, social support, and alcohol involvement: A longitudinal test of the buffering hypothesis in a general population study. *Health Psychology, 15,* 38–47.

Peterson, Christopher. (2000). Optimistic explanatory style and health. In Jane E. Gillham (Ed.), *The science of optimism and hope: Research essays in honor of Martin E. P. Seligman.* Philadelphia: Templeton Foundation Press.

Peterson, Christopher, & Bossio, Lisa M. (1993). Healthy attitudes: Optimism, hope, and control. In Daniel Goleman & Joel Gurin (Eds.), *Mind/body medicine: How to use your mind for better health.* Yonkers, NY: Consumer Reports Books.

Peterson, Christopher, & Bossio, Lisa M. (2001). Optimism and physical well-being. In Edward C. Chang (Ed.), *Optimism and pessimism: Implications for theory, research, and practice.* Washington, DC: American Psychological Association.

Peterson, Christopher; Seligman, Martin E. P.; & Vaillant, George E. (1988). Pessimistic explanatory style as a risk factor for physical illness: A thirty-five-year longitudinal study. *Journal of Personality and Social Psychology, 55,* 23–27.

Petrovic, Predrag; Kalso, Eija; Petersson, Karl Magnus; & Ingvar, Martin. (2002, March 1). Placebo and opioid analgesia—Imaging a shared neuronal network. *Science, 295,* 1737–1740.

Pillow, David R.; Zautra, Alex J.; & Sandler, Irwin. (1996). Major life events and minor stressors: Identifying mediational links in the stress process. *Journal of Personality and Social Psychology, 70,* 381–394.

Rahe, Richard H. (1972). Subjects' recent life changes and their near-future illness reports. *Annals of Clinical Research, 4,* 250–265.

Rejeski, W. Jack; Gregg, Edward; Thompson, Amy; & Berry, Michael. (1991). The effects of varying doses of acute aerobic exercise on psychophysiological stress responses in highly trained cyclists. *Journal of Sport and Exercise Psychology, 13,* 188–199.

Rejeski, W. Jack; Thompson, Amy; Brubaker, Peter H.; & Miller, Henry S. (1992). Acute exercise: Buffering psychosocial responses in women. *Health Psychology, 11,* 355–362.

Repetti, Rena L. (1989). Effects of daily workload on subsequent behavior during marital interaction: The roles of withdrawal and spouse support. *Journal of Personality and Social Psychology, 57,* 651–659.

Repetti, Rena L. (1993). Short-term effects of occupational stressors on daily mood and health complaints. *Health Psychology, 12,* 125–131.

Repetti, Rena L., & Wood, Jenifer. (1997). The effects of daily stress at work on mothers' interactions with preschoolers. *Journal of Family Psychology, 11,* 90–108.

Robbins, Ann S.; Spence, Janet T.; & Clark, Heather. (1991). Psychological determinants of health and performance: The tangled web of desirable and undesirable characteristics. *Journal of Personality and Social Psychology, 61,* 755–765.

Rodin, Judith. (1986, September 19). Aging and health: Effects of the sense of control. *Science, 233,* 1271–1275.

Rodin, Judith, & Langer, Ellen. (1977). Long-term effects of a control-relevant intervention with the institutionalized aged. *Journal of Personality and Social Psychology, 35,* 897–902.

Rook, Karen S. (1992). Detrimental aspects of social relationships: Taking stock of an emerging literature. In Hans O. F. Veiel & Urs Baumann (Eds.), *The meaning and measurement of social support.* New York: Hemisphere.

Rosenman, Ray H., & Chesney, Margaret A. (1982). Stress, Type A behavior, and coronary disease. In Leo Goldberger & Shlomo Breznitz (Eds.), *Handbook of stress: Theoretical and clinical aspects.* New York: Free Press.

Russek, Linda G., & Schwartz, Gary E. (1997). Perceptions of parental caring predict health status in midlife: A 35-year follow-up to the Harvard Mastery of Stress Study. *Psychosomatic Medicine, 59,* 144–149.

Sacks, Michael H. (1993). Exercise for stress control. In Daniel Goleman & Joel Gurin (Eds.), *Mind/body medicine: How to use your mind for better health.* Yonkers, NY: Consumer Reports Books.

Segerstrom, Suzanne C.; Taylor, Shelley E.; Kemeny, Margaret E.; & Fahey, John L. (1998). Optimism is associated with mood, coping, and immune change in response to stress. *Journal of Personality and Social Psychology, 74,* 1646–1655.

Seligman, Martin E. P. (1990). *Learned optimism.* New York: Knopf.

Seligman, Martin E. P. (1992). *Helplessness: On development, depression, and death.* New York: Freeman.

Selye, Hans. (1956). *The stress of life.* New York: McGraw-Hill.

Selye, Hans. (1976). *The stress of life.* (Rev. ed.). New York: McGraw-Hill.

Shumaker, Sally A., & Hill, D. Robin. (1991). Gender differences in social support and physical health. *Health Psychology, 10,* 102–111.

Shuval, Judith T. (1993). Migration and stress. In Leo Goldberger & Shlomo Breznitz (Eds.), *Handbook of stress: Theoretical and clinical aspects* (2nd ed.). New York: Free Press.

Smith, Timothy W. (1992). Hostility and health: Current status of a psychosomatic hypothesis. *Health Psychology, 11,* 139–150.

Spiegel, David. (1993b). Social support: How friends, family, and groups can help. In Daniel Goleman & Joel Gurin (Eds.), *Mind/body medicine: How to use your mind for better health.* Yonkers, NY: Consumer Reports Books.

Spiegel, David; Bloom, J. R.; Kraemer, H. C.; & Gottheil, E. (1989). Effect of psychosocial treatment on survival of patients with metastatic breast cancer. *Lancet, 2,* 888–891.

Stanton, Annette L., & Snider, Pamela R. (1993). Coping with a breast cancer diagnosis: A prospective study. *Health Psychology, 12,* 16–23.

Stone, Arthur A.; Neale, John M.; Cox, Donald S.; Napoli, Anthony; Valdimarsdottir, Heiddis; & Kennedy-Moore, Eileen. (1994). Daily events are associated with a secretory immune response to an oral antigen in men. *Health Psychology, 13,* 440–446.

Taylor, Shelley E. (2000, July/August). Quoted in Beth Azar, A new stress paradigm for women. *APA Monitor on Psychology, 31,* 42–43.

Taylor, Shelley E., & Aspinwall, Lisa G. (1993). Coping with chronic illness. In Leo Goldberger & Shlomo Breznitz (Eds.), *Handbook of stress: Theoretical and clinical aspects* (2nd ed.). New York: Free Press.

Taylor, Shelley E.; Helgeson, Vicki S.; Reed, Geoffrey M.; & Skokan, Laurie A. (1991). Self-generated feelings of control and adjustment to physical illness. *Journal of Social Issues, 47,* 91–109.

Taylor, Shelley E.; Klein, Laura Cousino; Lewis, Brian P.; Guenewald, Tara L.; Gurung, Regan A.; & Updegraff, John A. (2000). Biobehavioral responses to stress in females: Tend-and-befriend, not fight-or-flight. *Psychological Review, 107,* 411–429.

Thompson, Suzanne C.; Nanni, Christopher; & Levine, Alexandra. (1994). Primary versus secondary and central versus consequence-related control in HIV-positive men. *Journal of Personality and Social Psychology, 67,* 540–547.

Thompson, Suzanne C., & Spacapan, Shirlynn. (1991). Perceptions of control in vulnerable populations. *Journal of Social Issues, 47,* 1–21.

Toews, John A.; Lockyer, Jocelyn M.; Dobson, Deborah J. G.; & Simpson, Elizabeth (1997). Analysis of stress levels among medical students, resident, and graduate students at four Canadian schools of medicine. *Academic Medicine, 72*(11), 997–1002.

Tomaka, Joe; Blascovich, Jim; Kelsey, Robert M.; & Leitten, Christopher L. (1993). Subjective, physiological, and behavioral effects of threat and challenge appraisal. *Journal of Personality and Social Psychology, 65,* 248–260.

Tversky, Amos, & Shafir, Eldar. (1992). Choice under conflict: The dynamics of deferred decision. *Psychological Science, 3,* 358–361.

Uchino, Bert N.; Cacioppo, John T.; & Kiecolt-Glaser, Janice K. (1996). The relationship between social support and physiological processes: A review with emphasis on underlying mechanisms and implications for health. *Psychological Bulletin, 119,* 488–531.

Vitkovic, Ljubisa. (1995). Neuroimmunology and neurovirology. In Stephen H. Koslow (Ed.), *The neuroscience of mental health II: A report on neuroscience research: Status and potential for mental health and mental illness* (NIMH Publication No. 95–4000). Rockville, MD: National Institute of Mental Health.

Ward, Colleen, & Rana-Deuba, Arzu. (1999). Acculturation and adaptation revisited. *Journal of Cross-Cultural Psychology, 30*(4), 422–442.

Watson, David, & Pennebaker, James W. (1989). Health complaints, stress, and distress: Exploring the central role of negative affectivity. *Psychological Review, 96,* 234–254.

Weisse, Carol Silvia. (1992). Depression and immunocompetence: A review of the literature. *Psychological Bulletin, 111,* 475–489.

Weisz, John R.; Rothbaum, Fred M.; & Blackburn, Thomas C. (1984). Standing out and standing in: The psychology of control in Japan and America. *American Psychologist, 39,* 955–969.

Wethington, Elaine; McLeod, Jane D.; & Kessler, Ronald C. (1987). The importance of life events for explaining sex differences in psychological distress. In Rosalind C. Barnett, Lois Biener, & Grace K. Baruch (Eds.), *Gender and stress.* New York: Free Press.

Williams, Carolyn L., & Berry, John W. (1991). Primary prevention of acculturative stress among refugees. *American Psychologist, 46,* 632–641.

Wortman, Camille B.; Sheedy, Collette; Gluhoski, Vicki; & Kessler, Ron. (1992). Stress, coping, and health: Conceptual issues and directions for future research. In Howard S. Friedman (Ed.), *Hostility, coping, and health.* Washington, DC: American Psychological Association.

York, Janine; Nicholson, Thomas; Minors, Patricia; & Duncan, David F. (1998). Stressful life events and loss of hair among adult women: A case-control study. *Psychological Reports, 82,*(3, Pt. 1). 1044–1046.

Practicing Your Textbook Reading Skills

1. Examine the "Chapter Outline" on page 537 to determine which of the following is not a *major* topic of the chapter.

   a. "Physical Effects of Stress: The Mind-Body Connection"

   b. "Mind, Body, and the Mysterious Placebo Effect"

   c. "Individual Factors That Influence the Response to Stress"

   d. "Coping: How People Deal with Stress"

2. The chapter prologue ("Katie's Story") on page 537–39

   a. provides a historical overview of the study of stress.

   b. summarizes the chapter's main points.

   c. outlines the chapter's organization.

   d. introduces an example that is used throughout the chapter to explain stress.

3. What is the meaning of the word *bizarre* as it is used in the seventh paragraph of the chapter prologue ("Katie's Story")?

   a. a Middle Eastern market   c. mildly amusing

   b. eerily unfamiliar   d. chaotic

4. Which sentence summarizes the main idea of the first section of the chapter ("What Is Stress?")?

   a. "When events are perceived as exceeding your ability to cope with them, you experience an unpleasant emotional and physical state—stress."

   b. "What is health psychology, and what is the biopsychosocial model?"

   c. "How do life events, daily hassles, and conflict contribute to stress?"

   d. "What are some social and cultural sources of stress?"

5. According to Table 13.1, which of the following events is the most stressful?

   a. death of a close friend

   b. marriage

   c. change in work responsibilities

   d. minor violations of the law

6. What pattern of organization dominates the boxed feature "Culture and Human Behavior 13.1: The Stress of Adapting to a New Culture"(p. 545)?

   a. cause and effect   c. classification

   b. example   d. definition

7. What kind of conflict is illustrated by the *Cathy* cartoon on page 544?
    a. approach-approach   c. approach-avoidance
    b. avoidance-avoidance   d. none of the above

8. Of the following psychologists, who is identified as a key person?
    a. Amos Tyversky   c. Janice Kiecolt-Glaser
    b. Sigmund Freud   d. Lisa F. Berkman

9. The specialized meaning of *distancing* for psychology is
    a. separating yourself physically from something.
    b. acknowledging a stressor but attempting to minimize or eliminate its emotional impact.
    c. measuring the length between two points.
    d. recording a period of time.

10. The boxed feature "Application: Providing effective Social Support" on page 567
    a. suggests how you might use the information in the chapter in your real life.
    b. describes an influential study.
    c. offers information on jobs in health psychology.
    d. includes statistics on psychological studies.

Testing Your Understanding

Identify the following statements as true or false.

1. Two people may respond very differently to the same potentially stressful event.

    T _____   F _____

2. The Social Readjustment Rating Scale accurately predicts how stressors will affect people's health.

    T _____   F _____

3. A person who has a sense of control over a potentially stressful situation will be less stressed by it than a person who does not feel a sense of control.

    T _____   F _____

4. Pessimistic people tend to be healthier than optimistic people.

    T _____   F _____

5. Research shows that loneliness can harm your health as much as smoking, having high cholesterol, being overweight, and not exercising.

    T _____   F _____

Select the best answer to each of the following questions.

6. According to the *biopsychosocial model,* health and illness are determined by

    a. our cognitive appraisal of an event and the resources we have to deal with it.

    b. the complex interaction of biological factors, psychological and behavioral factors, and social conditions.

    c. everyday occurrences that annoy and upset people.

    d. how people characteristically explain their failures and defeats.

7. Daily hassles strongly affect stress levels because they are

    a. annoying.

    b. unpredictable.

    c. cumulative.

    d. minor.

8. All of the following are types of conflict except

    a. approach-approach.

    b. avoidance-avoidance.

    c. approach-avoidance.

    d. vacillation.

9. Whose research in the 1970s revolutionized psychologists' understanding of the relationship between the mind and the immune system?

    a. Robert Ader and Nicholas Cohen

    b. Ron Glaser and Janice Kiecolt-Glaser

    c. Walter B. Cannon

    d. Hans Selye

10. Which of the following might explain why chronically negative people are more likely to suffer serious health problems than positive people are?

    a. Positive people are more likely to be affected by daily hassles.

    b. Positive people react more intensely to stressors.

    c. Negative people suffer from learned helplessness.

    d. Negative people experience more stress than positive people do.

11. All of the following are characteristics of Type A behavior except

    a. extreme confidence.

    b. exaggerated sense of time urgency.

    c. general sense of hostility.

    d. intense ambition and competitiveness.

12. Having friends can benefit your health because
    a. knowing that they support you can make a situation seem less threatening.
    b. their presence decreases the intensity of physical reactions to a stressor.
    c. loneliness increases levels of stress hormones and weakens the immune system.
    d. all of the above.

13. Which of the following is an example of an adaptive coping strategy?
    a. smoking
    b. maintaining self-esteem
    c. drinking
    d. hostile confrontation

14. Which of the following is more likely than the others to worsen the physical effects of stress?
    a. watching television
    b. exercising regularly
    c. avoiding stimulants
    d. practicing a relaxation technique

15. All of the following are examples of emotion-focused coping except
    a. escape-avoidance.
    b. seeking social support.
    c. planful problem solving.
    d. denial.

Using your own words, define the following terms as they are used in the chapter.

16. *conflict*

    _____

    _____

17. *acculturative stress*

    _____

    _____

18. *fight-or-flight response*

    _____

    _____

19. *corticosteroids*

_____

_____

20. *coping*

_____

_____

Answer each of the following questions using the space provided.

21. Identify two strategies for resolving an approach-avoidance conflict.

_____

_____

_____

22. What physical symptoms might occur when a person faces immediate danger?

_____

_____

_____

23. Outline and briefly describe the three stages of general adaptation syndrome.

_____

_____

_____

_____

24. Describe the differences in how men and women experience and cope with stress.

_____

_____

_____

_____

_____

25. Provide two examples of how Americans' and Asians' coping strategies differ.

_____

_____

_____

Making Thematic Connections

The history chapter reprinted in Unit 5 of this reader describes working conditions in late-nineteenth-century America and how different people and organizations responded to them. For example, as laborers found they had less control over their work, cheap forms of entertainment—such as movie theaters, amusement parks, and dance halls—became increasingly popular. (See pages 688–71 of that chapter for more information.) How would you categorize that development as a coping strategy? Is spending time on amusements an emotion-focused or a problem-focused coping strategy? Is it adaptive or maladaptive? Explain your answer. (Note that *adaptive* behavior helps people get everyday tasks done, while *maladaptive* behavior interferes with people's ability to perform such tasks.)

Mass Communication

"Public Relations and Framing the Message"

Introduction

Mass communication is the study of how individuals and groups spread information, ideas, and entertainment to a wide audience. Newspapers and magazines, television and radio, movies, the Internet, and advertising and public relations are all part of the media examined by mass communication scholars. As an academic discipline, mass communication seeks not only to understand the various channels of communication available to those who want to spread a message or entertainment but also to train students in how to work in one of the mass media industries.

Media and Culture: An Introduction to Mass Communication, Updated Third Edition, by Richard Campbell, Christopher R. Martin, and Bettina Fabos, is a popular introductory textbook used in hundreds of colleges across the United States. Because the media pervade almost every aspect of our lives, the book aims to teach its readers "to become critical consumers of the media and engaged citizens in the society that the media shape." As part of this effort, the authors take a "critical approach" and organize the book's chapters—including the one on public relations that you're about to read—into four parts: description, analysis, interpretation, and evaluation. Like any good introductory textbook, *Media and Culture* is carefully designed and written to teach the content it covers. It includes a number of features and tools to help you read it successfully. The chapter's opening story, photographs with captions, cartoons, and highlighted quotations in the margins show examples of public relations work in action and help to keep the material interesting. Paying attention to the chapter's different levels of headings will help you determine how the information is connected and what is most important. Tables and figures provide data and facts to back up or explain elements of the chapter's main discussion. The chapter also offers learning tools, such as bold-face glossary terms and "Review Questions," that will help you check your understanding.

This unit's textbook reading comes from *Media and Culture: An Introduction to Mass Communication,* Updated Third Edition, by Richard Campbell, Christopher R. Martin, and Bettina Fabos, Bedford/St. Martin's, 2003, Chapter 12, pages 422–51.

As you read, you'll come across a couple of highlighted sections: "Case Study" and "Examining Ethics." Remember that you aren't expected to read these boxed features in the same flow as the text itself; they provide additional information on and in-depth looks at the key points made in the text. And at the end of the chapter, sections called "Questioning the Media," "Searching the Internet," and "The Critical Process" are designed to help you review what you have learned and think critically about it, learn about Internet resources, and (if you were taking a course in mass communication) study for a quiz or a test.

How does the communication chapter fit into this reader's overall theme of work? First, it explores a field that may interest you as a potential career. As you're about to learn, public relations is a growing business with many job opportunities, ranging from researching to writing to making television appearances. At the same time, the chapter looks closely at how others have worked in this field, and it examines some of the ethical and practical issues that public relations workers face. The history of public relations that begins on page 426 of this chapter covers much of the same period (the late 1800s) that is discussed in the history chapter reprinted in Unit 5. Consider also that public relations tries to help different businesses win customers from a limited pool—a competition that is in many ways similar to the community interactions described in the biology chapter reprinted in Unit 4.

Preparing to Read the Textbook Chapter

1. Has your opinion of a company, a politician, or a product ever been influenced by a public relations campaign? How do you know?

2. Take a moment to scan through the chapter. Are any of the images familiar? Which ones capture your interest? Why?

3. Imagine that you work for a major clothing company. Its most recent line of children's play wear was defective—the seams fell apart on the first washing—and a competitor has been quick to emphasize the durability of its children's clothes in a recent round of ads. What would you recommend your employer do to regain your customers' confidence and their business?

public relations
and framing the message

CHAPTER 12

In the mid-1950s, the blue-jeans industry was in deep trouble. After hitting a postwar peak in 1953, jeans sales began to slide. The durable one-hundred-year-old denim product had become associated with rock and roll and teenage troublemakers. Popular movies, especially *The Wild One* and *Blackboard Jungle*, featured emotionally disturbed, blue-jeans-wearing "young toughs" terrorizing adult authority figures. A Broadway play about juvenile delinquency was even entitled *Blue Denim*. The worst was yet to come, however. In

1957, the public school system in Buffalo, New York, banned the wearing of blue jeans for all high-school students. Formerly associated with farmers, factory workers, and an adult work ethic, jeans had become a reverse fashion statement for teenagers—something many adults could not abide.

In response to the crisis, the denim industry waged a public relations (PR) campaign to eradicate the delinquency label and rejuvenate denim's image. In 1956, the nation's top blue-jeans manufacturers formed

the national Denim Council "to put schoolchildren back in blue jeans through a concerted national public relations, advertising, and promotional effort."[1] First the council targeted teens, but its promotional efforts were unsuccessful. The manufacturers soon realized that the problem was not with the teens but with the parents, administrators, teachers, and school boards. It was the adults who felt threatened by a fashion trend that seemed to promote

● The delinquent in jeans: Marlon Brando in *The Wild One* (1953).

● The good citizen in jeans: former president Jimmy Carter, working with Habitat for Humanity.

disrespect through casualness. In response, the council hired a public relations firm to turn the image of blue jeans around. Over the next five years, the firm did just that.

The public relations team determined that mothers were refusing to outfit their children in jeans because of the product's association with delinquency. To change this perception among women, the team encouraged fashion designers to update denim's image by producing new women's sportswear styles made from the fabric. Media outlets and fashion editors were soon inundated with news releases about the "new look" of durable denim.

The PR team next enlisted sportswear designers to provide new designs for both men's and women's work and utility clothes, long the backbone of denim sales. Targeting business reporters as well as fashion editors, the team transformed the redesign effort into a story that appealed to writers in both areas. They also planned retail-store promotions nationwide, including "jean queen" beauty contests, and advanced positive denim stories in men's publications.

The team's major PR coup, however, involved an association with the newly formed national Peace Corps. The brainchild of the Kennedy administration, the Peace Corps encouraged young people to serve their country by working with people from developing nations. Envisioning the Peace Corps as the flip side of delinquency, the Denim Council saw its opening. In 1961, it agreed to outfit the first group of two hundred corps volunteers in denim. As a result of all these PR efforts, by 1963 manufacturers were flooded with orders, and sales of jeans and other denim goods were way up. The delinquency tag disappeared, and jeans gradually became associated with a more casual, though not anti-social, dress ethic.

424

he blue-jeans story illustrates a major difference between advertising and public relations: Advertising is controlled publicity that a company or an individual buys; public relations attempts to secure favorable media publicity (which is more difficult to control) to promote a company or client. In advertising, clients buy space or time for their products or services, and consumers know who paid for the messages. But with public relations the process is more subtle, requiring news media to accept the premise or legitimacy of a PR campaign and to use it as news. The transformation of denim in the public's eye was achieved primarily without the purchase of advertising. The PR team restyled denim's image mainly by cultivating friendly relations with reporters who subsequently wrote stories associating the fabric with a casual, dedicated, youthful America.

Publicity refers to one type of PR communication: messages that spread information about a person, corporation, issue, or policy in various media. Public relations today, however, involves many communication strategies besides publicity. In fact, much of what PR specialists do involves dealing with negative or unplanned publicity. For example, when documents and audiotapes surfaced in the fall of 1996 revealing that certain top executives at Texaco had made racist remarks, an intense PR campaign began. It employed a range of tactics, including paid TV advertising, major news conferences, and meetings with regional Texaco distributors. The Denny's chain of restaurants encountered similar negative publicity throughout the 1990s, particularly after six African American Secret Service agents were refused service in one of the restaurants in 1993. However, by 2002 the chain had improved its image so much that *Fortune* magazine listed it as the country's best company for minority employees two years in a row.

Because it involves multiple forms of communication, **public relations** is difficult to define precisely. It covers a wide array of actions, such as shaping the image of a politician or celebrity, repairing the image of a major corporation, establishing two-way communication between consumers and companies, and molding wartime propaganda. Broadly defined, *public relations* refers to the entire range of efforts by an individual, an agency, or any organization attempting to reach or persuade audiences.[2]

The social and cultural impact of public relations, like that of advertising, has been immense. In its infancy, PR helped convince many American businesses of the value of nurturing the public, who had been redefined as purchasers rather than as producers of their own goods. PR also set the tone for the corporate image-building that characterized the economic environment of the twentieth century and transformed the profession of journalism by complicating the way "facts" could be interpreted. Perhaps PR's most significant effect, however, has been on the political process in which individuals and organizations—on both the Right and the Left—hire *spin doctors* to shape their media images.

> **❝** An **image** . . . is not simply a trademark, a design, a slogan or an easily remembered picture. It is a **studiously crafted personality profile** of an individual, institution, corporation, product or service. **❞**
>
> –Daniel Boorstin, *The Image,* 1961

Without public relations, the news profession would be hard-pressed to keep up with every upcoming event or complex issue. Although reporters and editors do not like to admit it, PR departments and agencies are a major source of story ideas and information. In this chapter, we will examine the impact of public relations and the historical conditions that affected its development as a modern profession—how it helped transform America into a more image-conscious society. We will begin by looking at nineteenth-century press agents and the role that railroads and utility companies played in developing corporate PR. We will then consider the rise of modern PR, particularly the influences of former reporters Ivy Lee and Edward Bernays.

In addition, we will explore the major practices and specialties of public relations, the reasons for the long-standing antagonism between journalists and members of the PR profession, and the social responsibilities of PR in a democracy.

Early developments in public relations

At the beginning of the twentieth century, the United States slowly shifted to a consumer-oriented, industrial society that fostered the rapid spread of advertising and publicity for new products and services. During this gradual transformation from farm to factory, PR emerged as a profession, partly because businesses needed to fend off increased scrutiny from muckraking journalists and emerging labor unions.[3]

Prior to this time, the first PR practitioners were simply theatrical **press agents**: those who sought to advance a client's image through media exposure, primarily via stunts staged for newspapers. The potential of these early PR techniques soon became obvious to business executives and to politicians. For instance, press agents were used by people like Daniel Boone, who engineered various land-grab and real-estate ventures, and Davy Crockett, who in addition to heroic exploits was also involved in the massacre of Native Americans. Such individuals often wanted to repair and reshape their reputation as cherished frontier legends or as respectable candidates for public office.

P. T. Barnum, Buffalo Bill, and the railroads

The most notorious theatrical agent of the 1800s was Phineas Taylor (P. T.) Barnum, who used gross exaggeration, fraudulent stories, and staged events to secure newspaper coverage for his clients, his American Museum, and later, his circus. Barnum's best-known acts included the "midget" General Tom Thumb, Swedish soprano Jenny Lind, Jumbo the Elephant, and Joice Heth, who Barnum claimed was the 161-year-old nurse of George Washington (although she was actually 80 when she died). These performers became some of the earliest nationally known celebrities because of Barnum's skill in using the media for promotion. Decrying outright fraud and cheating, Barnum understood that his audiences liked to be tricked. In newspapers and on handbills, he later often revealed the strategies behind his more elaborate hoaxes.

● Buffalo Bill's Wild West and Congress of Rough Riders of the World show, depicted in this 1899 poster, was internationally popular as a touring show for more than thirty years. William Frederick Cody (1846–1917) became popularly known as "Buffalo Bill" through dime-store novel stories adapted from his life by E. Z. C. Judson (under the pen name Ned Buntline). Prior to his fame as an entertainer, he worked as a Pony Express rider at age 14, and later as a buffalo hunter for the Kansas Pacific Railroad. Cody claimed that he killed 4,280 buffalo in one seventeen-month period.

From 1883 to 1916, former army scout William F. Cody, who once killed buffalo for the railroads, promoted himself in his "Buffalo Bill's Wild West and Congress of Rough Riders" traveling show. Cody's troupe—which featured bedouins, cossacks, and gauchos as well as "cowboys and Indians"—re-created dramatic gunfights, the Civil War, and battles of the Old West. The show employed sharpshooter Annie Oakley and Lakota medicine man Sitting Bull, whose own legends were partially shaped by Cody's nine publicity agents. These agents were led by John Burke, who promoted the show for its thirty-four-year run. Burke was one of the first PR agents to use a variety of media channels: promotional newspaper stories, magazine articles and ads, dime novels, theater marquees, poster art, and early films. Burke's efforts successfully elevated Cody's show, which was seen by more than fifty million people in a thousand cities in twelve countries.[4] Burke and Buffalo Bill shaped many of the lasting myths about rugged American individualism and frontier expansion. Along with Barnum, they were among the first to use publicity to elevate entertainment-centered culture to an international level.

During the 1800s, America's largest industrial companies, particularly the railroads, also employed press agents to win favor in the court of public opinion. Initially, government involvement in railroad development was minimal; local businesses raised funds to finance the spread of rail service. Around 1850, however, the railroads began pushing for federal subsidies, complaining that local fund-raising efforts took too long. In its drive for government support, for example, Illinois Central promoted the following public strategy: "The railroad line would be expensive to construct; it would open up new land for economic development; without subsidy, the line might not be built; with subsidy the public interest would be served."[5] Illinois Central was one of the first companies to use government lobbyists to argue that railroad service between the North and the South would ease tensions, unite the two regions, and prevent a war.

The railroads successfully campaigned for government support by developing some of the earliest publicity tactics. Their first strategy was simply to buy favorable news stories through direct bribes. By the late 1880s, this practice was so common that a Chicago news reporter published his tongue-in-cheek rates: "For setting forth of virtues (actual or alleged) of presidents, general managers, or directors, $2 per line.... For complimentary notices of the wives and children of railroad officials, we demand $1.50 per line. . . . Epic poems, containing descriptions of scenery, dining cars, etc., will be published at special rates."[6] In addition to planting favorable articles in the press, the railroads engaged in *deadheading*: the practice of giving reporters free rail passes with the tacit understanding that they would write glowing reports about rail travel. Eventually, wealthy railroads received federal subsidies and increased their profits, while the public shouldered much of the financial burden for rail expansion.

In terms of power and influence, companies like Illinois Central and the Pennsylvania Railroad in the late 1800s were comparable to American automakers in the 1950s. Having obtained construction subsidies, the larger rail companies turned their attention to bigger game—lobbying the government to control rates and reduce competition, especially from smaller, aggressive regional lines. Railroad lobbyists argued that federal support would lead to improved service and guaranteed quality, because the government would be keeping a close watch. These lobbying efforts, accompanied by favorable publicity, led to passage of the Interstate Commerce Act in 1881, authorizing railroads "to revamp their freight classification, raise rates, and eliminate fare reduction."[7] Historians have argued that the PR campaign's success actually led to the decline of railroads: Artificially maintained higher rates and burdensome government regulations forced smaller firms out of business and eventually drove many customers to other modes of transportation.

The modern public relations agent

Along with the railroads, utility companies such as Chicago Edison and AT&T also used PR strategies in the late 1800s to derail competition and eventually attain monopoly status. In fact, although both local and regional competitors existed at the time, AT&T's PR and lobbying efforts were so effective that they eliminated all telephone competition—with the government's blessing—until the 1980s.

The tactics of the 1880s and 1890s, however, would haunt public relations as it struggled to become a respected profession. In addition to buying the votes of key

> **"Public relations developed in the early part of the twentieth century as a profession which responded to, and helped shape, the public, newly defined as irrational, not reasoning; spectatorial, not participant; consuming, not productive."**
>
> –Michael Schudson, *Discovering the News,* **1978**

"Since crowds do not reason, they can only be organized and stimulated through **symbols and phrases.**"

–Ivy Lee, 1917

lawmakers, the utilities used a number of shady practices. These included hiring third-party editorial services, which would send favorable articles about utilities to newspapers; assigning company managers to become leaders in community groups; producing ghostwritten articles (often using the names of prominent leaders and members of women's social groups, who were flattered to see their names in print); and influencing textbook authors to write histories favorable to the utilities.[8]

As the promotional agendas of many companies escalated in the late 1800s, a number of reporters and muckraking journalists began investigating these practices. By the early 1900s, with an informed citizenry paying more attention, it became more difficult for large firms to fool the press and mislead the public. With the rise of the middle class, increasing literacy among the working classes, and the spread of information through print media, democratic ideals began to threaten the established order of business and politics—and the elite groups who managed them.

"Poison Ivy" Lee

Most nineteenth-century corporations and manufacturers cared little about public sentiment. By the early 1900s, though, executives realized that their companies could sell more products if they were associated with positive public images and values. Into this public space stepped Ivy Ledbetter Lee, considered one of the founders of modern public relations. Lee understood the undercurrents of social change. He counseled clients that honesty and directness were better PR devices than the deceptive practices of the 1800s, which had fostered a climate of suspicion and anti–big-business sentiment.

A minister's son and once an economics student at Princeton University, Lee, a former reporter, opened one of the first New York PR firms with a colleague in the early 1900s. Lee quit the firm in 1906 to work for the Pennsylvania Railroad, which, following a rail accident, wanted him to help downplay unfavorable publicity. Lee's advice, however, was that Penn admit its mistake, vow to do better, and let newspapers in on the story. These suggestions ran counter to what the utilities and railroads had been doing, yet Lee argued that an open relationship between the press and business would lead to a more favorable public image. In the end, Penn adopted Lee's strategies.

In 1914, Lee went to work for John D. Rockefeller, who by the 1880s controlled 90 percent of the nation's oil industry (Rockefeller once said, "It is my duty to make money and still more money").[9] Rockefeller suffered from periodic image problems, particularly after Ida Tarbell's powerful muckraking series in *McClure's* magazine about Rockefeller's Standard Oil trust. Despite his philanthropic work, Rockefeller was often depicted in the press as a tyrant, as were other corporate bosses. The Rockefeller and Standard Oil reputations reached a low point in April 1914, when tactics to stop union organizing erupted in tragedy at a fuel and iron company in Ludlow, Colorado. During a violent strike, fifty-three workers and their family members, including thirteen women and children, died.

Lee was hired to contain the damaging publicity fallout. He immediately distributed a series of "fact" sheets to the press, telling the corporate side of the story and discrediting the United Mine Workers, which had been trying to organize the Ludlow workers. As he had done for Penn, Lee brought in the press and staged photo opportunities. John D. Rockefeller Jr., who by then ran his father's company, donned overalls and a miner's helmet and posed with the families of workers and union leaders. While Lee helped the company improve conditions for workers, the publicity campaign also kept the union out of the Ludlow coal mines. This was probably the first use of a PR campaign in a labor-management dispute. Over the years, Lee completely transformed the wealthy family's image, urging the discreet Rockefellers to publicize their charitable work. To improve his image, the senior Rockefeller took to handing out dimes to children wherever he went—a strategic ritual that historians attribute to Lee.

Called "Poison Ivy" by newspaper critics and corporate foes, Lee had a complex understanding of facts. He realized, better than most journalists of his day, that facts were open to various interpretations. For Lee, facts were elusive and malleable, begging to be forged and shaped. Interpreting facts so as to shine the best light on a client was not viewed as a particularly honorable practice, however. In the Ludlow case, for instance, Lee noted that the women and children who died while retreating from the charging company-backed militia had overturned a stove, which caught fire and caused their deaths. His PR fact sheet implied that they had, in part, been victims of their own carelessness.

In the 1930s, Ivy Lee was investigated by Congress for counseling German industries during the Nazi regime and for fraternizing with the Soviet Union under Joseph Stalin. Some critics thought that Lee's interest in a communist nation represented a curious contradiction for an avowed capitalist. In Lee's earlier work for railroads and utilities, however, he had advocated an anticompetition, pro-consolidation theme that he believed was in the best interests of his clients. Lee had argued for corporate-controlled monopolies, which benefited from protective government regulation. Thus Lee did share some common ground with foreign governments that ran state-controlled, anticompetitive business monopolies.

Edward Bernays

The nephew of Sigmund Freud, former reporter Edward Bernays inherited the public relations mantle from Ivy Lee and dressed it up with modern social science. Bernays, who died in 1995 at age 103, was the first person to apply the findings of psychology and sociology to the business of public relations. He also referred to himself as a "public relations counselor" rather than as just a publicity agent. Over the years, Bernays's client list included General Electric, the American Tobacco Company, General Motors, *Good Housekeeping* and *Time* magazines, Procter & Gamble, RCA, the government of India, and the city of Vienna. In addition, he served as an adviser to President Coolidge in the 1920s, helping the president revamp his stiff, formal image.

Bernays made key contributions to public relations education.[10] He taught the first class called *public relations*—at New York University in 1923—and wrote the field's first textbook, *Crystallizing Public Opinion*. For many years, his definition of PR was a standard: "Public relations is the attempt, by information, persuasion, and

● Public relations pioneer Edward Bernays and his business partner and wife, Doris Fleischman, worked on behalf of a client, the American Tobacco Company, to make smoking socially acceptable for women. For one of American Tobacco's brands, Lucky Strike, they were also asked to change public attitudes toward the color green. (Women weren't buying the brand because surveys indicated that the forest-green package clashed with their wardrobes.) Bernays and Fleischman organized events such as green fashion shows and sold the idea of a new trend in green to the press. By 1934, green had become the fashion color of the season, making Lucky Strikes the perfect accessory for the female smoker. Interestingly, Bernays forbade his own wife to smoke, flushing her cigarettes down the toilet and calling smoking a nasty habit.

❝It was the astounding success of propaganda during the war which opened the eyes of the intelligent few in all departments of life to the possibilities of regimenting the public mind.**❞**

–Edward Bernays,
Propaganda, 1928

adjustment, to engineer public support for an activity, cause, movement, or institution." Bernays worked for the Committee on Public Information (CPI) during World War I, developing propaganda that supported America's entry into that conflict. Later, CPI helped create the image of President Woodrow Wilson as a peacemaker, among the first full-scale governmental attempts to mobilize public opinion.

Hired by the American Tobacco Company after World War I, Bernays was asked to develop a campaign that would make smoking more publicly acceptable for newly liberated women who had recently won the right to vote. Among other strategies, Bernays staged an event: placing women smokers in New York's 1929 Easter parade. He labeled cigarettes "torches of freedom" and encouraged women to smoke as a symbol of their newly acquired suffrage and independence from men. He also asked the women he placed in the parade to contact newspaper and newsreel companies in advance—to announce their symbolic protest. The campaign received plenty of free publicity from newspapers and magazines. Within five weeks of the parade, men-only smoking rooms in New York theaters began opening up to women.

Through much of his writing, Bernays suggested that emerging forms of social democracy threatened the established hierarchical order. He thought it was important for experts and leaders to keep business and society pointed in the right directions: "The duty of the higher strata of society—the cultivated, the learned, the expert, the intellectual—is therefore clear. They must inject moral and spiritual motives into public opinion."[11] Bernays saw a typical public relations campaign giving shape to public opinion—what he termed the "engineering of consent." Bernays believed that for any PR campaign to work, securing the consent of the people was the crucial ingredient.

Ivy Lee believed that public opinion was based on people's self-interests. Both Lee and Bernays thought that such opinion was pliant and not always rational: In the hands of the right experts, leaders, and PR counselors, public opinion was ready for shaping in forms that people could rally behind.[12] Walter Lippmann, the newspaper columnist who wrote *Public Opinion* in 1922, also believed in the importance of an expert class to direct the more irrational twists and turns of public opinion. But he saw the development of public relations as "a clear sign that the facts of modern life [did] not spontaneously take a shape in which they can be known."[13] Lippmann lamented that too often PR professionals with hidden agendas, rather than detached reporters, were giving only their own meaning to the facts.

Throughout Bernays's most active years, his business partner and later his wife, Doris Fleischman, worked on many joint projects as a researcher and coauthor. Beginning in the 1920s, she was one of the first women to work in advertising and public relations. She edited a pamphlet called *Contact*, which explained the emerging profession of public relations to America's most powerful leaders. Because it was a new quasi-profession not claimed entirely by men, PR was one of the few professions—apart from teaching and nursing—that were accessible to women who chose to work outside the home. By 2002, women outnumbered men by more than three to one in the profession.

Pseudo-events and manufacturing news

Armed with its new understanding of public psychology, modern public relations changed not only the relationship between corporations and the public but also that among corporations, politics, and journalism. In his influential book *The Image*, historian Daniel Boorstin coined the term **pseudo-event** to refer to one of the key contributions of PR and advertising in the twentieth century. Basically, a pseudo-event is any circumstance created for the purpose of gaining coverage in the media. In other words, if no news media show up, there is no event.[14]

Typical pseudo-events are interviews, press conferences, TV and radio talk shows, the Super Bowl pregame show, or any other staged activity aimed at drawing public attention and media coverage. Such events depend on the participation of clients and performers and on the media's recording of the performances. With regard to national politics, Theodore Roosevelt's administration set up the first White House pressroom and held the first presidential press conferences in the early 1900s. In the 1990s, Vice President Al Gore championed White House Internet sites, making it possible for larger public audiences to interact with reporters and leaders in electronic press conferences.

As powerful companies, savvy politicians, and activist groups became aware of the media's susceptibility to pseudo-events, these activities proliferated. For example, to get free publicity, companies began staging press conferences to announce new product lines. During the 1960s, antiwar and civil-rights protesters began their events only when the news media were assembled. One anecdote from that era aptly illustrates the principle of a pseudo-event: A reporter asked a student leader about the starting time for a particular protest; the student responded, "When can you get here?"

Politicians running for national office have become particularly adept at scheduling press conferences and interviews around 5 or 6 P.M. They realize that local TV news is live during these times, so they stage pseudo-events to take advantage of TV's appetite for live remote feeds and breaking news.

The practice of public relations

By 2002, there were more than 2,900 PR firms worldwide, including 2,200 in the United States; thousands of companies and organizations also had in-house departments devoted to public relations functions. In addition, the formal study of public relations, especially since the 1980s, experienced significant growth in colleges and universities. As certified PR programs expanded (often featuring journalism as a minor), the profession relied less and less on the ranks of reporters for its workforce. At the same time, new courses in professional ethics and issues management trained future practitioners to be more responsible.

The growth of formal PR education has been fairly dramatic. In the 1970s, the majority of students in communications and journalism programs indicated in surveys that they intended to pursue careers in news or magazine writing. By the late 1980s, however, similar surveys indicated that the majority of students wanted to enter public relations or advertising. Throughout the 1990s, entry-level salaries and opportunities were greater in the latter areas. By 2002, the Public Relations Student Society of America (PRSSA) had more than 6,000 members and chapters in 208 colleges and universities. Such growth parallels the general rise of business schools and majors throughout the 1970s and 1980s.

Approaches to organized public relations

In 1988, the Public Relations Society of America (PRSA) offered this useful definition of PR: "Public relations helps an organization and its publics adapt mutually to each other." To carry out this mutual communication process, the PR industry follows two main approaches. First, many agencies function as independent companies whose sole job is to provide various clients with PR services. (During the 1980s and 1990s, though, many large ad agencies acquired independent PR firms as subsidiaries.) Second, most companies, which may or may not buy the services of independent PR firms, maintain their own in-house staffs to handle routine PR tasks, such as writing press releases, managing various media requests, staging special events, and dealing with the public.

● **Table 12.1 The Top 15 Public Relations Firms, 2000**
(by Worldwide Net Fees in U.S. $)

Rank	Firm (parent firm)	2000 Net Fees	Number of Employees
1	Fleishman-Hillard (Omnicom)	$342,840,620	2,620
2	Weber Shandwick Worldwide (Interpublic)	334,960,755	2,672
3	Hill and Knowlton (WPP Group)	306,264,000	2,389
4	Burson-Marsteller (WPP Group)	303,860,000	1,955
5	Incepta (Citigate)	243,938,000	1,847
6	Edelman PR Worldwide	238,044,792	2,319
7	Porter Novelli Int'l (Omnicom)	208,157,000	1,812
8	BSMG Worldwide (True North)*	192,194,536	1,245
9	Ogilvy PR Worldwide (WPP Group)	169,453,900	1,534
10	Ketchum (Omnicom)	168,247,000	1,299
11	GCI Group/APCO Assocs. (Grey)	150,661,643	1,324
12	Golin/Harris Int'l (Interpublic)	136,993,000	913
13	Manning, Selvage & Lee (B Com3)	118,843,522	955
14	Euro RSCG (Havas)	107,959,000	859
15	Brodeur Worldwide (Omnicom)	84,200,000	750

*On July 10, 2001, Interpublic, which had earlier acquired True North Communications, announced that it would merge BSMG Worldwide with Weber Shandwick to form the largest global public relations firm.

Source: The J. R. O'Dwyer Company, 2001, <www.odwyerpr.com>.

Independent agencies   About 2,200 American companies identify themselves exclusively as public relations counseling firms. Two of the biggest, Burson-Marsteller and Hill and Knowlton, are now subsidiaries of the same global ad agency, the WPP Group (see Table 12.1). Founded in 1953, Burson-Marsteller remains one of PR's top-ranking firms, with revenue of more than $300 million annually. It has about 76 offices operating in 35 countries and about 2,000 employees worldwide. Among its major clients have been Boeing and McDonald's.

Hill and Knowlton employs more than 2,300 people in 170 offices in 33 countries. Its clients have included Microsoft, Motorola, Nintendo, Pepsi, Procter & Gamble, Xerox, former president Richard Nixon, and the royal family of Kuwait. By the late 1990s, most of the largest PR firms were owned by or affiliated with multinational ad agencies, such as WPP, Omnicom, and Interpublic, which have long provided PR as a part of their full-service operations.

In-house services   In contrast to independent agencies, the most common type of public relations is done in-house by individual companies and organizations. Although about a third of America's largest companies retain an external PR firm, almost every company involved in a manufacturing or service industry has an in-house department. Such departments are also a vital part of many professional organizations, such as the American Medical Association, the AFL-CIO, and the National Association of Broadcasters, as well as large nonprofit organizations, such as the American Cancer Society, the Arthritis Foundation, and most universities and colleges.

Performing public relations

Public relations, like advertising, pays careful attention to the various audiences and clients that it interacts with or serves. These groups include not only consumers and the general public but company employees, shareholders, media organizations, government agencies, and community and industry leaders. Among potential clients, which constitute another public, are politicians, small businesses, industries, and nonprofit organizations.

Public relations involves a multitude of practices and techniques. The PRSA identifies a number of general activities associated with PR: publicity, communication, public affairs, issues management, government relations, financial PR, community relations, industry relations, minority relations, advertising, press agentry, promotion, media relations, and propaganda. This last activity, **propaganda**, is communication strategically placed, either as advertising or publicity, to gain public support for a special issue, program, or policy, such as a nation's war effort.

The practice of public relations encompasses a wide range of activities. PR personnel produce employee newsletters, manage client trade shows and conferences, conduct historical tours, appear on news programs, organize damage control after negative publicity, and analyze complex issues and trends that may affect a client's future. Basic among these activities, however, are writing and editing, media relations, special events, research, and community and government relations. PR practice is generally divided into two roles: PR technicians, who handle daily short-term activities, and PR managers, who counsel clients and manage activities over the long term.

Writing and editing

One of the chief day-to-day technical functions in public relations is composing news releases, or **press releases**: announcements, written in the style of news reports, that give new information about an individual, company, or organization and pitch a story idea to the news media (see Figure 12.1). In issuing press releases, often called *handouts* by the news media, PR agents hope that their client information will be picked up and transformed into news. Through press releases, PR firms manage the flow of information; they often control which media get what material in which order. (Sometimes a PR agent will reward a cooperative reporter through the strategic release of information.)

News editors and broadcasters sort through hundreds of releases daily to determine which ones contain the most original ideas or the most currency for their readers and viewers. The majority of large media institutions rewrite and double-check

● During World War I, PR pioneer Edward Bernays (1891–1995) worked for the federal Committee on Public Information (CPI). One of the main functions of the CPI was to create the poster art and print ads that would persuade reluctant or isolationist Americans to support the war effort against Germany.

❝PR expands the public discourse, helps provide a wide assortment of news, and is essential in explaining the **pluralism** of our total communication system.❞

—John C. Merrill, *Media Debates*, 1991

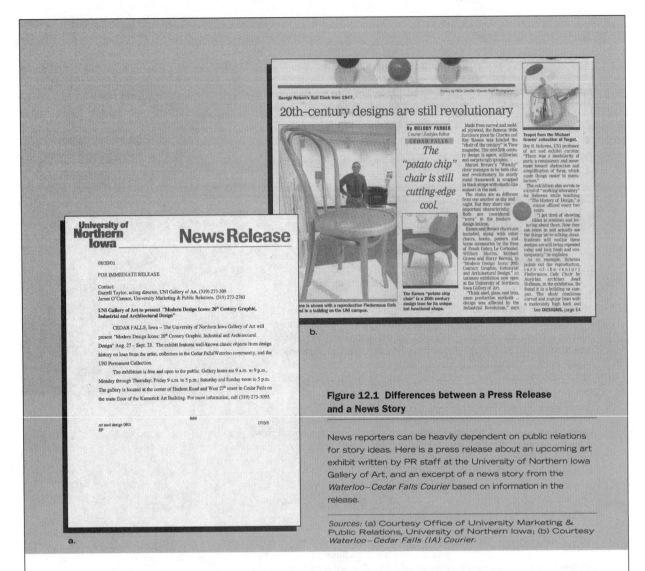

Figure 12.1 Differences between a Press Release and a News Story

News reporters can be heavily dependent on public relations for story ideas. Here is a press release about an upcoming art exhibit written by PR staff at the University of Northern Iowa Gallery of Art, and an excerpt of a news story from the *Waterloo–Cedar Falls Courier* based on information in the release.

Sources: (a) Courtesy Office of University Marketing & Public Relations, University of Northern Iowa; (b) Courtesy *Waterloo–Cedar Falls (IA) Courier.*

the information in news releases, but small media companies and small-town newspapers often use them verbatim, especially if their own editorial resources are limited or if they are under deadline constraints. Usually, the more closely a press release resembles actual news copy, the more likely it is to be used, which is why newspaper work is a good training ground for PR.

Since the 1970s and the introduction of portable video equipment, PR agencies and departments have been using **video news releases (VNRs)**, which are thirty- to ninety-second visual PR stories packaged to mimic the style of a broadcast news report. Many large companies now operate their own TV studios, which enable them to produce training videos for their employees and to create VNRs for their clients. Broadcast news stations in small TV markets regularly use video material from VNRs. Although large stations with more resources may get story ideas from VNRs, their news directors do not like to use video material obtained directly from PR sources; they prefer to assemble their own reports in order to maintain their independence. On occasion, news stations have been criticized for using bits of video footage from a VNR without acknowledging the source.

In addition to issuing press releases, nonprofit groups also produce **public-service announcements (PSAs)**: fifteen- to sixty-second reports or announcements for radio and television that promote government programs, educational projects, volunteer agencies, or social reform. As part of their requirement to serve the public interest, broadcasters historically have been encouraged to carry free PSAs. Since the deregulation of broadcasting began in the 1980s, however, there has been less pressure and no minimum obligation for TV and radio stations to air PSAs. When PSAs do run, they are frequently scheduled between midnight and 6 A.M., a less commercially valuable time slot with relatively few viewers or listeners.

The writing and editing part of PR also involves creating brochures and catalogues as well as company newsletters and annual reports for shareholders. It may include writing and editing speeches that aim to boost a politician's image or a company's stature. Major politicians and business leaders today seldom write their own speeches. Instead, they hire speechwriters or PR specialists.

Media relations

Through publicity, PR managers specializing in media relations promote a client or organization by securing favorable coverage in the news media. Media specialization often requires an in-house PR person to speak on behalf of an organization or to direct reporters to experts who can provide the best, or at least official, sources of information.

Media-relations specialists also perform *damage control* or *crisis management* when negative publicity occurs (see "Case Study: GM Trucks and NBC's *Dateline* Disaster" on page 438). Occasionally, in times of crisis—such as a virus outbreak at a hospital, a scandal at a university, or a safety recall by a car manufacturer—a PR spokesperson might be designated as the only source of information available to news media. Although journalists often resent being cut off from higher administrative levels and leaders, the institution or company wants to ensure that rumors and inaccurate stories do not circulate in the media. In these situations, a game often develops in which reporters attempt to circumvent the company spokesperson and induce a knowledgeable insider to talk *off the record,* providing background details without being named directly as a source.

> **❝**I get in **a lot of trouble** if I'm quoted, especially if the quotes are accurate.**❞**
>
> –A congressional staff person, explaining to the *Wall Street Journal* why he can speak only "off the record," 1999

PR agents who specialize in media relations also recommend advertising to their clients when it seems appropriate. Unlike publicity, which is sometimes outside a PR agency's control, paid advertising may help to focus a complex issue or a client's image. Publicity, however, carries the aura of legitimate news and thus has more credibility than advertising. In addition, media specialists cultivate associations with editors, reporters, freelance writers, and broadcast news directors to ensure that press releases or VNRs are favorably received.

Special events

Another public relations specialty involves coordinating special events. Since the late 1960s, for instance, the city of Milwaukee has run Summerfest, a ten-day music and food festival that attracts nearly a million people each year. As the festival's popularity grew, various companies sought to become sponsors of the event. Local manufacturers and the beer industry, for example, signed up to support different musical venues. The Miller Brewing Company sponsored a festival stage devoted to jazz. In exchange for sponsorship, the stage carried the Miller name, which also accompanied many items connected with Summerfest. In this way, Miller received favorable publicity by showing a commitment to the city that serves as the company's corporate headquarters.[15]

More typical of special-events publicity is the corporate sponsor that aligns its company image with a cause, or an organization that has positive stature among the general public. For example, for more than thirty years Mobil Oil (now ExxonMobil) has underwritten special programming such as *Masterpiece Theatre* on PBS. At the local level, companies often sponsor a community parade or a charitable fund-raising activity. When a new professional sports team arrives in a community, a host of local companies may compete to associate themselves with the new franchise. In this kind of situation, a team's PR specialist attempts to identify those companies that will provide the most favorable publicity for the client.

Research

Just as advertising is driven today by demographic and psychographic research, PR uses similar strategies to project a client's image to the appropriate audience. The research area is PR's fastest-growing segment as the profession attempts to bring new social-science techniques to its audience studies and image campaigns. Because historically it has been difficult to determine why particular campaigns succeed or fail, research has become the key ingredient in PR forecasting. Like advertising studies, PR research targets specific audiences. It makes use of mail and telephone surveys to get a fix on an audience's perceptions of a client's reputation.

As in advertising research, focus groups have become prominent in public relations campaigns. Although such groups are often unreliable because of small sample size, they are fairly easy to set up and do not require elaborate statistical designs. In 1990, for example, Gemstar Development Corporation introduced a remote-control technology that helps people program television codes into their VCRs more easily. This device, which employs a one-step recording technique using number codes printed in *TV Guide* and most newspaper TV supplements, was the end product of research initiated by a California PR firm, Rogers and Associates. The firm used three focus groups totaling forty-eight participants to learn that the majority of the nation's then seventy million VCR owners did not know how to tape movies or TV programs because the steps seemed too complicated. The research project concluded that users were most interested in "high-fidelity picture quality," one-step recording, and "a VCR that quickly locates a segment on your recorded tape for playback or editing." Not only did the participants help pick the name of the product—VCR Plus+— but 77 percent of them bought or ordered the device after their experience in the focus group.[16]

Community and consumer relations

Two other PR activities involve building relationships between companies and their communities. Companies have learned that sustaining close ties with their neighbors not only enhances their image but promotes the idea that the companies are good citizens. Such ties expose a business to potential customers through activities such as plant tours, open houses, participation in town parades, and special events such as a company's anniversary.

Besides encouraging client employees to get involved in community activities, many PR firms like their clients to make charitable donations that build local bonds. Some companies offer their work sites to local groups for meetings and help in fund-raising efforts. More progressive companies get involved in unemployment and job-retraining programs, and others donate equipment and workers to urban revitalization projects such as Habitat for Humanity.

In terms of customer relations, PR has become much more sophisticated since the 1960s, when Ralph Nader's *Unsafe at Any Speed* revealed safety problems concerning the Chevrolet Corvair. Nader's book gave General Motors a corporate migraine that resulted in the discontinuance of the Corvair line. More important, however, Nader's book lit the fuse that ignited a vibrant consumerism movement. During the

1960s, consumers became more sophisticated and, consequently, unwilling to readily accept the claims of those in power—including corporate leaders. Contributing to this movement was the trend toward large multinational corporate mergers and the rise of impersonal chain stores, both of which signaled a decreasing accountability to consumers.

For a while, the consumerism movement drew media attention. Many newspapers and TV stations hired consumer reporters, who tracked down the sources of customer complaints and often embarrassed companies by putting them in the media spotlight. Firms that were PR savvy responded by paying more attention to customers, establishing product and service guarantees and ensuring that all calls and mail from customers were answered promptly. The smartest companies produced consumer-education literature about specific products and developed close ties with local consumer groups.

Today, the impact of the consumer movement is especially evident in the resources devoted to carefully training employees in good customer relations. Many product and service companies have also developed customer-satisfaction questionnaires and "consumer creeds." For example, many restaurants and department stores go beyond asking consumers for advice, outlining what treatment customers should expect and what they should do when those expectations are not met. PR professionals routinely advise clients that satisfied customers mean not only repeat business but new business, based on a strong word-of-mouth reputation about a company's behavior and image.

● Socially conscientious PR firms encourage their employees and their clients to get involved in community projects, donating work and time that pay off by strengthening a firm's image. For example, the efforts of Habitat for Humanity—building low-income housing using volunteers and donated material—are often supported by progressive public relations companies.

CASE STUDY

GM Trucks and NBC's *Dateline* Disaster

On November 17, 1992, NBC's new *Dateline* program aired a report that showed two different full-size Chevy pickup trucks bursting into flames after being hit broadside by small cars. Along with the demonstration, *Dateline* implied that the trucks' side-mounted fuel tanks were extremely dangerous.

There was only one problem: The report was phony. For dramatic impact, *Dateline* had rigged the trucks with special igniters. With careful editing, the effect in each case was a big explosion and leaping flames, suggesting that drivers and passengers were at risk. In response, a General Motors crisis-management team fought back. During a thorough investigation, GM got a tip from an area news reporter who had found a witness to the enhanced presentation—a firefighter who had made his own video recording of each crash. GM investigators also located the rigged trucks in an Indiana junkyard.

A GM public relations team wrote a series of letters asking NBC to acknowledge the deception. When NBC executives continued to stand by the report, GM filed a lawsuit in February 1993. The defamation suit was announced at a press conference conducted by Harry Pearce, GM's general counsel. More than 150 reporters, photographers, and TV camera crews attended Pearce's own two-hour exposé of *Dateline*. Systematically critiquing the sixteen-minute report, Pearce convincingly showed that the only fires in both rigged sequences were brief grass fires ignited mainly by gasoline spurting from ill-fitting gas caps that came loose on impact. At the end of the conference, Pearce called on the assembled members of the news media to monitor the episodes of abuse in their own profession.

The day after the conference, NBC and GM entered negotiations, with GM demanding public repentance. On February 9, 1993, *Dateline* coanchors Jane Pauley and Stone Philips read a four-minute retraction and apology. Eventually, three *Dateline* producers were fired and an on-air reporter was demoted. Michael Gartner, NBC News president, resigned in disgrace. Up until the press conference, Gartner had claimed that NBC's report was accurate and responsible. NBC reimbursed GM $2 million for the costs of the company's investigation. In turn, GM dropped its defamation suit.

During its battle, GM's PR team also had to confront charges from national safety experts, many of whom were on NBC's payroll. GM was able to discredit these officials and also fend off a recall effort by the National Highway Traffic Safety Administration (NHTSA), which raised its own questions about truck safety. The NHTSA asked GM to recall the trucks in question even before the organization had finished its own investigation. GM refused and made convincing public arguments in two additional press conferences about the flawed conclusions of the NHTSA concerning the proficiency of GM's older trucks.

The NBC deception is a story that might not have been told had GM decided not to challenge the network. After all, it is very difficult for public individuals and companies to win damages in suits against the mainstream news media, which citizens count on to watch for abuses in politics and business. The strategy used by GM now serves as a crisis-management model for handling complicated cases that have both legal and ethical implications. Although GM is one of the world's largest companies and had the resources (and evidence) to fight back in this case, its PR strategy demonstrated that all citizens have a responsibility to watch over the watchdog.

Government relations and lobbying

Public relations also entails maintaining connections with government agencies that have some say in how companies operate in a particular community, state, or nation. The PR divisions of major firms are especially interested in making sure that government regulation neither becomes burdensome nor reduces their control over their businesses. Specialists in this area often develop self-regulatory practices, which either keep governments at some distance or draw on them for subsidies, as the railroads and utilities did in the nineteenth century. Such specialists also monitor new and existing legislation, create opportunities to ensure favorable publicity, and write press releases and direct-mail letters to educate the public on the pros and cons of new regulations.

In many firms, government relations has developed into **lobbying**: the process of attempting to influence the voting of lawmakers to support a client's or an organization's best interests. In seeking favorable legislation, some PR agents lobby government officials on a daily basis. In Washington, D.C., alone, more than twenty thousand registered lobbyists write speeches, articles, and position papers in addition to designing direct-mail campaigns, buying ads, and befriending editors.

Today, most major corporations, trade associations, labor unions, consumer groups, professional organizations, religious groups, and even foreign governments employ lobbyists. For instance, prior to the Persian Gulf War, lobbyists tried to justify U.S. and UN military action against Iraq, which had invaded Kuwait in 1990. To that end, the Kuwaiti royal family (who went into exile before Iraq invaded Kuwait) hired Hill and Knowlton to help rally public support for U.S. military intervention. The firm developed the idea of a "congressional human rights caucus," which in October 1990 reported acts of barbarism perpetrated by Iraqis on Kuwaitis. Later it was discovered that one witness, a fifteen-year-old Kuwaiti girl who testified at the caucus to seeing acts of cruelty, was

the daughter of the Kuwaiti ambassador to the United States and "had been witness to no such events." In January 1991 the United States invaded Iraq, with the majority of Americans, according to opinion polls, supporting the intervention.[17]

Public relations firms have had a hand in the public's understanding of a number of other international situations as well. For example, the Chinese government retained Hill and Knowlton to repair its image after the 1989 Tiananmen Square massacre that left more than 150 unarmed civilian protesters dead. In 2001, the U.S. Department of Defense hired the Rendon Group, a public relations firm in Washington, D.C., to help explain U.S. military airstrikes against the Taliban regime in Afghanistan to a worldwide audience. The firm's efforts included monitoring news media in nearly eighty nations, conducting focus groups, creating an informational Web site about the U.S. campaign against terrorism, and recommending ways in which the U.S. military can improve its global communications.

● Corporations, trade associations, labor unions, and special-interest groups are among the organizations that help to mobilize citizens to lobby government agencies and politicians to support their causes. For example, the Texas Motorcycle Rights Association directs its members to attend press conferences and legislative hearings that might concern motorcycle regulations.

❝Managing the **outrage** is more important than managing the hazard.❞

–Thomas Buckmaster, Hill and Knowlton, 1997

Tensions between pr and the press

In 1932, Stanley Walker, an editor at the *New York Herald Tribune,* compared public relations agents and publicity advisers to "mass-mind molders, fronts, mouthpieces, chiselers, moochers, and special assistants to the president."[18] Walker added that newspapers and public relations agencies would always remain enemies, even if PR professionals adopted a code of ethics (which they did in the 1950s) to "take them out of the red-light district of human relations."[19] Walker's tone captures the spirit of one of the most mutually dependent—and antagonistic— relationships across mass media.

Much of this antagonism, directed at public relations from the journalism profession, is historical. Reporters have long considered themselves part of an older public-service profession, whereas many regard PR as a pseudo-profession created to distort the facts that reporters work so hard to gather. Over time, reporters and editors developed a nationwide derogatory term for a PR agent—**flack**—which continues in usage to this day. The term derives from the military word *flak,* meaning the antiaircraft artillery shells fired to deflect aerial attack, and from the related *flak jacket,* the protective military attire worn to ward off enemy fire. For journalists, the word *flack* has come to mean PR people who insert themselves between their employers/clients and members of the press.

In the 1960s, an Associated Press manual for editors defined a *flack* as "a person who makes all or part of his income by obtaining space in newspapers without cost to himself or his clients." The AP depiction continued: "A flack is a flack. His job is to say kind things about his client. He will not lie very often, but much of the time he tells less than the whole story. You do not owe the PR man anything. The owner of the newspaper, not the flack, pays your salary. Your immediate job is to serve the readers, not the man who would raid your columns." This description, however, belies journalism's dependence on public relations. Many editors, for instance, admit that more than half of their story ideas each day originate with PR people.

Elements of professional friction

The relationship between journalism and PR is an important and complex one. Although journalism lays claim to independent traditions, the news media have become ever more reliant on public relations because of the increasing amount of information now available. Staff cutbacks at many papers, combined with television's need for local newscast events, have also expanded the news media's need for PR story ideas.

Further depleting journalism, PR firms routinely raid the ranks of reporting for new talent. Because most press releases are written in a style that imitates news reports, the PR profession has always sought good writers who are well connected to sources and savvy about the news business. For instance, the fashion industry likes to hire former style or fashion news writers for its PR staff, and university information offices seek reporters who once covered higher education. It is interesting to note that although reporters frequently move into PR, public relations practitioners seldom move into journalism; the news profession rarely accepts prodigal sons or daughters back into the fold once they have left reporting for public relations. According to many reporters and editors, any profession that shapes images is considered manipulative or self-serving—and its practitioners may not be redeemable. Nevertheless, the professions remain co-dependent: PR needs journalists for publicity, and journalism needs PR for story ideas. Several historical explanations shed light on this type of discord and on the ways in which different media professions interact.

Undermining facts and blocking access

Modern public relations redefined and complicated the notion of facts. PR professionals demonstrated that the same set of facts can be spun in a variety of ways, depending on what information is emphasized and what is downplayed. As Ivy Lee noted in 1925: "The effort to state an absolute fact is simply an attempt to achieve what is humanly impossible; all I can do is to give you *my interpretation of the facts.*"[20] With practitioners like Lee showing the emerging PR profession how facts and news could be manipulated, the journalist's role as a custodian of accurate information became much more difficult. In fact, a 2000 survey of PR professionals gave some credence to public relations' worst image: "25 percent admit to lying on the job, 39 percent say they had exaggerated the truth, and 44 percent were uncertain of the ethics of the task they were required to perform."[21]

Journalists have also objected to PR flacks who block press access to key leaders. At one time, reporters could talk to such leaders directly and obtain quotable information for their news stories. Now, however, PR people insert themselves between the press and the powerful, thus disrupting the old ritual in which reporters would vie for interviews with top government and business leaders. If PR agents today want to manipulate or use reporters, they may give information to journalists who are likely to cast a story in a favorable light in return for getting the information first. On rarer occasions, a reporter's access to key sources might be cut off altogether if that journalist has written unfavorably about a client.

Promoting publicity and business as news

Another explanation for the professional friction between the press and PR involves simple economics. The trade journal *Editor & Publisher* once called public relations agents "space grabbers"; what editors and publishers feared actually became a reality: PR agents helped companies "promote as news what otherwise would have been purchased in advertising."[22]

As Ivy Lee wrote to John D. Rockefeller after the oil magnate gave money to Johns Hopkins University: "In view of the fact that this was not really news, and that the newspapers gave so much attention to it, it would seem that this was wholly due to the manner in which the material was 'dressed up' for newspaper consumption. It seems to suggest very considerable possibilities along this line."[23] Many newspeople react strongly to this sort of manipulation. Critics worry that public relations is taking media space and time away from those who do not have the financial resources or the sophistication to become readily visible in the public eye. Beyond this lies another issue: If public relations can secure publicity for clients in the news, the added credibility of a journalistic context gives clients a status that the purchase of advertising cannot confer.

Today, however, something more subtle underlies journalism's contempt for public relations: Much of journalism actually functions in the same way. For instance, politicians, celebrities, and PR firms with abundant resources are clearly afforded more coverage by the news media than are their lesser-known counterparts. For example, workers and union leaders have long argued that the money that corporations allocate to PR leads to more favorable coverage for management positions in labor disputes. Standard news reports may feature subtle language choices, with "rational, cool-headed management making *offers*" and "hot-headed workers making *demands*." Walter Lippmann saw such differences in 1922 when he wrote: "If you study the way many a strike is reported in the press, you will find very often that [labor] issues are rarely in the headlines, barely in the leading paragraph, and sometimes not even mentioned anywhere."[24] Most newspapers now have business sections that focus on the work of various managers, but few have a labor, worker, or employee section. In fact, most large metro papers have eliminated the specialty beat of labor reporting.[25]

Business, economic, and stock "news" reports generated by corporate PR agents inundate newspapers and the evening news. A single business reporter at a large metro daily sometimes receives as many as a hundred press releases a day—far outnumbering the fraction of handouts generated by organized labor or grassroots organizations. This imbalance is particularly significant in that the great majority of workers are neither managers nor CEOs, and yet these workers receive little if any media coverage on a regular basis. Essentially, as a number of critics have pointed out, mainstream journalism best serves managers and the status quo.

Managing the press

Public relations, by making reporters' jobs easier, has often helped reporters become lazy. PR firms now supply what reporters used to work hard to gather for themselves. Instead of going out to beat the competition, many journalists have become content to wait for a PR handout or a good tip before following up on a story. Small community groups, social activists, and nonprofit organizations often cannot afford elaborate publicity. These groups argue that because of PR, large corporations and well-connected politicians enjoy easier access to reporters and receive more frequent news coverage. Occasionally, also because of PR, powerful firms and individuals receive less critical scrutiny. Some members of the news media, grateful for the reduced workload that occurs when they are provided with handouts, may be hesitant to criticize a particular PR firm's clients.

Dealing with both a tainted past and journalism's hostility has often preoccupied the public relations profession, leading to the development of several image-enhancing strategies. Over the years, for example, as public relations has subdivided itself into specialized areas, it has used more positive descriptive phrases, such as "institutional relations," "corporate communications," and "news and information services." With the development of its own professional organization, PRSA, the PR industry has also enhanced its standing among the public and even the news media.[26] PRSA functions as an internal watchdog group that accredits individuals, maintains a code of ethics, and publishes newsletters and trade publications. Most PRSA local chapters and national conventions also routinely invite reporters and editors to speak to PR practitioners about what the news media expect from their rival professionals. In addition, independent agencies, devoted to uncovering shady or unethical public relations activities, publish their findings in publications like *PR Tactics, PR Week,* or *PR Watch*. Ethical issues have become a major focus of the PR profession, with self-examination of these issues routinely appearing in PR textbooks as well as in various professional newsletters (see Table 12.2).

Public relations' best press strategy, however, may be the limitations of the journalism profession itself. For most of the twentieth century, many reporters and editors clung to the ideal that journalism is, at its best, an objective institution that gathers information on behalf of the public. Reporters have only occasionally turned their pens, computers, and cameras on themselves to examine their own practices or their vulnerability to manipulation. Thus, by not challenging PR's more subtle strategies, many journalists have allowed PR professionals to interpret "facts" to their clients' advantage.

● **Table 12.2 Public Relations Society of America Ethics Code**

In 2000, the PRSA approved a completely revised Code of Ethics, which included core principles, guidelines, and examples of improper conduct. Below is one section of the code.

PRSA Member Statement of Professional Values

This statement presents the core values of PRSA members and, more broadly, of the public relations profession. These values provide the foundation for the Member Code of Ethics and set the industry standard for the professional practice of public relations. These values are the fundamental beliefs that guide our behaviors and decision-making process. We believe our professional values are vital to the integrity of the profession as a whole.

ADVOCACY

We serve the public interest by acting as responsible advocates for those we represent.

We provide a voice in the marketplace of ideas, facts, and viewpoints to aid informed public debate.

HONESTY

We adhere to the highest standards of accuracy and truth in advancing the interests of those we represent and in communicating with the public.

EXPERTISE

We acquire and responsibly use specialized knowledge and experience.

We advance the profession through continued professional development, research, and education.

We build mutual understanding, credibility, and relationships among a wide array of institutions and audiences.

INDEPENDENCE

We provide objective counsel to those we represent. We are accountable for our actions.

LOYALTY

We are faithful to those we represent, while honoring our obligation to serve the public interest.

FAIRNESS

We deal fairly with clients, employers, competitors, peers, vendors, the media, and the general public.

We respect all opinions and support the right of free expression.

Source: The full text of the PRSA Code of Ethics is available at <http://www.prsa.org/codeofethics.html>.

Limited by its reluctance or failure to identify and evade savvy public relations tactics, conventional journalism remains vulnerable. Consider this hypothetical situation: A wealthy and powerful development corporation decides to raze a homeless shelter to build a condo. The firm uses public relations resources that overwhelm the protests of a few homeless activists. The major newspaper in town attempts to remain neutral on the issue. However, the strength of the corporation's PR unit has already tipped the balance of the issue in all of the town's media outlets. To recenter the scales, the newspaper in this case would have to take an advocacy position on behalf of the activists. But in conventional journalism, detachment prohibits this, and thus the corporate point of view triumphs—or, at least, gains most of the space and time in the news coverage. Although many alternative newspapers and advocacy reporters

Crude oil from the tanker Exxon *Valdez* swirls on the surface of Alaska's Prince William Sound on April 9, 1989, 16 days after the tanker ran aground, spilling millions of gallons of oil and causing widespread environmental damage.

444

do a fine job of critiquing the limits of some questionable public relations activities, conventional journalism has few mechanisms for rebalancing the scales tipped by PR embellishment, whether advanced by government or business leaders.

Alternative voices   Because public relations professionals work so closely with the press, their practices are not often the subject of media reports or investigations. Indeed, the multibillion-dollar industry remains virtually invisible to the public, most of whom have never heard of Burson-Marsteller, Hill and Knowlton, or Ketchum. John Stauber and Sheldon Rampton, investigative reporters who work for the Center for Media and Democracy in Washington, D.C., are concerned about the invisibility of PR practices and have sought to expose the hidden activities of large PR firms. As editors of *PR Watch*, a quarterly publication they launched in 1995, they publish investigative reports on the PR industry that never appear in mainstream mass media outlets. "*PR Watch* seeks to serve the public rather than PR," they explain. "With the assistance of whistleblowers and a few sympathetic insiders, we report about the secretive activities of an industry which works behind the scenes to control government policy and shape public opinion."[27]

Stauber and Rampton have also written books targeting public relations practices having to do with industrial waste (*Toxic Sludge Is Good for You: Lies, Damn Lies and the Public Relations Industry*), mad cow disease (*Mad Cow USA: Could the Nightmare Happen Here?*), and PR uses of scientific research (*Trust Us, We're Experts: How Industry Manipulates Science and Gambles with Your Future*). The work of Stauber and Rampton helps to bring an alternative angle to the well-monied battles over public opinion. "You know, we feel that in a democracy, it's very, very critical that everyone knows who the players are, and what they're up to," Stauber says.[28]

Public relations, social responsibility, and democracy

Although the image of public relations professionals may not be as negative as that of advertisers, a cynical view of the profession nonetheless exists beyond the field of journalism. Given the history of corporate public relations, many concerned citizens believe that when a company or an individual makes a mistake or misleads the public, too often a PR counsel is hired to alter the image rather than to admit the misdeed and correct the problem. An anecdote about a lawn-service/weed-control company illustrates this scenario: "A PR manager for a company named ChemLawn complained that the entire city of Columbus, Ohio, its headquarters, hated the company because it makes . . . chemicals. 'But what can you do?' she asked a couple of colleagues. They replied immediately—and in unison—'Change the name.'"[29] Although ChemLawn did not change its name, a company's decision to simply alter an image rather than deal with a problem highlights a dilemma for many PR agencies and their clients.

Let's look at a more familiar PR dilemma. In the aftermath of one of the largest environmental disasters of the twentieth century—the Exxon *Valdez* oil spill along the Alaskan coast in 1989—the multinational corporation eventually changed the name of the tanker *Valdez* to the *Mediterranean* in the 1990s. The name change was just a small tactic in a series of damage-control strategies that Exxon enacted to cope with the oil spill. Such disaster management may reveal the worst—or best—attributes of the PR profession. How to enhance a company's image and, at the same time, encourage the company to be a socially responsible corporate citizen remains a major challenge for public relations.

> **"The Exxon *Valdez* Story: How to Spend a Billion or Two and Still Get a Black Eye in Public."**
>
> —Business school conference title, Fordham University, 1990

EXAMINING ETHICS

Levi Strauss and Anti-Sweatshop Public Relations

In the late 1990s, a growing tide of Americans focused on the problems of outsourcing: using the production, manufacturing, and labor resources of foreign companies to produce American brand-name products, sometimes under deplorable working conditions. Since 1998, more than 180 university chapters of United Students Against Sweatshops have formed, and at several universities—including Duke, Georgetown, the

446

University of Wisconsin, and some Ivy League schools—students staged rallies and sit-ins to urge administrators to take a hard line against companies that use overseas sweatshops to make apparel bearing university logos. At many of these schools, administrators complied by instituting tougher guidelines for overseas licensing.

In 1996, outsourcing was pushed into the public eye after major media attention focused on morning talk-show host Kathie Lee Gifford when human-rights groups revealed that part of her clothing line, made and distributed by Wal-Mart, came from sweatshops in New York and Honduras. The sweatshops paid less than minimum wages, and some employed child laborers. Human-rights activists claimed that in the overseas sweatshops in particular, children were being exploited in violation of international child-labor laws.

Many global companies now comply with international guidelines that protect children and pay workers living wages. Many countries, however, including the United States, still tolerate sweatshop conditions in which workers take home minimal pay, sometimes less than a dollar an hour for working ten- to twelve-hour shifts six days a week.

As labor unions, the national media, and human-rights groups began tracking the problem of sweatshops, stories about worker exploitation were exposed. One U.S. firm, Levi Strauss & Company, pioneered an institutional public relations program to guard against sweatshop

● Thousands rally in New York City in a National Labor Committee protest against sweatshops and child labor.

practices. With more than seven hundred sewing contractors making jeans and other clothing in fifty countries, Levi Strauss developed the first set of international, anti-sweatshop guidelines for its contractors. The guidelines were the company's response to early criticism about its moving some of its manufacturing overseas in search of low-cost labor markets.

The Levi Strauss plan focused on balancing "the company's merchandising and production needs with corporate social responsibility." Managers at Levi Strauss studied various ways of dealing with the cultural values and differences in the countries where they had manufacturing interests.[1]

To execute the plan, Levi Strauss instituted a training program involving more than a hundred "in-country" managers who understood the language, culture, and values of their workforces. The company met with apparel workers' unions to get input and support; the trained managers then regularly monitored and audited their plants. The Levi Strauss media

plan succeeded in positioning the company as a leader in global business practices while "distinguishing itself from other companies as the 'bright spot' in otherwise negative sourcing stories."[2]

By 1993, all of Levi Strauss's worldwide contractors had been audited. About 70 percent met the anti-sweatshop standards set by company policy. About 25 percent of the contractors promised to make mandated improvements in the treatment of their workers. Five percent of the contractors were dropped for violating anti-sweatshop agreements. The company withdrew outsourcing from both Burma and China after human-rights violations persisted. It also suspended its contract with Peruvian plants because of employee safety concerns. In 1993, *Fortune* magazine ranked Levi Strauss as "America's most admired apparel company," and *Business Ethics* magazine honored the jeans company with its Award for Excellence in Ethics.

In 2002, even as sales of Levi's clothing had fallen, the company's executives held fast to their code of conduct. "Levi Strauss & Co. is committed to ensuring compliance with our code of conduct at all facilities that manufacture or finish our products around the world," executives said. "If a contractor fails to meet the corrective action plan committment, Levi Strauss & Co. will terminate the business relationship."[3] Meanwhile, several other clothing sellers, including Wal-Mart, still struggled with charges that they use sweatshop labor in hundreds of garment factories in places like China, Saipan, Bangladesh, and Honduras.[4]

> **❝The burden is on us to earn your trust all over again. But it will take more than words. It will only be through our actions that people will once again think well of Firestone.❞**
>
> – John Lampe, CEO, Bridgestone/ Firestone, 2000

The Exxon *Valdez* case was a corporate as well as an environmental disaster, despite the company's outlay of $2 billion to clean up both its image and the spill. When eleven million gallons of crude oil spilled into Prince William Sound, contaminating fifteen hundred miles of Alaskan coastline and killing countless birds, otters, seals, and fish, Exxon was slow to react to the crisis and even slower to accept responsibility. Although its PR advisers had encouraged a quick response, the corporation failed to send any of its chief officers immediately to the site to express concern. Many critics believed that Exxon was trying to duck responsibility by laying the burden of the crisis on the shoulders of the tanker's captain. A former president of NBC News, William Small, maintained that Exxon "lost the battle of public relations" and suffered "one of the worst tarnishings of its corporate image in American history."[30]

A decidedly different approach was taken in the 1982 tragedy involving Tylenol pain-relief capsules. Seven people died in the Chicago area after someone tampered with several bottles and laced them with poison. Like the oil spill, the case was a major news story. Discussions between the parent company, Johnson & Johnson, and its PR and advertising representatives focused on whether withdrawing all Tylenol capsules might send a signal that corporations could be intimidated by a single deranged person. Nevertheless, Johnson & Johnson's chairman, James E. Burke, and the company's PR agency, Burson-Marsteller, opted for full disclosure to the media and the immediate recall of the capsules nationally, costing the company an estimated $100 million. Before the incident, Tylenol had a market share of 37 percent, making it the leading pain-relief medicine. After the capsule withdrawal, Tylenol's share was cut nearly in half.

As part of its PR strategy to overcome the negative publicity and to restore Tylenol's market share, Burson-Marsteller tracked public opinion nightly through telephone surveys and organized satellite press conferences to debrief the news media. In addition, emergency phone lines were set up to take calls from consumers and health-care providers, who altogether sent two million messages to Johnson & Johnson. When the company reintroduced Tylenol three months after the tragedy began, it did so with tamper-resistant bottles that were soon copied by almost every major drug manufacturer. Burson-Marsteller, which received PRSA awards for its handling of the crisis, found that the public thought Johnson & Johnson had responded admirably to the crisis and did not hold Tylenol responsible for the deaths. In fewer than three years, Tylenol recaptured its former share of the market.

The Exxon and Tylenol incidents—and the more recent crises of Odwalla fruit juice contamination and the Bridgestone/Firestone–Ford Explorer tire problems—demonstrate both dim and bright aspects of public relations, a profession that continues to provoke concern (see "Examining Ethics: Levi Strauss and Anti-Sweatshop Public Relations" on page 446). The bulk of the criticism leveled at public relations argues that the crush of information produced by PR professionals overwhelms traditional journalism. In one example, former president Richard Nixon, who resigned from office in 1974 to avoid impeachment hearings regarding his role in the Watergate scandal, hired Hill and Knowlton to restore his post-presidency image. Through the firm's guidance, Nixon's writings, mostly on international politics, began appearing in Sunday op-ed pages. Nixon himself started showing up on *Nightline* and spoke frequently before groups such as the American Newspaper Publishers Association and the Economic Club of New York. In 1984, after a media blitz by Nixon's PR handlers, the *New York Times* announced: "After a decade, Nixon is gaining favor," and *USA Today* trumpeted: "Richard Nixon is back." Before his death in 1994, Nixon, who never publicly apologized for his role in Watergate, saw a large portion of his public image shift from that of an arrogant, disgraced politician to that of a revered elder statesman.[31] Many media critics have charged that the press did not balance the scales and treated Nixon too reverently after the successful PR campaign.

In terms of its immediate impact on democracy, the information crush delivered by public relations is at its height during national election campaigns. In fact, PR's most significant impact may be on the political process, especially when organizations hire spin doctors to favorably shape or reshape a candidate's media image. During the 1998 governor's race in Minnesota, former pro wrestler and navy SEAL Jesse "the Body" Ventura successfully combined a third-party PR and ad campaign to defeat the leading Democratic and Republican candidates. Ventura's strategy—which targeted independent voters and young adults—transformed his image as an evil, cross-dressing, "dumb rassler" into that of a patriotic, rugged individualist. Minnesota's registered-voter turnout—more than 60 percent—was the highest in the nation in 1998. And during the 2000 presidential campaign, Democratic candidate Al Gore, drawing on advice from his PR handlers, decided to combat his wooden public image by wearing earth tones to appear more reassuring and by behaving like a commanding, leading, "alpha male" in order to appeal to more women voters.

Though public relations often provides political information and story ideas during an election, the PR profession probably bears only part of the responsibility for manipulating the news media; after all, it is the job of an agency to spin the news favorably for its candidate. PR professionals should certainly police their own ranks (and usually do) for unethical or irresponsible practices, but the news media should also monitor the public relations industry, as they do other government and business activities. This media vigilance should be on behalf of citizens, who are entitled to robust debates on important social and political issues.

In a democracy, journalism and public relations need to retain their guarded posture toward each other. But journalism itself may need to institute changes that will make it less dependent on PR and more conscious of how its own practices play into the hands of spin strategies. Especially during elections, journalists need to become more vigilant in monitoring questionable PR tactics. A positive example of change on this front is that many major newspapers and news networks now offer regular critiques of the facts and falsehoods contained in political advertising.

Like advertising and other forms of commercial speech, publicity campaigns that result in free media exposure raise a number of questions regarding democracy and the expression of ideas. Large PR agencies and product companies, like well-financed politicians, have money to invest to figure out how to obtain favorable publicity. The question is not how to prevent that but how to ensure that other voices, less well financed and less commercial, receive an adequate hearing. To that end, journalists need to become less willing conduits in the distribution of publicity. PR agencies, for their part, need to show clients that participating in the democratic process as responsible citizens can serve them well and enhance their image.

> ❝In politics, **image** [has] replaced action.❞
>
> –Randall Rothenberg,
> *Where the Suckers Moon,* 1994

REVIEW QUESTIONS

Early Developments in Public Relations

1. What did people like P. T. Barnum and Buffalo Bill Cody contribute to the development of modern public relations in the twentieth century?

2. How did railroads and utility companies give the early forms of corporate public relations a bad name?

3. What contributions did Ivy Lee make toward the development of modern PR?

4. How did Edward Bernays affect public relations?

5. What is a pseudo-event? How does it relate to the manufacturing of news?

The Practice of Public Relations

6. What are two approaches to organizing a PR firm?

7. What are press releases, and why are they important to reporters?

8. What is the difference between a VNR and a PSA?

9. What special events might a PR firm sponsor to build stronger ties to its community?

10. Why have research and lobbying become increasingly important to the practice of PR?

Tensions between PR and the Press

11. Explain the historical background of the antagonism between journalism and public relations.

12. How did PR change old relationships between journalists and their sources?

13. In what ways is conventional news like public relations?

14. How does journalism as a profession contribute to its own manipulation at the hands of competent PR practitioners?

Public Relations, Social Responsibility, and Democracy

15. What are some socially responsible strategies that a PR specialist can use during a crisis to help a client manage unfavorable publicity?

16. In what ways does the profession of public relations serve democracy? In what ways can it impede democracy?

QUESTIONING THE MEDIA

1. What do you think of when you hear the term *public relations*? What images come to mind? Where did these impressions come from?

2. What might a college or university do to improve public relations with homeowners on the edge of a campus who have to deal with noisy student parties and a shortage of parking spaces?

3. What steps can reporters and editors take to monitor PR agents who manipulate the news media?

4. Can and should the often hostile relationship between the journalism and PR professions be mended? Why or why not?

5. Besides the Exxon *Valdez* and Tylenol cases cited in this chapter, investigate and research a PR crisis (such as the Bridgestone/Firestone–Ford Explorer tire problems, the mad cow disease beef scare in Europe, the contamination of Odwalla fruit juice, or the proposed General Electric Hudson River cleanup in upstate New York). How was the crisis handled?

SEARCHING THE INTERNET

http://www.prsa.org

The official site of the Public Relations Society of America, the leading U.S. professional PR organization. Provides information on membership, awards, conferences, PR publications, and links to other PR-related sites.

http://www.prssa.org

This site of the Public Relations Student Society of America gives information on local student chapters around the United States.

http://www.online-pr.com

An online catalogue of PR, media, and marketing resources.

http://www.odwyerpr.com

This site, linked to an influential and independent publisher of PR news and directories of PR firms, includes information about the field and statistics on numerous firms.

http://silveranvil.org

A resource center and archive for case studies of award-winning PR campaigns.

http://www.prwatch.org

This site is the online presence of the Center for Media and Democracy, a nonprofit, public interest organization dedicated to investigative reporting on the PR industry.

THE CRITICAL PROCESS

■ IN BRIEF

Imagine that you work for a high-powered PR firm, and a controversial client (e.g., a tobacco company, Bridgestone/Firestone, Microsoft, etc.) hires your firm to reshape the client's image. To perform this job, what are the strategies you would employ and why? (Before you begin, your class may want to discuss clients you would refuse to work for.)

■ IN DEPTH

Split the class into groups of three or four for a bit of investigative work to be done over a three- to four-week period. Each group should try to identify one or two press releases that were converted into a substantial news story by a local paper. In the newspaper, look for articles that highlight a particular organization or profile a prominent business or government leader. The business section of most papers is a particularly good source for PR-influenced stories.

The goal is to get a copy of the original press release and compare it with the article that appears in the paper (see example on page 434). Here are some strategies your group might use:

- Call a local reporter (ideally, the person who wrote the story), explain the assignment, and see if he or she will provide your group with the original release to compare against the news story.
- Call a public relations department at a local company, explain your assignment, and see if someone will provide your group with a copy of the original release.

Another part of this assignment is to interview both a PR agent and a reporter about the use and success of news releases. Your group should devise a questionnaire for each professional. The questions listed here may be helpful.

To the reporter:

1. What determines whether a PR release will be used?
2. How does a reporter go about rewriting press releases? What information should be kept? Eliminated?
3. What is the newspaper's policy on rewriting press releases? Does the paper ever print releases verbatim? Why or why not?

To the PR agent:

1. What determines whether a PR release will be used? What are some writing tips for composing a good release?
2. Do newspapers ever print releases verbatim? Should they?

Feel free to develop other questions.

After the releases and news stories have been gathered and the subjects interviewed, your group should address the following:

- What changes, if any, were made between each public relations release and the corresponding news story? Why do you think these changes were made?
- Which version represented the best story—the press release or the news story? Why? (Keep in mind that each story has a different purpose and audience.)

Each group should report its findings to the entire class.

KEY TERMS

publicity, 425
public relations, 425
press agents, 426
pseudo-event, 430

propaganda, 433
press releases, 433
video news releases (VNRs), 434

public-service announcements (PSAs), 435
lobbying, 439
flack, 440

BIBLIOGRAPHY

1. Matthew J. Culligan and Dolph Greene, *Getting Back to the Basics of Public Relations & Publicity* (New York: Crown Publishers, 1982), 90.

2. Ibid., 100.

3. See Stuart Ewen, *PR! A Social History of Spin* (New York: Basic Books, 1996).

4. Suzanne Heck, "Multimedia Sharpshooter Brought Buffalo Bill Fame," *Public Relations Journal* (October–November 1994): 12.

5. Marvin N. Olasky, "The Development of Corporate Public Relations, 1850–1930," *Journalism Monographs*, no. 102 (April 1987): 3.

6. Quoted in Alfred McClung Lee, *The Daily Newspaper in America* (New York: Macmillan, 1937), 436.

7. Olasky, "The Development of Corporate Public Relations," 14.

8. Ibid., 15.

9. See Ewen, *PR!*, 47.

10. See Scott M. Cutlip, *The Unseen Power: Public Relations—A History* (Hillsdale, N.J.: Lawrence Erlbaum, 1994).

11. Edward Bernays, *Crystallizing Public Opinion* (New York: Horace Liveright, 1923), 217.

12. Michael Schudson, *Discovering the News* (New York: Basic Books, 1978), 136.

13. Walter Lippmann, *Public Opinion* (New York: The Free Press, 1922/1949), 218

14. See Daniel Boorstin, *The Image: A Guide to Pseudo-Events in America* (New York: Atheneum, 1961), 11–12, 205–210.

15. The author of this book, Richard Campbell, worked briefly as the assistant PR director for Milwaukee's Summerfest in the early 1980s.

16. Susan Lucarelli, "Public Relations Research," in Michael Singletary, ed., *Mass Communication Research* (New York: Longman, 1995), 357–359.

17. See Ewen, *PR!*, 28–29; and John R. McArthur, *The Second Front: Censorship and Propaganda in the Gulf War* (New York: Hill & Wang, 1992), 58–59.

18. Stanley Walker, "Playing the Deep Bassoons," *Harper's* (February 1932): 365.

19. Ibid., 370.

20. Ivy Lee, *Publicity* (New York: Industries Publishing, 1925), 21.

21. Luke Timmerman, "Are PR Firms Going Too Far? Survey Asks," *Seattle Times*, May 17, 2000, p. D2.

22. Schudson, *Discovering the News*, 136.

23. Ivy Lee, quoted in Ray Eldon Hiebert, *Courtier to the Crowd: The Story of Ivy Lee and the Development of Public Relations* (Ames: Iowa State University Press, 1966), 114.

24. See Lippmann, *Public Opinion*, 221.

25. See Jonathan Tasini, "Lost in the Margins: Labor and the Media," *Extra!* (Summer 1992): 2–11.

26. See J. David Pincus et al., "Newspaper Editors' Perceptions of Public Relations: How Business, News, and Sports Editors Differ," *Journal of Public Relations Research* 5, no. 1 (1993): 27–45.

27. John Stauber and Sheldon Rampton, "Flack Attack," *PR Watch* 4, no. 1 (1997), <http://www.prwatch.org/prw_issues/1997-Q1/index.html>.

28. John Stauber, "Corporate PR: A Threat to Journalism?" Radio National/Australian Broadcasting Association, March 30, 1997, <http://www.abc.net.au/rn/talks/bbing/stories/s10602.htm>.

29. Bill Walker, "Green Like Me," in Ray Eldon Hiebert, ed., *Impact of Mass Media: Current Issues*, 3rd ed. (White Plains, N.Y.: Longman, 1995), 177.

30. William Small, quoted in Walker, "Playing the Deep Bassoons," 174–175.

31. See Alicia Mundy, "Is the Press Any Match for Powerhouse PR?" in Hiebert, ed., *Impact of Mass Media*, 179–188.

EXAMINING ETHICS: LEVI STRAUSS AND
ANTI-SWEATSHOP PUBLIC RELATIONS, P. 446

1. Public Relations Society of America, *PRSA Silver Anvil Awards* (New York: PRSA, 1994), 9–10.

2. Ibid., 10.

3. Karl Schoenberger, "Tough Jeans, a Soft Heart and Frayed Earnings," *New York Times*, June 25, 2000, sec. 3, p. 1.

4. See the National Labor Committee, <www.nlcnet.org>.

Practicing Your Textbook Reading Skills

1. According to the chapter-opening story, popular attitudes toward denim changed in the 1950s and 1960s because of

   a. popular movies.   c. the Peace Corps.

   b. public schools.   d. a public relations campaign.

2. Note the quotation in the margin on page 428: "Since crowds do not reason, they can only be organized and stimulated through symbols and phrases" (Ivy Lee, 1917). How does this statement relate to the text?

   a. It repeats a comment made in the text.

   b. It highlights the most important point of the text.

   c. It illustrates Lee's approach to public relations.

   d. There is no relationship between the quotation and the text.

3. The advertisement and caption on page 429 are provided to

   a. illustrate how public relations campaigns fail.

   b. show an example of the work of Edward Bernays.

   c. prove that Edward Bernays was an unprincipled hypocrite.

   d. demonstrate how easily fooled consumers are.

4. Which sentences in the following paragraph (from p. 431) provide minor supporting details to support the paragraph's main point?

   (1) Typical pseudo-events are interviews, press conferences, TV and radio talk shows, the Super Bowl pregame show, or any other staged activity aimed at drawing public attention and media coverage. (2) Such events depend on the participation of clients and performers and on the media's recording of the performances. (3) With regard to national politics, Theodore Roosevelt's administration set up the first White House pressroom and held the first presidential press conferences in the early 1900s. (4) In the 1990s, Vice President Al Gore championed White House Internet sites, making it possible for larger public audiences to interact with reporters and leaders in electronic press conferences.

   a. sentences 1 and 2   c. sentences 3 and 4

   b. sentences 2 and 3   d. sentences 1 and 3

5. What is the relationship between the following two sentences from page 431? "In the 1970s, the majority of students in communications and journalism programs indicated in surveys that they intended to pursue careers in news or magazine writing. By the late 1980s, however, similar surveys indicated that the majority of students wanted to enter public relations or advertising."

   a. The second sentence shows a contrast to the idea of the first sentence.

   b. The second sentence provides an example of the point made in the first sentence.

   c. The first sentence introduces the second sentence.

   d. The first sentence clarifies the second sentence.

6. According to Table 12.1, approximately how many people, in total, are employed by the five PR firms that earned the most money in 1999?

   a. 5,000   c. 10,000

   b. 8,250   d. 12,000

7. The purpose of the "Case Study" on page 438 is to

   a. make NBC look bad.

   b. warn students about the dangers of GM trucks.

   c. argue that the news media need to be monitored as closely as public relations firms do.

   d. provide a reading break for students.

8. The boxed feature "Examining Ethics" on pages 446–47 provides a real-world illustration of the ideas in which titled section of the chapter?

   a. "Tensions between PR and the Press"

   b. "Public Relations, Social Responsibility, and Democracy"

   c. "Community and Consumer Relations"

   d. "Performing Public Relations"

9. Which of the shaded sections at the end of the chapter would best help you prepare for a quiz or an exam on the subject of public relations?

   a. "Review Questions"

   b. "Questioning the Media"

   c. "Searching the Internet"

   d. "The Critical Process"

10. On which of the following Internet sites would you be most likely to find information on the tensions between public relations and journalism?

    a. www.pprsa.org   c. www.silveranvil.org

    b. www.online-pr.com   d. www.prwatch.org

Testing Your Understanding

Identify the following statements as true or false.

1. Public relations has little social or cultural impact in the United States.

   T _____   F _____

2. Daniel Boone and Davy Crockett hired press agents to help shape their reputations.

   T _____   F _____

3. More women work in public relations than men do.

   T _____   F _____

4. Some news organizations print press releases as newspaper articles, exactly as they were distributed by a public relations firm.

   T _____   F _____

5. Most major business leaders and politicians write their own speeches.

   T _____   F _____

Select the best answer to each of the following questions.

6. Which of the following statements applies to public relations?

   a. It is controlled publicity that a company or an individual buys.

   b. It attempts to secure favorable media publicity to promote a company or client.

   c. Clients buy space or time for their products or services.

   d. Consumers know who paid for the messages.

7. Who among the following was *not* an early influence on the practice of public relations?

   a. P. T. Barnum   c. John Burke

   b. Buffalo Bill   d. Tom Thumb

8. What behavior did PR agent "Poison Ivy" Lee recommend to the Pennsylvania Railroad after a rail accident?

   a. Downplay the story and try to cover it up.

   b. Avoid talking to the press.

   c. Admit its mistake to reporters.

   d. Deny responsibility.

9. Which of the following definitions of *public relations* was written by the Public Relations Society of America in 1988?

   a. "Broadly defined, public relations refers to the entire range of efforts by an individual, an agency, or any organization attempting to reach or persuade audiences."

   b. "Public relations is the attempt, by information, persuasion, and adjustment, to engineer public support for an activity, cause, movement, or institution."

   c. "Public relations helps an organization and its publics adapt mutually to each other."

   d. "Public relations expands the public discourse, helps provide a wide assortment of news, and is essential in explaining the pluralism of our total communication system."

10. IBM, Kodak, Nintendo, Pepsi, Procter & Gamble, Xerox, Richard Nixon, and the royal family of Kuwait have all used the public relations services of

    a. Hill and Knowlton.   c. Fleishman-Hillard.

    b. Burson-Marsteller.   d. BSMG Worldwide.

11. All except which of the following jobs are available to public relations personnel?

    a. conducting historical tours

    b. purchasing advertising space and time

    c. appearing on news programs

    d. coordinating special events

12. In times of crisis, why do institutions or companies sometimes make a PR spokesperson the only contact for the news media?

    a. They believe that the PR spokesperson will have more authority with the press.

    b. It is difficult to schedule experts for press conferences.

    c. They want to make sure that rumors or inaccurate stories do not get picked up by the media.

    d. All of the above.

13. What is the fastest-growing area of public relations?

    a. research   c. editing

    b. writing   d. video production

14. For companies, what is one of the benefits of community and consumer relations?

    a. It provides a source of potential new employees.

    b. It provides a source of potential new customers.

    c. It helps companies get around federal safety regulations.

    d. It offers inexpensive employee training.

15. The public relations firm Hill and Knowlton helped gain Americans' support for the Persian Gulf War by

    a. spreading rumors about Saddam Hussein.

    b. working with Congress to report stories of Iraqi cruelty toward Kuwaitis.

    c. revealing that a witness to the cruelty was lying.

    d. funding the U.S. invasion of Iraq.

Using your own words, define the following terms as they are used in the chapter.

16. *publicity*

_____

_____

17. *pseudo-event*

_____

_____

18. *propaganda*

_____

_____

19. *lobbying*

_____

_____

20. *flack*

_____

_____

Answer each of the following questions using the space provided.

21. Explain how the major American railroads convinced the U.S. government to subsidize their business in the nineteenth century.

_____

_____

_____

_____

_____

_____

_____

22. List four PR practices of late-nineteenth-century utilities that contributed to the bad reputation of public relations as a profession.

_____

_____

_____

23. According to the text, why do politicians tend to schedule press conferences and interviews between five and six o'clock in the evening?

_____

_____

_____

24. Identify and describe the two primary sources of public relations jobs.

_____

_____

_____

_____

25. Why is there tension between public relations and journalism?

_____

_____

_____

_____

_____

_____

_____

_____

_____

Making Thematic Connections

Invitation to Biology (the textbook from which the Unit 4 chapter was excerpted) defines *symbiosis* as "a close and long-term association between organisms of two different species" (p. 802). The authors, Helena Curtis and N. Sue Barnes, break symbiotic relationships into three categories: *parasitism,* *mutualism,* and *commensalism.* (Read or reread pages 802–05 in the biology chapter for more information.) Which of these categories best describes the working relationship between public relations agents and journalists? Explain your answer.

Biology

"Interactions in Communities"

Introduction

Biology is the study of life. Biologists examine how living things—from microscopic cells to humans to communities of mammals—function and coexist. They attempt to understand the natural world and to classify all forms of life into organized categories. Like other sciences, biology focuses on things that can be observed and tested. Scientists ask questions and look for answers to them by experimenting. They also consider what others before them have discovered. Sometimes they add to the scientific body of knowledge; sometimes they learn things that change what they and their colleagues had believed: these findings in turn lead to new questions. In other words, biologists observe details, make connections, make inferences, and draw conclusions. They think critically about what they do and what they know. As a student and a critical reader, you must do the same.

Invitation to Biology, Fifth Edition, by Helena Curtis and N. Sue Barnes, introduces students to the science of biology and aims to provide a grounding in the basics of the field. A major focus of *Invitation to Biology* is the theory of evolution and natural selection. Natural selection is Charles Darwin's famous theory that those living things that are best adapted to their surroundings have the best chance of surviving and producing offspring. This theory has also been called "survival of the fittest." Natural selection is an important concept behind evolution—the idea that all living things developed by a process of gradual change, over millions of years, from earlier life forms. In the chapter you're about to read, "Interactions in Communities," Curtis and Barnes apply these ideas to the study of how animals, plants, and other organisms coexist and adapt to one another over time. In particular, they look at competition, predation or hunting, and symbiosis or living together.

As you read the chapter you'll see that a variety of elements will help you understand its content. The photograph and caption that open the chapter provide a dramatic example of how the ideas in the chapter apply to a specific biological community: grazing animals on Africa's Serengeti plain. The

---

This unit's textbook reading comes from *Invitation to Biology*, Fifth Edition, by Helena Curtis and N. Sue Barnes, Worth Publishers, 1994, Chapter 44, pages 792–813.

first paragraph briefly summarizes the chapter. In addition, figures, graphs, and photographs present biological concepts visually, reinforcing the main text and making complex information easier to understand. Important terms are printed in boldface and defined. The chapter concludes with a summary and questions to help test your understanding.

The chapter's explanations of how some scientists have made their discoveries will give you an idea of what the work of a biologist is like. At the same time, understanding how groups in nature compete and coexist will give you an important insight into how businesses and other human communities compete and coexist. The natural world and the working world, it turns out, aren't so very different.

Preparing to Read the Textbook Chapter

1. The theories of evolution and natural selection are controversial to some religious groups who believe instead in creationism, or the Bible's explanation that the world and all of its living inhabitants were created by God. The idea of evolution is so controversial that the Kansas Board of Education voted in 1999 to make the teaching of evolution optional (the decision was reversed in 2001). What is your opinion? Should evolution and creationism be given equal time in public schools? Why or why not?

2. Skim through the chapter, focusing your attention on the headings, the photographs and figures, and the terms in bold print. Without reading anything closely, list the main ideas of the chapter.

3. You may have heard a ruthless businessperson referred to as a "shark" or a person who depends on others to provide money or food called a "leech." Or perhaps you've heard the phrase "survival of the fittest" used to explain why some companies succeed and others fail. Why do you think people use these kinds of scientific expressions to describe human social interactions?

The Serengeti, the vast plain that spans northern Tanzania and southern Kenya, is home to the largest herds of grazing animals in the world. Zebras, wildebeest, and Thomson gazelles—affectionately known as "tommies"—move through the plains, following the annual cycle of rainfall. Ecologists have been able to demonstrate that species like these, which appear to be competitors, actually partition their resources—not only sharing but also, in some cases, facilitating each other's existence.

Zebras are the first animals to move into long-grass areas. Like horses, zebras have large incisors on both their top and bottom jaws and heavy grinding molars. They eat the long, tough grass stalks and the older leaves. By removing the coarse top stems, they make the more nutritious leaves accessible to the animals that follow.

The wildebeest—large, ungainly looking antelopes with long manes and a distinct beard—come next. A wildebeest feeds like a cow, wrapping its tongue around the long grass stems and drawing them across the saw-like ridge of its lower incisors. The great herds of wildebeest remove so much of the grass that new shoots of grass and tiny soft-stemmed dicots spring up.

The tommies come last. These exquisite little antelopes are only about 2 feet high at the shoulder and weigh about 40 pounds. With their tiny muzzles, they nibble at the new grass leaves and the small herbs that grow between them.

Grazing stimulates new growth, as do the trampling of the soil and the feces that the animals leave behind. Grazing also makes room for a variety of species, where otherwise only one or two species might dominate. Although each zebra, each wildebeest, each tommie, and every plant on the Serengeti is acting in its own self-interest, their combined activities have produced a vast, self-sustaining system that has operated to the benefit of all of its inhabitants for millennia—and perhaps will continue to do so for years to come.

Interactions in Communities

Populations are made up of individual organisms. Communities are made up of populations. Ecologically speaking, a **community** consists of all the populations of organisms inhabiting a common environment and interacting with one another. These interactions are major forces of natural selection. They also influence the number of individuals in each population and the number and kinds of species in the community. The interactions among different populations are enormously varied and complex, but they can generally be categorized as competitive, predatory, or symbiotic.

Competition

Competition is the interaction between individual organisms of the same species (**intraspecific competition**) or of different species (**interspecific competition**) using the same resource, often present in limited supply. As a result of competition, the overall fitness—that is, the reproductive success—of the interacting individuals may be reduced. Among the many resources for which organisms may compete are food, water, light, or living space, including nesting sites or burrows.

Competition is generally greatest among organisms that have similar requirements and life styles. Plants often compete with other plants for sunlight and water. **Herbivores**, animals that eat plants and algae, may compete with other herbivores. **Carnivores**, animals that eat animals, may compete with other carnivores. Moreover, within these categories, the more similar two species are in their requirements and life style, the more intense the competition between them is likely to be.

For many years, competition has been invoked as a major force in determining the composition and structure of communities—that is, the number and kinds of species present and their arrangement in space and time within the community. Recently, however, a number of ecologists have come to question the importance of competition as an influence on community composition and structure. The debate—at times acrimonious—that has ensued concerns not only the role of competition but also the methods to be used in testing ecological hypotheses.

We shall begin our consideration of competition—and of the controversies surrounding it—with the principle that, until very recently, dominated the study of competition and the kinds of questions that ecologists asked about it.

The Principle of Competitive Exclusion

In 1934, the Russian biologist G. F. Gause formulated what became known as the principle of **competitive exclusion**. According to this principle, if two species are in competition for the same limited resource, one or the other will be more efficient at utilizing or controlling access to this resource and will eventually eliminate the other in situations in which the two species occur together.

Gause demonstrated the validity of his principle in his own, now classic, experiments involving laboratory cultures of two species of *Paramecium: Paramecium aurelia* and *Paramecium caudatum*. When the two species were grown under identical conditions in separate containers, both grew well. *Paramecium aurelia*, however, multiplied much more rapidly than *P. caudatum*, indicating that the former used the available food supply more efficiently than the latter. When the two were grown together, *P. aurelia* rapidly outmultiplied *P. caudatum*, which soon died out (Figure 44–1).

In laboratory experiments, the fastest growing species is not always the most successful competitor, how-ever, as observed with two species of duckweed, *Lemna gibba* and *Lemna polyrrhiza*. In pure culture, *L. gibba* grows more slowly than *L. polyrrhiza*, yet *L. gibba* always replaces *L. polyrrhiza* when they are grown together. The plant bodies of *L. gibba* have air-filled sacs that serve as little pontoons, so that these plants form a mass over the other species, cutting off the light. As a consequence, the shaded *L. polyrrhiza* dies out (Figure 44–2).

It is possible to devise different culture conditions so that the outcomes of both the *Paramecium* and *Lemna* experiments are reversed. However, as long as the conditions of a particular experiment are held constant, one species always wins and the other is always eventually eliminated.

44–1   *The results of Gause's experiments with two species of* Paramecium *demonstrate the principle that if two species are in direct competition for the same limited resource—in this case, food—one eliminates the other.* (a) Paramecium aurelia *and* (b) Paramecium caudatum *were first grown separately under controlled conditions and with a constant food supply. As you can see,* P. aurelia *grew much more rapidly than* P. caudatum, *indicating that* P. aurelia *uses available food supplies more efficiently.* (c) *When the two protists were grown together, the more rapidly growing species outmultiplied and eliminated the slower-growing species.*

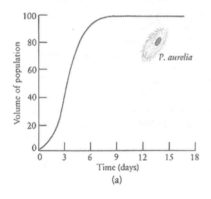

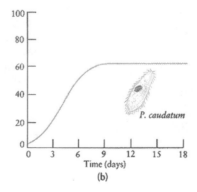

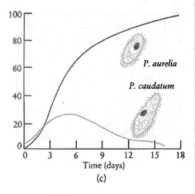

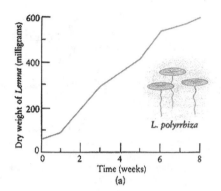

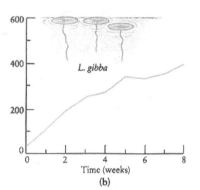

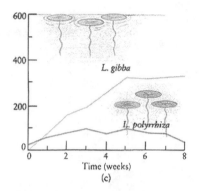

44–2 *An experiment with two species of floating duckweed, tiny angiosperms found in ponds and lakes. One species, Lemna polyrrhiza (a), grows more rapidly in pure culture than the other species, Lemna gibba (b). But L. gibba has tiny air-filled sacs that float it on the surface. When the two species are grown together, L. gibba shades L. polyrrhiza and is the victor in the competition for light (c).*

The Ecological Niche

Gause's competitive exclusion principle would lead you to expect that only dissimilar species would be found coexisting in natural communities. Yet, in fact, species with similar requirements and life styles are often found in the same community.

This observation raised the question of how similar two or more species can be and still continue to coexist in the same place at the same time, which led, in turn, to the concept of the ecological niche. This term is somewhat misleading because the word "niche" has the connotation of a physical space. An ecological niche, however, is not the space occupied by an organism but rather the role that it plays. The simplest analogy is that the niche is an organism's profession, as distinct from its habitat, which is its address.

A working definition of the niche is more complex, however, and includes many more factors than the way in which an organism makes its living. A niche is, in fact, the total environment and way of life of all the members of a particular species of organism in the community. Its description includes physical factors, such as the temperature limits within which the organisms can survive and their requirements for moisture. It includes biological factors, such as the nature and amount of required food sources. And, it also includes aspects of the behavior of the organisms, such as patterns of movement and daily and seasonal activity cycles. Although only a few of these factors can be studied at any one time, all are likely to influence the interactions of the members of a species with the members of other species in the community.

Resource Partitioning

The concept of the ecological niche suggested that when similar species are found coexisting together, a close examination will reveal that their niches are, in fact, different. An example is provided by the grazing animals of the Serengeti with which we began this chapter. Although the zebras, wildebeest, and gazelles appear to be sharing and competing for the same resources, they are not.

Numerous studies of different types of organisms have revealed that such dividing up, or partitioning, of resources occurs frequently among ecologically similar members of a community. The cause of the partitioning is a matter of considerable disagreement among ecologists, as we shall see shortly. First, however, let us consider two other examples.

796

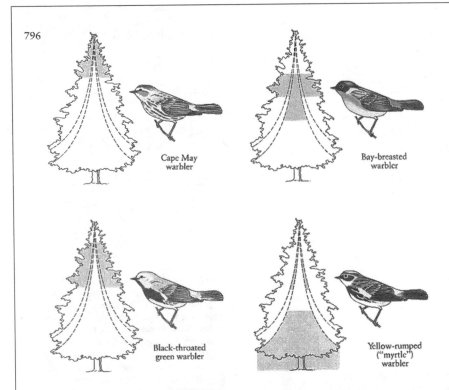

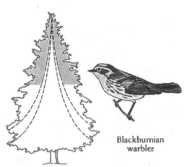

Cape May warbler

Bay-breasted warbler

Blackburnian warbler

Black-throated green warbler

Yellow-rumped ("myrtle") warbler

44–3   *The feeding zones in a spruce tree of five species of North American warblers. The colored areas in the tree indicate where each species spends at least half its feeding time. This partitioning of resources allows all five species to feed in the same trees.*

44–4   *Mosses of the genus* Sphagnum, *which form extensive bogs in both temperate and cold regions of the world. Peat is formed from the accumulation and compression of the mosses themselves, as well as the sedges, reeds, and other grasses that grow among them. In Ireland, dried peat is widely used as an industrial fuel, as well as for home heating. It is estimated that peat bogs cover at least 1 percent of the Earth's land surface, an enormous area equivalent to half of the United States.*

Woodland Warblers

Some New England forests are inhabited by five closely related species of warblers, all about the same size and all insect eaters. The late Robert MacArthur, a brilliant and innovative young ecologist, meticulously observed and timed where the warblers fed within the trees. His data showed that the five species have different feeding zones (Figure 44–3). Because they exploit slightly different resources—that is, insects in different parts of the trees—the species can coexist.

Bog Mosses

In bogs, mosses of the genus *Sphagnum* (Figure 44–4) often appear to form a continuous cover, and several species are usually involved. How can these species, apparently very similar, continue to coexist?

When the situation is examined in detail, it is found that semiaquatic species grow along the bottoms of the wettest hollows. Other species grow in drier places on the sides of the hummocks, which they help to form. Still other species grow only in the driest conditions on the tops of the hummocks, where they are eventually succeeded by one or more species of flowering plants. Therefore, although all the species of *Sphagnum* coexist, in the sense that they are all present in the same bog, they actually occupy different microenvironments and continually replace one another as the characteristics of each microenvironment change.

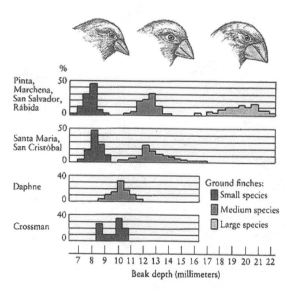

44–5 *Beak sizes in three species of ground finch found on the Galapagos Islands. Beak measurements are plotted horizontally, and the percentage of specimens of each species is shown vertically. Daphne and Crossman, which are very small islands, each have only one species of ground finch. These species have beak sizes halfway between those of the medium-sized and small finches on the larger islands.*

The Role of Past Competition in Resource Partitioning

The resource partitioning observed among African herbivores, woodland warblers, *Sphagnum* mosses, and many other organisms was long considered to be the result of competition. In some cases, such as the warblers, the competition was thought to be occurring in the present. In other cases, such as the mosses and the herbivores, it was thought to have occurred in the evolutionary past, leading to the differing adaptations that enable the organisms to coexist. This phenomenon, in which species that live together in the same environment tend to diverge in those characteristics that overlap, is known as character displacement.

One of the most frequently cited examples of character displacement is provided by the beaks of Darwin's finches. As we saw in Chapter 21, the large, medium, and small ground finch species are very similar except for differences in overall body size and in the sizes and shapes of their beaks. The differences in the beaks are correlated with the sizes of the seeds the birds eat. On islands such as Pinta and Marchena (see page 364), where all three species of ground finch exist together, there are clear-cut differences in beak size (Figure 44–5). On Santa Maria and San Cristóbal Islands, the large species is not found, and the beak sizes of the medium ground finches on these islands are larger and overlap the beak sizes of the large finches found on

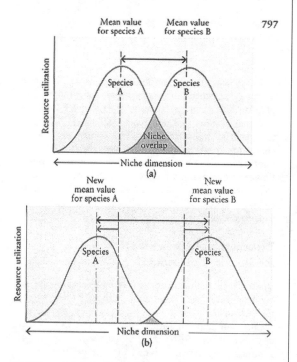

44–6 *Overlap in one dimension of an ecological niche. (a) The two bell-shaped curves represent utilization of a resource by two species in a community. The niche dimension might represent living space, as in the case of Sphagnum mosses; foraging space, as in the case of warblers; size of seeds eaten, as in the case of the Galapagos finches; and so on. Competition between the two species is potentially most intense in areas of niche overlap, leading to restriction of one or both species in living space, foraging space, or the size of seeds eaten, and so on. (b) It is hypothesized that such competition results in selection against individuals with overlapping characteristics, leading to divergence in the niches of the two species.*

Pinta and Marchena. Daphne and Crossman, which are very small islands, each have only one species. Daphne has the medium-sized finch and Crossman, the small finch. These two populations have similar beak sizes, which are intermediate between those of the medium-sized and small finches on the larger islands.

These data have been interpreted in two different ways by ecologists. Some ecologists maintain that the observed differences in beak size are the result of the selection pressures exerted by interspecific competition. According to this interpretation, competition between organisms whose ecological niches overlap causes selection against individuals with overlapping characteristics, leading to the observed divergence between the species (Figure 44–6).

Other ecologists point out that it is impossible to determine if the differing beak sizes are the result of competition that occurred at times when the different species were coexisting on the same islands or if they are the result of adaptations to local conditions that occurred at times when the species were isolated from one another on different islands. Both groups of ecologists, however, agree that whatever their evolutionary cause, the differences in beak size and shape enable the different finch species to exploit different food sources and thus to coexist.

Experimental Approaches to the Study of Competition

Virtually all ecologists agree that competition does occur in nature, with the degree of intensity varying according to the particular species involved, the sizes of the interacting populations, and the abundance or scarcity of resources. Although the analysis of resource partitioning may provide clues as to the occurrence and importance of competition in a particular situation, experiments involving changes in community composition are required to demonstrate that competition is actually taking place. At their best, laboratory experiments, such as those performed by Gause, can only approximate natural conditions, which are invariably much more complex.

Barnacles in Scotland

One of the clearest experimental demonstrations of competition in a natural community was a study of barnacles performed by Joseph Connell. Barnacles are crustaceans. When they change from their free-swimming, larval form into their adult, sedentary form, they cement themselves to rocks and secrete protective calcium-containing plates. Once attached, barnacles remain fixed, so that by making careful observations over time, one can determine the dynamics of a particular population. One can identify exactly which barnacles have died and which new ones have arrived between visits to the study site.

Connell studied two barnacle species, *Chthamalus stellatus* and *Semibalanus balanoides,* that live on the coasts of Scotland. *Chthamalus* is found in the high part of the intertidal seashore. As the tides go in and out, these barnacles are exposed to wide fluctuations of temperature and salinity and to the hazards of desiccation. The other species, *Semibalanus,* occurs in the lower intertidal zone, where conditions are more constant.

Although *Chthamalus* larvae, after their period of drifting in the plankton, often attach to rocks in the lower, *Semibalanus*-occupied zone, adults are rarely

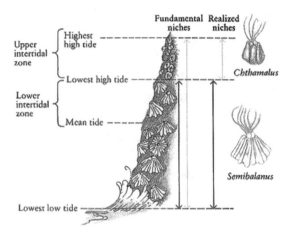

44–7 *Interspecific competition between* Semibalanus *and* Chthamalus *barnacles. The larvae of both species settle over a wide range, but the adults live in precisely restricted areas. The upper limits of the* Semibalanus *area are determined by physical factors such as exposure to air, which can lead to desiccation. Such exposure occurs at specific times during the month when the high tide covers only the lower portion of the intertidal zone, leaving the upper intertidal zone exposed.* Chthamalus *barnacles, however, are prevented from living in the* Semibalanus *area not by physical factors (they would probably thrive there since the area is less physically limiting) but by the* Semibalanus *barnacles.* Semibalanus *grows faster, and whenever it comes upon* Chthamalus *in the* Semibalanus *area, it either pries it off the rocks or grows right over it.*

found there. Connell showed that in the lower zone, *Semibalanus,* which grows faster, ousts *Chthamalus* by crowding it off the rocks and growing over it or undercutting it. When Connell experimentally removed *Semibalanus* from the lower portion of the intertidal zone, *Chthamalus* invaded the area and thrived there. In the control areas, where barnacles were not removed, each species remained in its own zone.

As this experiment demonstrates, *Chthamalus* is not restricted to the upper intertidal zone by a physiological inability to live elsewhere. It is restricted by competition with *Semibalanus.* There is no evidence, however, that competition with *Chthamalus* keeps *Semibalanus* in the lower zone. Because *Semibalanus* lacks the physiological adaptations required for life in the upper, drier zone, it cannot successfully invade it.

This study, and others like it, have generated the concepts of fundamental niche and realized niche. The **fundamental niche** describes the physiological limits of tolerance of the organism. It is the niche occupied by an organism in the absence of interactions with other organisms. The **realized niche** is that portion of the fundamental niche actually utilized. It is determined by physical factors and also by interactions with other organisms.

In its fundamental niche, *Chthamalus* can occupy both the high and low intertidal zones, but because of niche overlap with *Semibalanus, Chthamalus* actually occupies a smaller area, its realized niche (Figure 44–7). Because *Semibalanus* is restricted by physiological limits, it can occupy only the lower intertidal zone. Its fundamental niche is narrower than that of *Chthamalus* and is totally included within it. In such a situation, the species with the narrow, included fundamental niche must be a superior competitor or it will be driven to extinction. *Semibalanus* can survive in the same intertidal community as *Chthamalus* because it is the superior competitor. *Chthamalus* can survive, despite its competitive inferiority, because its fundamental niche is broader, providing it with a refuge that cannot be invaded by *Semibalanus*.

Winner Takes All

Most studies of competition have emphasized the adaptations and the partitionings of resources that make possible the coexistence of similar species within a community. This is, however, a biased view, for it is difficult to study the interactions between species after one of the protagonists has left. Just as competition within species leads to the elimination of the great majority of individual organisms, as Darwin observed, competition between species may lead to elimination of a species from the community.

One example is the disappearance from many localities of bluebirds (Figure 44–8). This is thought to have been caused, in part, by the usurpation of their nesting sites by starlings. Starlings were introduced into Central Park in New York City in 1891 and are now found throughout the United States, whereas some of us have never seen a bluebird.

Predation

Predation is the consumption of live organisms, including plants by animals, animals by animals, and even, as we have seen, animals by plants (page 741) or by fungi (page 437). Predators use a variety of techniques—known as **foraging strategies**—to obtain their food. Foraging strategies are under intense selection pressure. Those individuals that forage most efficiently are likely to leave the most offspring. From the standpoint of po-

tential prey, those individuals that are most successful at avoiding predation are likely to leave the most offspring. Thus, predation affects the evolution of both predator and prey.

Predation also affects the number of organisms in a population and the diversity of species within a community.

Predation and Numbers

For many populations, predation is the major cause of death, yet, paradoxically, it is not at all clear that predation necessarily reduces the numbers of a prey population below the carrying capacity of its environment. However, when predation is heavier on certain age groups—juveniles versus adults, for instance—or certain life stages—such as caterpillars versus butterflies—it can alter the structure of a prey population and promote adjustments in life-history patterns.

44–8   *A male mountain bluebird at the entrance of a nesting box in Denver, Colorado. For more than 25 years, the U.S. Fish and Wildlife Service has been monitoring the breeding populations of the three bluebird species native to North America. A significant increase in the size of the populations began to occur in the mid-1980s. This increase is attributed, in large part, to a concerted effort by the North American Bluebird Society and others to encourage people to provide suitable nesting boxes for the birds in potential bluebird habitats. An important factor in the design of the nesting boxes is that the entrance holes be large enough to admit bluebirds but small enough to exclude starlings.*

800   SECTION 8   Ecology

44–9   (a) *Prickly-pear cactus growing on a pasture in Queensland, Australia, in November of 1926. Such rapid and environmentally destructive spread often occurs when alien organisms are introduced into a region where they have no competitors or predators. (b) The same pasture in October of 1929, slightly less than three years after the introduction of the cactus moth.*

(a)   (b)

Predation, especially on large herbivores, tends to cull animals in poor physical condition. Wolves, for instance, have great difficulty overtaking healthy adult moose or even healthy calves. A study of Isle Royale, an island in Lake Superior, showed that in some seasons more than 50 percent of the animals the wolves killed had lung disease, although the incidence of such individuals in the population was less than 2 percent. Thus, many of the animals killed by predators, according to this study, are animals that would have died soon anyway. (Modern human hunters, however, with their superior weapons and their desire for a "prize" specimen, are more likely to injure or destroy strong, healthy animals.)

In some situations, however, predators do limit their prey species. This has been most clearly demonstrated in cases involving the introduction of alien species into areas where they have no natural predators. When prickly-pear cactus, for instance, was brought to Australia from South America, it escaped from the garden of the gentleman who imported it and spread into fields and pastureland until more than 12 million hectares were so densely covered with prickly pears that they could support almost no other vegetation (Figure 44–9). The cactus then began to take over the rest of Australia at the rate of about 400,000 hectares a year. It was not brought under control until a natural predator was imported—a South American moth, whose caterpillars feed only on the cactus. Now only an occasional cactus and a few moths can be found. (Note, however, that the introduction of the alien moth was, in itself, risky.)

Few predator-prey relationships are this simple. Most predators have more than one prey species, al-

though one prey species may be preferred. Characteristically, when one prey species becomes less abundant, predation on other species increases so the proportions of each in the predator's diet fluctuate.

Although predators may not always limit prey populations, the availability of prey constitutes a major component of the carrying capacity for predator populations, often stringently affecting their size. This is evident in relatively simple situations, such as when a bloom of phytoplankton (mostly microscopic algae) results from an upwelling of nutrients due to ocean currents and then is followed by a corresponding increase in zooplankton (animal plankton).

A more complex example is that of the lynx and the snowshoe hare. The data (Figure 44–10) are based on pelts received yearly by the Hudson's Bay Company over a period of almost 100 years. As you can see, there are oscillations in population density that occur about every 10 years. Generally speaking, a rise in the hare population is followed by a rise in the lynx population. The hare population then plummets, and the lynx population follows.

This example, which has been studied by ecologists over the last 50 years, can be interpreted in a variety of ways. The traditional explanation is that overpredation by the lynx reduces the snowshoe hare population. The lynx population, heavily dependent on the snowshoe hare as prey, is reduced in turn. The reduction in predation then permits the snowshoe hares to increase in number, followed by an increase in the number of lynx, and so on.

A second explanation is that the hare population undergoes a regular 10-year cycle caused, perhaps, by diseases associated with crowding or the effects of its own

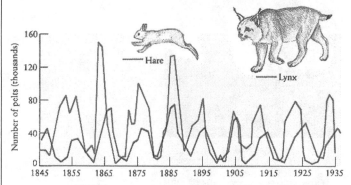

44–10   *The number of lynx and snowshoe hare pelts received yearly by the Hudson's Bay Company over a period of almost 100 years, indicating a pattern of 10-year oscillations in population density. The lynx reaches a population peak every 9 or 10 years, and these peaks are followed in each case by several years of sharp decline. The snowshoe hare follows a similar cycle, with a peak abundance generally preceding that of the lynx by a year or more.*

predatory activities on the vegetation it consumes. This latter hypothesis is supported by two discoveries: (1) when overbrowsed, certain types of plants put out new shoots and leaves that contain chemicals toxic to hares, and (2) on an island where there are no lynx, the hare population undergoes similar cycles.

A third possibility is that the lynx undergo a regular cycle, independent of the hares, perhaps associated with some other factor, such as changes in the habits of their own predators, the human hunters. A decrease in the lynx population may permit growth of the hare population, or the two populations may oscillate independently. Thus, whereas the lynx and the hare used to serve as a simple model of predator-prey relationships, it is now perhaps more instructive as an example of the difficulties in dealing with ecological variables.

Predation and Species Diversity

The number and kinds of species in a community can be greatly influenced by predation. Although predation may occasionally eliminate a prey species, many experimental studies have shown that it is often an important factor in maintaining species diversity in a community.

For example, R. T. Paine studied a community on the rocky coast of Washington. In this community, the principal predator was the starfish *Pisaster* (Figure 44–11). At the beginning of the experiment, there were 15 prey species, including several species of barnacles and several kinds of mollusks, including mussels, limpets, and chitons. Paine systematically removed the starfish from one area of the community, 8 meters by 2 meters in size. By the end of the experiment, the number of prey species in the area from which the starfish were removed had declined to eight, and the community was dominated by one species of mussel. In the undisturbed community, starfish predation kept the densities of the prey populations low, reducing competition between the species and permitting all to survive. In the absence of the predator, the mussels were clear victors in the competition for living space.

Organisms, such as *Pisaster*, that are of exceptional importance in maintaining the diversity of a community are known as **keystone species**. When the keystone is removed from a stone arch, the arch falls apart. Similarly, when a keystone species is lost from a community—as a result, for example, of pollution, disease, or competition from an alien organism—the diversity of the community decreases and the structure of the community is significantly altered.

In another series of experiments, Jane Lubchenco showed that the herbivorous marine snail *Littorina lit-*

44–11   *Photographed off the coast of California, this starfish of the genus* Pisaster *is opening a mussel, one of its favorite foods. Studies have shown that predation by* Pisaster, *particularly on mussels and barnacles, is an important factor in maintaining species diversity in the rocky coastal communities in which it lives.*

torea controls the abundance and type of algae in the higher intertidal pools on the New England coast. In such pools, the snails' preferred food (the green alga *Enteromorpha*) is competitively superior, and its removal by the snails permits the growth of other algal species (Figure 44–12). However, in areas exposed to the air at high tide as well as at low tide, *Enteromorpha* is competitively inferior. Its removal by the snails from those areas facilitates the growth of algal species that are competitively superior under exposed conditions. The result is domination by those species and a decrease in the total number of species in the exposed areas.

As this example illustrates, although predation often plays an important role in maintaining species diversity, it does not always do so. Even when the same predator and prey species are involved, the effect of predation on species diversity depends on the particular situation.

Symbiosis

As we saw in Chapter 25, **symbiosis** ("living together") is a close and long-term association between organisms of two different species. Long-continued symbiotic relationships can result in profound evolutionary changes in the organisms involved, as in the case of lichens (page 439), one of the oldest and most ecologically successful symbioses.

Although there is some disagreement among ecologists as to precisely what constitutes a symbiotic relationship, and the details of the relationship between two closely associated species are often difficult to determine, symbiotic relationships are generally considered to be of three kinds. If one species benefits and the other is harmed, the relationship is known as **parasitism**. If the relationship is beneficial to both species, it is called **mutualism**. Less common is **commensalism**, a relationship that is beneficial to one species and that neither benefits nor harms the other.

An example of commensalism is the relationship between the marine annelid *Chaetopterus* and tiny crabs of the genus *Pinnixa*, which live in the intertidal mud flats along the Atlantic coast of the United States. Each *Chaetopterus* constructs a U-shaped tube in which it lives (Figure 44–13), and the tube usually also contains two crabs, one male and one female. Both worm and crabs feed on particles of organic matter carried in water currents moved through the tube by fanlike appendages of the worm's body. The crabs obtain shelter and a steady food supply, and, as best anyone has been able to determine, their presence neither benefits nor harms the worm.

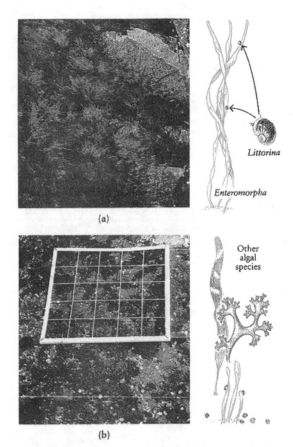

(a)

(b)

44–12 *An example of the effects of predation on species diversity. (a) In this high intertidal pool on the New England coast, the density of the herbivorous marine snail* Littorina lit- torea *is very low (between one and five individuals per square meter). The competitively superior green alga* Enteromorpha *dominates the pool, excluding other algae. (b) In a neighboring pool, less than a meter away, the density of* Littorina *is much higher—more than 250 individuals per square meter. The snails have grazed heavily on* Enteromorpha, *permitting the growth of other algal species that are, for* Littorina, *inedible. The aluminum grid at the top of the photograph was used to estimate the density of the snails.*

Parasitism

Parasitism may be considered a special form of predation in which the predator is considerably smaller than the prey. The plants and animals in a natural community support hundreds of parasitic species—in fact, certainly thousands and perhaps millions if one were to count nematodes and viruses.

As with more obvious forms of predation, parasitic diseases are most likely to wipe out the very young, the very old, and the disabled—either directly or, more often, indirectly, by making them more susceptible to other predators or to the effects of climate or food

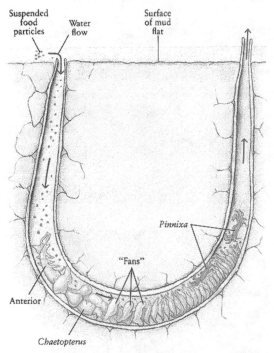

44–13 Chaetopterus, *a marine annelid, lives in a parchment tube, constructed by the worm itself, with two commensal crabs of the genus* Pinnixa. *Modified parapodia ("side feet") of the worm function as fans, pulling water through the tube. Both the worm and the crabs are nourished by food particles carried into the tube with the moving water.*

44–14 *Rabbits crowd a water hole in Australia. Imported from Europe as potentially valuable herbivores, they soon overran the countryside. The myxoma virus was introduced to control them, and now host and parasite are coexisting.*

shortages. It is predictable that a parasite-caused disease should not be too virulent or too efficient. If a parasite were to kill all the hosts for which it is adapted, it too would perish.

This principle is particularly well illustrated by a series of further misadventures on the continent of Australia. There were no rabbits in Australia until 1859, when an English gentleman imported a dozen from Europe to grace his estate. Six years later he had killed a total of 20,000 on his own property and estimated he had 10,000 remaining. In 1887, in New South Wales alone, Australians killed 20 million rabbits. By 1950, Australia was being stripped of its vegetation by the rabbit hordes (Figure 44–14).

In that year, rabbits infected with myxoma virus were released on the continent. Myxoma virus, which is carried from host to host by mosquitoes, causes only a mild disease in South American rabbits, its normal hosts, but is usually fatal to the European rabbit. At first, the effects were spectacular, and the rabbit population steadily declined, yielding a share of pasture-

land once more to the sheep herds on which much of the economy of the country depends. But then occasional rabbits began to survive the disease, and their litters also showed resistance to the myxoma virus.

A double process of selection had taken place. The original virus was so rapidly fatal that often a rabbit died before there was time for it to be bitten by a mosquito and thereby infect another rabbit. The virus strain then died with the rabbit. Strains less drastic in their effects, on the other hand, had a better chance of survival since they had a greater opportunity to spread to a new host. So selection began to work in favor of a less virulent strain of the myxoma virus. Simultaneously, rabbits that were resistant to the original virus began to proliferate. Now, as a result of coevolution, the host-parasite relationship seems to be stabilizing.

Mutualism

If the current hypothesis as to the origin of eukaryotic cells (page 419) is correct, we owe our very origins to

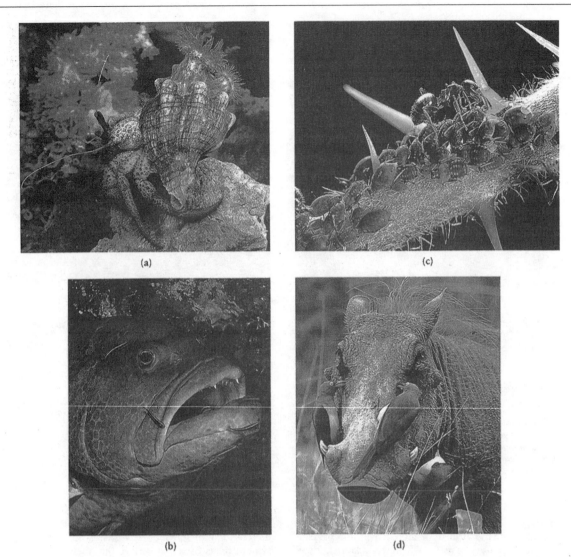

(a)

(c)

(b)

(d)

44–15 *Mutualism. (a) Sea anemones on the back of a whelk shell occupied by a red hairy hermit crab. The anemones protect and camouflage the crab and, in turn, gain mobility—and so a wider feeding range—from their association with the crab. Hermit crabs, which periodically move into new, larger shells, will coax their anemones to move with them.*

(b) Cleaner fish, removing parasites from a tiger grouper. Throughout the process of having its mouth cleaned, the grouper holds its mouth perfectly still. Cleaner fish are permitted to approach larger fish with impunity because of the service they render as they feed off the algae, fungi, and other microorganisms on the fish's body. Larger fish recognize the cleaners by their brilliant colors and distinctive markings. Other species of fish, by closely resembling the cleaners, are able to get close enough to the large fish to remove big bites of flesh. What would probably happen if the number of cleaner mimics began to approach the number of true cleaners?

(c) Aphids suck sap from the phloem, removing certain amino acids, sugars, and other nutrients from it and excreting most of it as "honeydew," or "sugar-lerp," as it is called in Australia, where it is harvested as food by the aborigines. Some species of aphids have been domesticated by some species of ants. These aphids do not excrete their honeydew at random, but only in response to caressing movements of the ants' antennae and forelimbs. The aphids involved in this symbiotic association have lost all their own natural defenses, including even their hard outer skeletons, relying upon their hosts for protection.

(d) Oxpeckers live on the ticks they remove from their hosts. Like cleaner fish, they perform an essential service. An oxpecker forms an association with one particular animal, such as the warthog shown here, conducting most of its activities, including courtship and mating, on the body of its host.

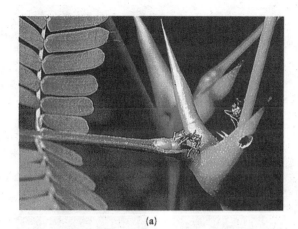

(a)

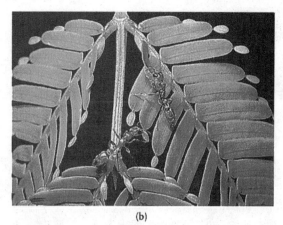

(b)

44–16 *Ants and acacias. (a) A worker ant, drinking from a nectary of a bull's-horn acacia. At the left is an entrance hole into a thorn that was cut by the queen ant. After she had hollowed out the thorn, the queen raised her brood* *within it. (b) Worker ants collecting Beltian bodies from the tips of acacia leaflets. Rich in proteins and oils, the Beltian bodies are an important food source for both adult and larval ants.*

mutualism. Examples of present-day mutualistic associations are so abundant that we must limit ourselves to only a few. Perhaps among the most significant are those that take place underground, between roots and nitrogen-fixing bacteria (page 751) and in mycorrhizae (page 440).

Some particularly colorful examples of mutualism are illustrated in Figure 44–15. Another example is the interaction of ants and acacias.

Ants and Acacias

Trees and shrubs of the genus *Acacia* grow throughout the tropical and subtropical regions of the world. In Africa and tropical America, where plants are preyed upon by large herbivores, acacia species are protected by thorns. (Acacias that evolved where there are no large browsers—Australia, for instance—lack thorns.)

On one of the African species of *Acacia,* ants of the genus *Crematogaster* gnaw entrance holes in the walls of the thorns and live permanently inside them. Each colony of ants inhabits the thorns on one or more trees. The ants obtain food from nectar-secreting glands on the leaves of the acacias and eat caterpillars and other small herbivores they find on the trees. Both the ants and the acacias appear to benefit from this association.

In the lowlands of Mexico and Central America, the ant-acacia relationship has been extended to even greater lengths. The bull's-horn acacia is found frequently in cutover or disturbed areas, where it grows extremely rapidly. This species of acacia has a pair of greatly swollen thorns, several centimeters in length, at the base of most leaves. The petioles bear nectaries, and at the very tip of each leaflet is a small structure, rich in oils and proteins, known as a Beltian body. Thomas

Belt, the naturalist who first described these bodies, noted that their only apparent function was to nourish the ants. Ants live in the thorns, obtain sugars from the nectaries, eat the Beltian bodies, and feed them to their larvae.

Worker ants, which swarm over the surface of the plant, are very aggressive toward other insects and, indeed, toward animals of all sizes. They become alert at the mere rustle of a passing mammal, and when their tree is brushed by an animal, they swarm out and attack at once, inflicting painful, burning bites. Moreover, and even more surprising, other plants sprouting within as much as a meter of occupied acacias are chewed and mauled, and their bark is girdled. Twigs and branches of other trees that touch an occupied acacia are similarly destroyed. Not surprisingly, acacias inhabited by these ants grow very rapidly, soon overtopping other vegetation.

Daniel Janzen, who first analyzed the ant-acacia relationship in detail, removed ants from acacias either by insecticides or by removing thorns or entire occupied branches. Acacias without their ants grew slowly and usually suffered severe damage from insect herbivores. They were soon overshadowed by competing species of plants and vines. As for the ants, according to Janzen, these particular species live only on acacias.

There is an epilogue to the ant-acacia story. Three new species—a fly, a weevil, and a spider—have been discovered that mimic the ants that inhabit the acacias. So expert is their mimicry (probably involving chemical recognition signals as well as appearance) that the patrolling ants do not recognize them as interlopers, and so they enjoy the hospitality and protection of the ant-acacia complex.

Conservation Biology and the Island Biogeography Model

As the human demand for natural resources increases, ecological communities are being fragmented at an accelerating rate. Formerly large and continuous natural communities are being reduced to isolated "islands," often surrounded by areas that are unsuitable for most of the species involved. The most dramatic examples of this destruction of natural communities are occurring in tropical forests. However, the destruction of wildlife habitat is not unique to tropical forests. Whenever a marsh is cut by a new roadway, a forest is cleared for agriculture or a housing development, or a river is interrupted by a dam, the result is a subdivision of ecological communities into smaller, increasingly isolated habitat islands.

As discussed on the facing page, the equilibrium hypothesis of island biogeography predicts higher rates of extinction on and lower rates of immigration to small, isolated islands. According to this model, as natural communities are reduced to smaller and more isolated fragments, they can be expected to support fewer and fewer species.

This prediction of reduced species numbers in small, isolated habitat fragments has been supported by research in a number of different regions. One of the most thoroughly studied sites is Barro Colorado Island, an area of tropical rain forest located in Lake Gatun in Panama. The lake was created early in the twentieth century by the completion of the Panama Canal, isolating what is now Barro Colorado Island from the previously contiguous forest. Since that time, more than 50 species of birds have disappeared from the island, although they remain abundant on the mainland, only half a kilometer away.

A similar pattern of extinction has been observed in the 86-hectare woodland of the Bogor Botanical Garden in Java, Indonesia. Fifty years ago, this woodland was isolated by the destruction of the surrounding woodlands. Since that time, it has lost 20 of the 62 species of birds originally breeding there—more than

(a)

(b)

30 percent of the original community—and another four species are close to extinction.

It has been suggested that isolation of ecological communities may be reduced—and dispersal rates increased—by maintaining natural corridors between isolated communities. This possibility is being explored in the Netherlands, where studies are examining the role of hedgerows ("paths" of trees and shrubs, ranging from 1 to 10 meters in width) in increasing the rates of colonization of forest fragments. The hedgerows appear to increase the rate of dispersal of most forest species and may play a role in maintaining animal diversity in otherwise isolated patches of forest.

One of the most ambitious ecological projects currently underway was inspired by the equilibrium hypothesis of island biogeography. Known as the Minimum Critical Size of Ecosystems Project, it is a cooperative investigation by Brazilian and North American scientists in the Amazon rain forests. The project has revealed that forest fragmentation can have substantial effects on the physical environment. Hot, dry winds blowing across surrounding cleared areas reduce the relative humidity along the edges of the forest fragments

by as much as 20 percent. Moreover, increased light penetration at the edges of the forest fragments has elevated the temperatures there as much as 4.5°C (8.1°F) above the temperature in the forest interior. These physical changes may be responsible for some of the initial biological changes in the forest fragments: more trees die, more leaves drop from the remaining trees, and both the number of bird species and their population density decrease.

Although the equilibrium hypothesis of island biogeography began as a purely theoretical exercise to explain the maintenance of species diversity on islands, it has inspired research that is providing information vital for conservation biology, for the design and management of nature reserves, and for informed land-use planning. Some of the results of this research were not predicted by the original model. However, one of the most important predictions has held up: reductions in species diversity can be expected within nature reserves as they become increasingly isolated. For most groups of organisms, the numbers of species lost will depend upon both the size of the reserves and their degree of isolation.

(c)

(a) *The tropical rain forest of Barro Colorado Island, Panama, as seen from an observation tower above the forest canopy. The island is in the foreground, and the Panamanian mainland is in the background. Biologists affiliated with the Smithsonian Tropical Research Institute, assisted by Earthwatch volunteers, are conducting detailed studies of the forest and its occupants.* (b) *For North American visitors, one of the most familiar animals of the forest is the bay-breasted warbler, which summers in the forests of New England but winters on Barro Colorado Island— and nowhere else in the world.* (c) *The forest interior.*

Community Composition and the Question of Stability

Viewed from a global perspective, ecological communities often seem to be at equilibrium, with many species persisting for many generations over large areas. However, when communities are examined on a local scale, it becomes apparent that they, like the individual populations of which they are composed, undergo many fluctuations. Two questions concerning community composition have long perplexed ecologists. First, what determines the number of species in a community? And, second, what factors underlie the changes in a community that occur with the passage of time?

The Island Biogeography Model

Because of their size and relative isolation, small islands are often excellent natural laboratories for the study of evolutionary and ecological processes. In a classic study published in 1963, Robert MacArthur and E. O. Wilson used small islands as models to explore questions of community composition and stability.

MacArthur and Wilson hypothesized that the number of species on any given island remains relatively constant through time but that the identity of the species present is continually changing. According to their proposal, known as the **equilibrium hypothesis of island biogeography**, there is a balance between the rate at which new species immigrate to an island and the rate at which species already present become locally extinct. Although the number of species is in equilibrium, the species composition is *not* in equilibrium, because when a species becomes locally extinct it is usually replaced by a different species.

The island biogeography model was tested in an ingenious way by Wilson and Daniel Simberloff. They selected a number of small mangrove islands off the Florida Keys and counted the number of species of arthropods on each. They then destroyed all the animal life (mostly insects and other small arthropods) by covering the islands with plastic tents and fumigating them. Their plant life intact, the islands were soon colonized again from the mainland, and the recolonization process was monitored.

As predicted by the model, the total number of species present on an island after recolonization tended to be the same as the total number before the island was disturbed. However, and this is an important point, the species composition was often quite different from what it had been previously. Moreover, once the equilibrium number had been reached, the species composition con-

808   SECTION 8   Ecology

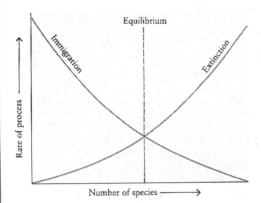

44–17   *Equilibrium model of the diversity of species on an island. The immigration rate declines as more species reach the island because species that arrived earlier have had time to become established. Thus, they are better able to compete against species that arrive later. Also, fewer immigrants will belong to new species. The extinction rate increases more rapidly at high species number because there is more competition between species. The equilibrium number of species (dashed line) is determined by the intersection of the immigration and extinction curves.*

44–18   *(a) Living sea fans, a coral that grows best in warm, clean water with a low level of nutrients. (b) The limestone remains of a sea fan of the same species that has been killed, most likely by parasites or polluted water. Reef-building corals are keystone species (page 801). When the living coral animals are destroyed, the structure of the reef community disintegrates. The diversity of other organisms that were once part of the community (page 460) must move elsewhere if they are to survive. When enormous areas of coral reef die, as is happening today in many parts of the world, there is no "elsewhere" for the other organisms.*

(a)

(b)

tinued to change, with extinction and immigration balancing one another out (Figure 44–17).

According to the island biogeography model, the two most important variables influencing species diversity are the size of the island and its distance from a source, usually the mainland, that can provide colonists. Distant islands tend to have fewer species than islands closer to the mainland. This is thought to be a result of lower rates of immigration, which appear to be a function of the distance that potential colonists must travel. Smaller islands are thought to reach equilibrium with a smaller number of species than larger islands, primarily because extinction rates are higher on smaller islands. This may be because populations tend to be smaller on such islands and thus are more susceptible to the effects of both predation and environmental disturbances.

This model applies not only to true islands but also to fragmented terrestrial areas. Thus it has important implications for conservation efforts (see essay).

The Intermediate Disturbance Hypothesis

Different types of communities vary widely in the number and diversity of species present. Among the most diverse are tropical rain forests and coral reefs. Until recently, it was thought that the species composition of these communities was relatively constant, and they were frequently cited as prime examples of an equilibrium state. Their high species diversity was thought to be a function of their stability. It now appears, however, that their diversity may be a function not of their stability but rather of the frequency and magnitude of the disturbances to which they are subjected.

Disturbances can take many forms. In the tropical forest, for example, trees are killed or severely damaged by storms, landslides, lightning strikes, and insect outbreaks. The corals that form the basis of the coral reef community can be destroyed by predators or parasites, by the severe waves that accompany tropical storms, and by influxes of polluted water (Figure 44–18).

Soon after a disturbance, open areas—of forest or reef—are invaded by immature forms—seeds, spores, larvae, or even gametes. Initially, diversity in a newly colonized area is low. Only species that are close to the disturbed area and that are reproducing at the time are able to exploit the newly available area. If disturbances are frequent, the community will consist only of those species that can invade, mature, and reproduce before the next disturbance occurs.

According to the **intermediate disturbance hypothesis**, as the interval between disturbances increases, so does species diversity. Species that are excluded by frequent disturbances (because they are slow to mature or have limited dispersal abilities) now have an opportunity to colonize. However, if the interval between disturbances increases still further, species diversity may begin to decline (Figure 44–19). The primary factor in this decline is thought to be competition, but even if all species were competitively equal, the species most resistant to ill effects from physical extremes, predation, or disease would eventually come to dominate the community.

Among the smallest self-contained communities are those found on boulders located in the intertidal zones of rocky coasts. These communities, which are dominated by the algae growing on the rock surface, are often subjected to massive disturbances as a result of severe waves. The waves may either strip the algae away or actually overturn the boulders. As a result, bare rock becomes available for colonization. In a series of observations in intertidal zones of southern California, Wayne Sousa found that large boulders, which are infrequently overturned, and small boulders, which are frequently overturned, are typically dominated by one or a few algal species. By contrast, medium-sized boulders, which are subjected to an intermediate number of disturbances, tend to have a greater diversity of species.

Ecological Succession

Numerous observations have revealed that, if the interval between disturbances is relatively long, gradual changes occur in the composition of a community following the initial recolonization. The photosynthetic organisms that are usually the first colonists (Figure 44–20) are generally replaced in time by other types, which gradually crowd out the earliest species and

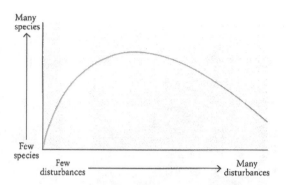

44–19   *According to the intermediate disturbance hypothesis, the diversity of species in a community is determined by the frequency of environmental disturbances. When disturbances occur either very seldom or very often, the number of species is low. By contrast, when the frequency of disturbances is somewhere in between, the number of species is high.*

44–20   *When Mt. St. Helens in the state of Washington exploded on May 18, 1980, shock waves leveled all of the trees in an area of about 21,000 hectares, and a deep layer of ash was deposited. Fireweed (Epilobium augustifolium) and grasses, as seen here four months after the eruption, were among the first plants to recolonize the area.*

(a)

(b)

44–21 (a) *Boulders in a low intertidal zone on the southern California coast. Those with bare upper surfaces have recently been overturned by the waves, while those covered with algae have remained undisturbed.* (b) *A collection of intertidal boulders covered with different successional stages of algae. The boulder in the center was overturned by wave action during the winter before this photograph was taken and has been colonized by the green alga* Ulva. *The surrounding boulders, which are larger, have not been disturbed as recently and are covered with later successional stages that are dominated by red algae.*

which may themselves be subsequently replaced. As the photosynthetic components of the system change, the accompanying animal life changes as well. This process is known as **ecological succession.**

An example of succession is provided by an abandoned field surrounded by other vegetation. Such an area is bombarded by the seeds of numerous plants and is rapidly covered by seedlings of those species whose seeds germinate the most rapidly. In an open field, the survivors among the seedlings will be those plants that can survive the sunlight and drying winds—weeds and grasses and, in many regions of North America, trees such as cedars, white pines, poplars, and birch. For a while, these plants dominate the community, but eventually they are replaced by other trees—oaks, red maples, white ash, and tulip trees. These trees are, in turn, replaced by hemlock, beech, and sugar maple, which, in the absence of major disturbances, dominate the forest indefinitely.

In many communities, the sequence of photosynthetic organisms is so regular and predictable that ecological succession was at one time viewed as analogous to the developmental processes of a single organism, with each stage "preparing the way" for the next by altering the local conditions of temperature, light, humidity, soil content, and so on. Ultimately, the com-

munity would, according to this view, reach a "mature," stable state, known as the climax community. This concept of succession, formulated in 1916 by the plant ecologist F. E. Clements, is known as the **facilitation hypothesis.** For many years, it dominated the study of ecological succession.

Recent studies, however, have suggested that there are alternative mechanisms by which succession may occur. According to the **inhibition hypothesis,** the early species prevent—rather than assist—colonization by other species. Eventually, however, the earliest colonizers are replaced by later arrivals, and those species may, in turn, prevent colonization by others, until they too are replaced or a subsequent disturbance lowers their numbers.

Another model, the **tolerance hypothesis,** suggests that the earliest species neither facilitate nor inhibit colonization by later species. The species dominant at any given time are those that can best tolerate the existing physical conditions and availability of resources.

In a continuation of his earlier studies, Wayne Sousa charted the patterns of algal succession on intertidal boulders by scraping boulders clean of algae and by adding bare rocks to the intertidal zone. The first colonists on the bare rock were the green algae *Ulva* (Figure 24–18d, page 430) and *Enteromorpha* (Figure

44–12a). These pioneer species grow rapidly and, within a short period of time, fully occupy the available space on the boulders (Figure 44–21). Later, large perennial brown and red algae become established, replacing the green algae. Ultimately, the dominant organism is *Gigartina,* a red alga.

To determine the mechanism by which this successional sequence occurred, Sousa removed algae at various stages of the process. For example, when he removed *Ulva,* he found that *Gigartina* was then able to colonize the boulders. Similarly, when he removed the middle successional species of red algae, *Gigartina* was also able to colonize. These results support the inhibition hypothesis, but they raise the question as to how the later species ever gain a foothold. The answer, it turns out, is that *Ulva* and the other early colonizers are subjected to heavy predation and have high mortality rates. As a consequence, small areas of space open up on the boulders, which are then seized by the later species.

Other experiments, however, have supported the facilitation hypothesis, suggesting that there are no simple answers that apply in all situations. Each community is a unique assemblage of organisms, the product of a unique and ever-changing history involving both physical and biological factors.

The world of living organisms is so vast and diverse—and ecologists are, relatively speaking, so few—that it may be many years before enough information is available to provide a thorough understanding of community ecology. Paradoxically, the processes that occur at the next level of ecological complexity—the ecosystem—are in many respects more clearly understood than those occurring within either populations or communities. These processes, which involve the flow of energy and the recycling of minerals, will be the subject of the next chapter.

Summary

Populations live as part of a community—an assemblage of organisms of different species inhabiting a common environment and interacting with one another. Three major types of interaction in communities are competition, predation, and symbiosis.

The more similar organisms are in their requirements and life styles, the more intense the competition between them is likely to be. As a result of competition, the overall fitness of the interacting individuals may be reduced. The importance of competition as an influence on community composition and structure is currently a matter of debate among ecologists.

The competitive exclusion principle, formulated by Gause, states that if two species are in competition for the same limited resource, one or the other will eventually be eliminated in situations in which they occur together. Similar species are able to coexist in the same community because they occupy different ecological niches. The ecological niche of a species is defined by the resource requirements and total life style of the members of that species, including their interactions with members of other species. Analyses of situations in which similar species coexist have demonstrated that resources are often subdivided, or partitioned, by the coexisting species.

Niche overlap describes the situation in which members of more than one species utilize the same limited resource. In communities in which niche overlap occurs, natural selection may result in an increase in the differences between the competing species, a phenomenon known as character displacement. Although the adaptations that enable various organisms to partition resources have often been attributed to character displacement, it is difficult, if not impossible, to distinguish between adaptations that occurred in response to competition and those that were the result of differing local conditions.

Competition has been demonstrated in numerous experimental studies. Experiments in which potential competitors were removed from a study site have given rise to the concepts of the fundamental niche and the realized niche. A fundamental niche represents the resources that would be utilized by a species in the absence of interactions with other organisms. A realized niche describes the resources actually utilized.

Predation is the consumption of live organisms. Predator-prey interactions influence population dynamics and may increase species diversity by reducing competition among prey species. The size of a predator population is often limited by the availability of prey. However, predation is not necessarily the major factor in regulating the population size of prey organisms, which may be influenced more by their own food supply.

Symbiosis is a close and long-term association between organisms of different species. It may be beneficial to one species and harmless to the other (commensalism), beneficial to one and harmful to the other (parasitism), or beneficial to both species (mutualism).

Two important questions regarding community composition and structure remain unanswered. First, what determines the number of species in a community? And, second, what factors underlie the changes in community composition with time? According to the island biogeography hypothesis, the number of species on islands reaches an equilibrium determined by the balance between immigration and extinction. Species composition may vary widely over time but the number of species remains approximately the same. For new species to gain a foothold, established species must become extinct, leading to a continual turnover in species composition.

According to the intermediate disturbance hypothesis, the greatest species diversity is found in communities, such as tropical rain forests and coral reefs, that are subjected to environmental disturbances at an intermediate frequency. Communities in which disturbances occur either very seldom or very often generally have a lower species diversity.

Following environmental disturbances, communities are recolonized by dispersal of immature forms from neighboring communities. If enough time elapses before the next major disturbance, a community typically goes through a process of ecological succession in which the earliest colonizers are replaced by other species that may, in turn, be replaced by still others. The mechanism of succession appears to vary from community to community. Communities, like the populations of which they are composed, are dynamic, continually changing as conditions change.

Questions

1. Distinguish among the following: population/community; competitive exclusion/resource partitioning; habitat/niche; niche overlap/character displacement; fundamental niche/realized niche; symbiosis/commensalism/parasitism/mutualism.

2. Compare the effects of interspecific (between species) and intraspecific (within species) competition. What is the principal reason for the differences?

3. Compare the results of MacArthur's study of the warblers with Connell's experiment with the barnacles. What step did Connell perform that MacArthur did not? Why is the step important?

4. In the American southwest, grasses and mesquite compete with each other for dominance of the landscape. Mesquite, however, was rare before cattle were introduced into the western United States. How have cattle affected the competition between the two types of plant? Suppose all cattle were removed from a large area. What change would you predict in the competition between grasses and mesquite?

5. Introducing a new species into a community can have a number of possible effects. Name some of these possible consequences both to the community and to the introduced species. What types of studies should be done before the im-

portation of an "alien" organism? Some states and many countries have laws restricting such importations. Has your own state adopted any such laws? Are they, in your opinion, ecologically sound?

6. In the long and ruthless war between coyotes and sheep herders, studies have shown that (a) coyotes kill sheep, and (b) the percentage of sheep lost from herds in areas where coyotes have been exterminated is about the same as the percentage lost in areas where coyotes are still present. How could you explain this finding?

7. In the opinion of some ecologists, animals that eat seeds, such as the Galapagos ground finches, should be regarded as predators, while animals that eat leaves, such as deer, should be regarded as parasites. Justify this classification of herbivores as either predators or parasites.

8. A national park or a game preserve can be considered an island, from the point of view of the species living there. What lesson in the management of such a park or preserve can be learned from the experiment carried out on the mangrove islands by Simberloff and Wilson?

9. Compare the three hypotheses (facilitation, inhibition, and tolerance) that have been proposed to explain the process of ecological succession.

Suggestions for Further Reading

Arehart-Treichel, Joan: "Science Helps the Bluebird," *Science News*, June 11, 1983, pages 376–377.

Bergerud, Arthur T.: "Prey Switching in a Simple Ecosystem," *Scientific American*, December 1983, pages 130–141.

Birkeland, Charles: "The Faustian Traits of the Crown-of-Thorns Starfish," *American Scientist*, vol. 77, pages 154–163, 1989.

Brown, Barbara E., and John C. Ogden: "Coral Bleaching," *Scientific American*, January 1993, pages 64–70.

Case, Ted J., and Martin L. Cody: "Testing Theories of Island Biogeography," *American Scientist*, vol. 75, pages 402–411, 1987.

Connell, Joseph H.: "Diversity and the Coevolution of Competitors, or the Ghost of Competition Past," *Oikos*, vol. 35, pages 131–138, 1980.

Connell, Joseph H., and Ralph O. Slatyer: "Mechanisms of Succession in Natural Communities and Their Role in Community Stability and Organization," *American Naturalist*, vol. 111, pages 1119–1144, 1977.

Connor, Edward F., and Daniel Simberloff: "Competition, Scientific Method, and Null Models in Ecology," *American Scientist*, vol. 74, pages 155–162, 1986.

DeVries, Philip J.: "Singing Caterpillars, Ants and Symbiosis," *Scientific American*, October 1992, pages 76–83.

Diamond, Jared M.: "Niche Shifts and the Rediscovery of Interspecific Competition," *American Scientist*, vol. 66, pages 322–331, 1978.

Diamond, Jared M., K. David Bishop, and S. Van Balen: "Bird Survival in an Isolated Javan Woodland: Island or Mirror?" *Conservation Biology*, vol. 1, pages 132–142, 1987.

Horn, Henry S.: "Forest Succession," *Scientific American*, May 1975, pages 90–98.

Karr, James R.: "Avian Extinction on Barro Colorado Island, Panama: A Reassessment," *American Naturalist*, vol. 119, pages 220–237, 1982.

Larson, Douglas: "The Recovery of Spirit Lake," *American Scientist*, vol. 81, pages 166–177, 1993.

Lubchenco, Jane: "Plant Species Diversity in a Marine Intertidal Community: Importance of Herbivore Food Preference and Algal Competitive Abilities," *American Naturalist*, vol. 112, pages 23–29, 1978.

O'Brien, W. John, Howard I. Browman, and Barbara I. Evans: "Search Strategies of Foraging Animals," *American Scientist*, vol. 78, pages 152–160, 1990.

Owen, Jennifer: *Feeding Strategy*, University of Chicago Press, Chicago, 1982.*

> This short, beautifully illustrated book explores the variety of ways in which animals obtain food. It considers not only herbivorous and carnivorous animals but also filter-feeders, parasites, and scavengers.

Peterson, Charles H.: "Intertidal Zonation of Marine Invertebrates in Sand and Mud," *American Scientist*, vol. 79, pages 236–249, 1991.

Rennie, John: "Living Together," *Scientific American*, January 1992, pages 122–133.

Rinderer, Thomas E., Benjamin P. Oldroyd, and Walter S. Sheppard: "Africanized Bees in the U.S.," *Scientific American*, December 1993, pages 84–90.

Romme, William H., and Don G. Despain: "The Yellowstone Fires," *Scientific American*, November 1989, pages 36–46.

Schaller, George: *The Serengeti Lion: A Study of Predator-Prey Relations*, University of Chicago Press, Chicago, 1976.*

> One of the first, best, and most comprehensive of the modern field studies in animal ecology and behavior. Winner of the National Book Award.

Schoener, Thomas W.: "The Controversy over Interspecific Competition," *American Scientist*, vol. 70, pages 586–595, 1982.

Sousa, Wayne P.: "Experimental Investigations of Disturbance and Ecological Succession in a Rocky Intertidal Algal Community," *Ecological Monographs*, vol. 49, pages 227–254, 1979.

Storer, John H.: *The Web of Life*, New American Library, Inc., New York, 1956.*

> One of the first books ever written on ecology for the general public. In its simple presentation of the interdependence of living things, it remains a classic.

Terborgh, John: "Why American Songbirds Are Vanishing," *Scientific American*, May 1992, pages 98–105.

Wilson, Edward O.: "Threats to Biodiversity," *Scientific American*, September 1989, pages 108–116.

Winkler, William G., and Konrad Bögel: "Control of Rabies in Wildlife," *Scientific American*, June 1992, pages 86–93.

Young, James A.: "Tumbleweed," *Scientific American*, March 1991, pages 82–87.

*Available in paperback.

Practicing Your Textbook Reading Skills

1. What is the purpose of the chapter-opening description of the Serengeti?

    a. It outlines the main points of the chapter.

    b. It provides an example of the chapter's topic.

    c. It identifies the chapter's learning objectives.

    d. None of the above.

2. What are the major topics covered by the chapter?

    a. competition, predation, symbiosis, and stability

    b. the principle of competitive exclusion, the ecological niche, resource partitioning, experimental approaches to the study of competition, and winner takes all

    c. parasitism and mutualism

    d. the island biogeography model, the intermediate disturbance hypothesis, and ecological succession

3. Of the following statements, what is the textbook's definition of *competition*?

    a. "Competition is the interaction between individual organisms of the same species . . . or of different species . . . using the same resource, often present in limited supply."

    b. "Competition is generally greatest among organisms that have similar requirements and life styles."

    c. "For many years, competition has been invoked as a major force in determining the composition and structure of communities—that is, the number and kinds of species present and their arrangement in space and time within the community."

    d. "We shall begin our consideration of competition—and of the controversies surrounding it—with the principle that, until very recently, dominated the study of competition and the kinds of questions that ecologists asked about it."

4. The authors use the following analogy (explaining something unfamiliar by showing how it is like something familiar) to explain the concept of "ecological niche": ". . . The niche is an organism's profession, as distinct from its habitat, which is its address" (p. 795). How does this analogy best translate into biological terms?

    a. Organisms go to work and then return to their homes.

    b. An organism's niche is the function it serves, not its home.

    c. Organisms can be found in zoos.

    d. None of the above.

5. How does Figure 44–3 (p. 796) explain the concept of resource partitioning?

   a. The highlighted sections of the trees show where each kind of North American warbler spends most of its feeding time. Because each species relies on a different section of the tree, all five of them are able to feed from the same trees without cutting into the resources available to the others.

   b. The highlighted sections of the trees show where each kind of North American warbler tends to nest. Because each species lives in a different section of the tree, all five of them are able to reside in it without conflict.

   c. The illustrations of Cape May, bay-breasted, Blackburnian, black-throated, and yellow-throated ("myrtle") warblers indicate that these birds have distinctive appearances, which prevents them from competing for the same resources.

   d. None of the above.

6. According to Figure 44–7 (p. 798), what is the realized niche of *Chthamalus*?

   a. lowest low tide   c. upper intertidal zone
   b. highest high tide   d. lower intertidal zone

7. What concept is illustrated by Figures 44–20 (p. 809) and 44–21 (p. 810)?

   a. conservation biology   c. predation
   b. commensalism   d. ecological succession

8. Which of the following statements presents the main idea of the section "Predation and Species Diversity" (pp. 801–2)?

   a. "Although predation may occasionally eliminate a prey species, many experimental studies have shown that it is often an important factor in maintaining species diversity in a community."

   b. "For example, R. T. Paine studied a community on the rocky coast of Washington."

   c. ". . . when a keystone species is lost from a community—as a result, for example, of pollution, disease, or competition from an alien organism—the diversity of the community decreases and the structure of the community is significantly altered."

   d. "Even when the same predator and prey species are involved, the effect of predation on species diversity depends on the particular situation."

9. Why is the section "Conservation Biology and the Island Biogeography Model" (pp. 806–7) presented in a shaded box?

    a. It is unimportant and reading it is optional.

    b. It summarizes the chapter and is highlighted so that readers will be able to find it easily.

    c. It is an extended example of a concept discussed in the main text; although you don't have to read it to understand the discussion, the example applies the concept from the main text to real life.

    d. It presents an idea that conflicts with the information provided in the main text.

10. Judging by what's discussed in the chapter summary on pages 811–12, what topics from the chapter are important to understand?

    a. the competitive exclusion principle

    b. niche overlap

    c. predation

    d. all of the above

Testing Your Understanding

Identify the following statements as true or false.

1. Only dissimilar species are found coexisting in natural communities.
   T _____   F _____

2. Similar members of a community often share the resources available to them.
   T _____   F _____

3. Ecologists agree that the differing beak sizes of Darwin's finches are the result of competition within the species.
   T _____   F _____

4. It is impossible for laboratory experiments to perfectly replicate what happens under natural conditions.
   T _____   F _____

5. Predation affects the evolution of both predator and prey.
   T _____   F _____

Select the best answer to each of the following questions.

6. Which of the following terms is *not* a category of interaction among populations?

   a. predatory

   b. ecological

   c. competitive

   d. symbiotic

7. According to G. F. Gause's principle of competitive exclusion, what will happen when two different species compete for the same resource, such as food, water, or habitat?

   a. Both species will adapt and be able survive on smaller quantities of the resource.

   b. Neither species will have enough of the resource it needs to survive, causing both to die out.

   c. One of the two species will be more successful in obtaining and/or using the resource, causing the other species to adapt.

   d. One of the two species will be more successful in obtaining and/or using the resource, causing the other species to die out.

8. What do contemporary ecologists think of Gause's principle of competitive exclusion?

   a. They agree with it and allow it to dominate their study of competition.

   b. They have determined that it is completely wrong.

   c. They believe that although the principle is helpful in understanding competition among species, it doesn't fully explain the interaction between them.

   d. They have found that laboratory experiments disprove Gause's theory.

9. According to Figure 44–1 (p. 794), what happened when two species of *Paramecium* were grown together?

   a. They formed a community.

   b. The more rapidly growing species outmultiplied and eliminated the slower-growing species.

   c. Both species were eliminated.

   d. None of the above.

10. Which of the following examples illustrates the concept of resource partitioning?

   a. zebras, wildebeest, and gazelles in the Serengeti

   b. woodland warblers

   c. bog mosses

   d. all of the above

11. Which is the most likely explanation of the changing lynx and snow-shoe hare populations described on pages 800–1?

    a. As the lynx kill large numbers of hares, their food source diminishes, and the lynx population declines. As the lynx die off from lack of food, the hares are then able to survive in greater numbers.

    b. Unaffected by the actions of lynx, the hare population regularly increases and decreases. As the availability of food rises and falls, the lynx population increases and decreases in response.

    c. Unaffected by the size of the hare population, the lynx population regularly increases and decreases. As the risk of being killed by lynx rises and falls, the hare population increases and decreases in response.

    d. Although they have several theories, biologists do not know what the cause-and-effect relationship is.

12. Which of the following is an example of parasitism?

    a. the relationship between the marine annelid *Chaetopterus* and tiny crabs of the genus *Pinnixa*

    b. rabbits infected with myxoma virus

    c. cleaner fish

    d. ants and acacias

13. Which of the following is an example of mutualism?

    a. sea anemones and hermit crabs

    b. aphids and ants

    c. oxpeckers and warthogs

    d. all of the above

14. According to the equilibrium hypothesis of island biogeography, what will most likely happen if a species is removed from an island?

    a. It will be replaced by a different species, keeping the number of species on the island constant.

    b. It will return to the island, keeping the number of species on the island constant.

    c. The number of species on the island will decrease.

    d. The number of species on the island will increase.

15. According to the intermediate disturbance hypothesis, what kinds of species are most likely to thrive in an environment that experiences frequent disturbances?

    a. species that can invade, mature, and reproduce before the next disturbance occurs

    b. species that are slow to mature or have limited dispersal abilities

c. species that are close to the area and that are reproducing at the time of the disturbances

d. species most resistant to ill effects from physical extremes, predation, or disease

Using your own words, define the following terms as they are used in the chapter.

16. *character displacement*

_____

_____

17. *predation*

_____

_____

18. *keystone species*

_____

_____

19. *symbiosis*

_____

_____

20. *island*

_____

_____

Answer each of the following questions using the space provided.

21. Explain the difference between a fundamental niche and a realized niche.

_____

_____

_____

22. List the three types of symbiotic relationship and briefly explain what they are.

_____

_____

_____

23. Briefly explain the mutualistic relationship between ants and acacias.

_____

_____

_____

24. List three hypotheses of ecological succession and briefly explain them.

_____

_____

_____

_____

_____

25. What books and articles might you refer to first if you were assigned to write a paper about the evolution of birds?

_____

_____

_____

_____

Making Thematic Connections

Many of the concepts described in this biology chapter are often used to describe corporate relationships and practices. *Competition, parasitism, symbiosis,* and *niche,* for example, are discussed (if not always in these exact terms) in most business, marketing, and advertising books. Pick one of these terms and, considering what you now understand to be its definition in biology, discuss how well the term applies to the working world. In what ways is it appropriate for this usage? In what ways does it fall short?

History

"America through the Eyes of the Workers, 1870–1890"

Introduction

History is more than a collection of facts about the past. Although names and dates are important, the historian's primary job is to make connections among events and interpret what happened. In many ways, the study of history is detective work. And because interpretation and analysis are central to the field, historians often disagree. New pieces of information—even new questions—lead scholars to revise their ideas. As a result, reading history demands critical and active reading. Historians report their findings and express their opinions; as with any opinion, what they write is open to debate. Both historians and the people who read their work, then, must observe details, make connections and inferences, and draw conclusions.

The American Promise: A History of the United States, Second Edition, by James L. Roark, Michael P. Johnson, Patricia Cline Cohen, Sarah Stage, Alan Lawson, and Susan M. Hartmann, is a survey of United States history. It outlines for students the major events and actors of America's past. At the same time, it devotes a lot of attention to the lives of everyday people "to create a vivid and compelling narrative that captures students' interest and sparks their historical imagination." As you read the following chapter about workers at the end of the nineteenth century, be aware that the stories of individual people are provided as examples: The authors don't expect you to memorize the name of every person mentioned in the chapter.

The authors all teach introductory history courses, so they were careful to provide features and tools to help new students like you understand the subject. To help you distinguish between major players and colorful examples, for instance, they provide a timeline at the end of the chapter. Every photograph was selected because of the way it illustrates everyday life. Maps are accompanied by captions and questions designed to help you interpret visual information. Call-outs—the italicized statements placed between lines

---

This unit's textbook reading comes from *The American Promise: A History of the United States,* Second Edition, by James L. Roark, Michael P. Johnson, Patricia Cline Cohen, Sarah Stage, Alan Lawson, and Susan M. Hartmann, Bedford/St. Martin's, 2002, Chapter 18, pages 650–82.

in the middle of the text—work the way they do in magazine articles: They capture your attention while giving you a general sense of what the section is about. Two boxed features—"The Promise of Technology" and "Historical Question"—highlight especially interesting developments and encourage critical thinking. References to the book's online study guide tell you where you can find extra help with important topics. The bibliography helps you find sources of additional information. Even the running heads at the top of each page will help you read successfully: The dates in the lower bar remind you where in the chapter's chronology you are.

The chapter you're about to read, "America through the Eyes of the Workers, 1870–1890," puts today's work issues into historical perspective. In the section "Immigration, Ethnic Rivalry, and Racism," you'll learn about social Darwinism, which was a direct response to the theories of Charles Darwin so central to biology (see Unit 4 for more on these theories). The business developments discussed under "Managers and White Collars" apply directly to the history of public relations you read about in Unit 3. Think also about the psychological concerns regarding stress and how changes in the American workforce more than a century ago illustrate the coping mechanisms discussed in Unit 2. Notice in particular the work difficulties that made people unhappy and prompted them to fight for changes, and think about how contemporary human resource management (see Unit 1) tries to respond to history's lessons.

Preparing to Read the Textbook Chapter

1. Are working conditions today better or worse than they were a century ago? Explain your answer.

2. Throughout the chapter, you'll find photographs and illustrations of everyday objects, such as lunch pails, and everyday people, such as visitors to Coney Island. How do these images confirm or contradict your ideas about history as an academic subject?

3. In recent years, resident assistants and teaching assistants on many campuses have joined unions to protect themselves from what they argue are unfair university employment practices. Are their complaints legitimate? Can organizing help them improve their working conditions?

DINNER PAILS

The dinner pail or lunch bucket, the universal symbol of the working class, took many sizes and shapes. Designed to carry a midday meal for workers who did not have time to go home to eat, it might hold bread, leftovers, a sandwich, coffee, or whatever else fit easily into the container. Some cities such as Riverside, California, prohibited workers from carrying dinner pails on downtown streets. Presumably sidewalks were meant only for the middle class and well to do.

Anthracite Heritage Museum.

AMERICA THROUGH THE EYES OF THE WORKERS

CHAPTER

18

1870–1890

FOR TWO WEEKS DURING THE SUMMER of 1877, President Rutherford B. Hayes faced an insurrection greater than any since the Civil War. Hayes met daily with his cabinet to plan military strategy and sat up late into the night receiving reports from his generals. He dispatched federal troops to nine states, ordered warships to protect the nation's capital, and threatened to declare martial law. Not since the Confederates fired on Fort Sumter had the nation witnessed such an alarm. Who posed this threat to the Republic? Not former rebels or foreign armies, but American workers engaged in the first nationwide labor strike in the country's history.

Economic depression following the panic of 1873 had thrown as many as three million people out of work. Those who were lucky enough to keep their jobs watched as pay cuts eroded their wages until they could no longer feed their families. When a Cincinnati cigar worker with a wife and three children was asked how he lived on $5 a week, he replied, "I don't live. I am literally starving. We get meat once a week, the rest of the week we have dry bread and black coffee."

The burden of the depression fell disproportionately on the backs of the country's working class. So that they could continue paying dividends to their shareholders, corporations laid off workers and cut wages. When the Baltimore and Ohio (B&O) Railroad announced a 10 percent wage reduction in the summer of 1877 at the same time it declared a 10 percent dividend to its stockholders, the brakemen in West Virginia, whose wages had already fallen from $70 to $30 a month, walked out on strike. One B&O worker described the hardship that had driven him to take such desperate action: "We eat our hard bread and tainted meat two days old on the sooty cars up the road, and when we come home, find our children gnawing bones and our wives complaining that they cannot even buy hominy and molasses for food."

The strike by brakemen in West Virginia touched off the Great Railroad Strike, a nationwide uprising that spread rapidly to Pittsburgh and Chicago, St. Louis and San Francisco. Within a few days, nearly 100,000 railroad workers went out on strike. The spark of rebellion soon fired other workers to action. An estimated 500,000 laborers joined the striking train workers. Steelworkers, longshoremen, workers from all industries, often with their wives and children, made common cause with the railroad strikers. Violence erupted as the strikers clashed with state militia. President Hayes, after hesitating briefly, called up federal troops. In three weeks it was over. "The strikes have been put down by force," Hayes noted in his diary on August 5. "But now for the real remedy. Can't something be done by education of the strikers, by judicious control of the capitalists, by wise general policy to end or diminish the evil? The railroad strikers, as a rule, are good men, sober, intelligent, and industrious."

HARPER'S WEEKLY.
JOURNAL OF CIVILIZATION

Vol. XXI.—No. 1073.]   NEW YORK, SATURDAY, AUGUST 11, 1877.   [WITH A SUPPLEMENT. PRICE TEN CENTS.

THE GREAT RAILROAD STRIKE
The August 11, 1877 cover of Harper's Weekly *featured an illustration of the great railroad strike depicting the sixth Maryland regiment firing its way through Baltimore. Notice the fixed bayonets of the soldiers and the brick-throwing strikers fighting in close quarters. Such scenes of violence frightened many middle-class Americans who initially had sympathized with the strikers. Public opinion shifted as a result of news coverage as many blamed the strikers for the bloodshed and damage to property that accompanied the strike.*
Harper's Weekly, August 11, 1877.

The uprising of the workers in 1877 underscored the tensions produced by rapid industrialization and pointed to many legitimate grievances on the part of labor. The unprecedented industrial growth that occurred after the Civil War came about as a result of the labor of millions of men, women, and children who toiled in workshops and factories, in sweatshops and mines, on the railroads and construction sites across America. Their stories provide a different perspective from that of the great industrialists and the politicians. Through their eyes it is possible to gauge how corporate capitalism transformed old work patterns and affected the social and cultural—as well as the economic and political—life of the United States.

America's New Industrial Workers

America's industrial growth in the years following the Civil War brought about a massive redistribution of population as agricultural workers moved to the city and became recruits in the industrial labor force. Burgeoning industrial centers such as

Pittsburgh, Chicago, New York, and Detroit acted like giant magnets, attracting workers from the countryside (Map 18.1). The movement from the rural periphery to industrial centers was not just American in scope. Farm boys and girls from western Pennsylvania who left for the mills of Pittsburgh were part of a global migration that included rural immigrants from Ireland, southern Italy, Russia, Japan, and China. As labor historian David Montgomery has pointed out, "The rural periphery of the nineteenth century industrial world became the primary source of supply for 'human machines.'"

Workers from the Rural Periphery

By the 1870s, the world could be seen as divided into three interlocking geographic regions forming roughly concentric circles (Map 18.2). At the center stood an industrial core bounded by Chicago and St. Louis in the west; Toronto, Glasgow, and Berlin

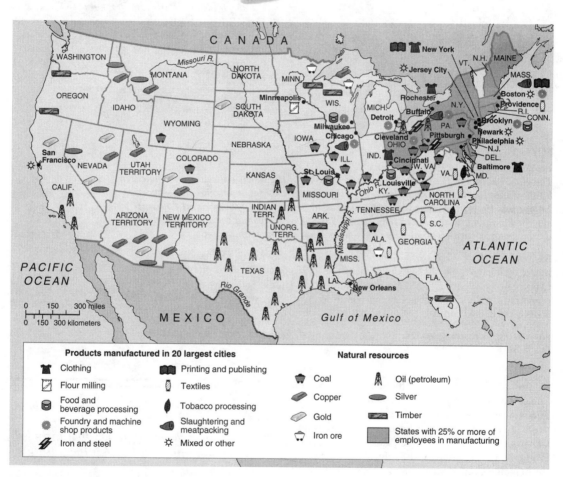

MAP 18.1

Industrialization, 1865–1900

Industrial development between 1865 and 1900 shows the clustering of industry in the Northeast and Great Lakes states. Only in these regions did industry employ 25 percent or more of the labor force. The West supplied raw materials—oil, minerals, and timber— while in the South and the Midwest agriculture and attendant industries such as tobacco processing and meatpacking dominated. Note, however, the concentration of textile manufacturing in the South.

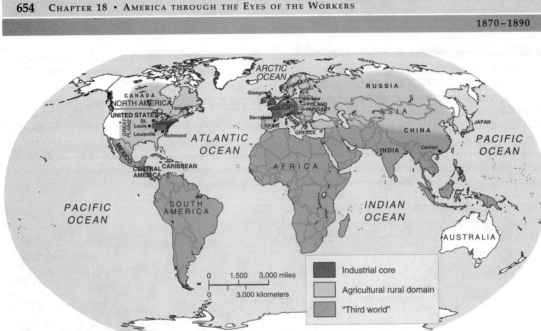

MAP 18.2

Economic Regions of the World
The global nature of the world economy at the turn of the twentieth century is indicated by three interlocking geographic regions. At the center was the industrial core—western Europe and the northeastern United States; the agricultural periphery (rural domain) supplied immigrant laborers to the industries in the core. Beyond these two regions lay a "third world" tied economically to the industrial core by colonialism.

READING THE MAP: What parts of the world did not belong to one of these three economic regions? Where did the United States fit in this economic division of the globe?
CONNECTIONS: What does this characterization of the United States say about its stage of economic development in the late nineteenth century? How would you characterize the areas outside the economic regions specified?

www.bedfordstmartins.com/tap   SEE THE ONLINE STUDY GUIDE for more help in analyzing this map.

[handwritten margin note: It is in the constitution that if you were from the free States you where worth 2/3 more as a African made vs 1/3 from so... States]

in the north; Warsaw in the east; and Milan, Barcelona, Richmond, and Louisville in the south. Surrounding the industrial core and its urban outposts lay a vast agricultural domain encompassing Canada, much of Scandinavia, Russia and Poland, Hungary, Greece, Italy and Sicily, southern Spain, the defeated Confederate states and the Great Plains of America, central and northern Mexico, the hinterlands of Canton, China, and later the southern islands of Japan. Capitalist development in the late nineteenth century shattered traditional patterns of economic activity in this rural periphery. As old patterns broke down, the rural areas exported, along with other raw materials, new recruits for the industrial labor force.

Farm boys and girls from western Pennsylvania who left for the mills of Pittsburgh were part of a global migration that included rural immigrants from Ireland, Italy, Russia, Japan, and China.

Beyond this second circle lay an even larger area including the Caribbean, Central and South America, the Middle East, Africa, India, and most of Asia. This third area too became increasingly tied to the industrial core in the late nineteenth century,

[handwritten note at bottom: China Poland Italy Ireland Japan Russia (Farmers former Slaves Soldier)   1870's workers]

1870–1890

but its peoples largely stayed put. They worked on the plantations and railroads, in the mines and ports as part of a huge export network managed by foreign powers that staked out spheres of influence and colonies, often with gunboats and soldiers.

Beginning in the 1870s, railroad expansion and low steamship fares gave the world's peoples a newfound mobility that enabled industrialists to draw on a worldwide population for cheap labor. The Carnegie steel mills outside Pittsburgh provide a good example. When Andrew Carnegie opened his first mill in 1872, his superintendent hired workers he called "buckwheats"—young American boys just off the farm. By the 1890s, however, Carnegie's workforce was liberally sprinkled with other rural boys—Hungarians and Slavs who had migrated to the United States, willing to work for low wages. The ability to draw on cheap labor on a global scale helps explain why, in spite of the soaring demand for laborers after the Civil War, the wages of unskilled workers in the United States remained relatively stagnant. Their pay fell dramatically during the depressions of 1873–1878 and 1893–1896, and did not regain 1872 levels before the end of the century.

Immigration, Ethnic Rivalry, and Racism

Ethnic diversity played a role in dividing skilled workers (those with a craft or specialized ability) from the unskilled (those who supplied muscle and brawn). As managers increasingly mechanized to replace skilled craftsworkers with lower-paid, unskilled labor, they drew on immigrants from southern and eastern Europe. The skilled workers, mostly from northern or western Europe, found it easy to criticize the newcomers. As one Irish worker complained, "There should be a law . . . to keep all the I-talians from comin' in and takin' the bread out of the mouths of honest people."

The Irish worker's resentment of the new Italian immigrants brings into focus the importance of the ideology and practice of racism in the experience of America's immigrant laborers. Throughout the nineteenth century, members of the educated elite as well as workers viewed ethnic and even religious differences as racial characteristics—referring to the Polish "race" or the Jewish "race." Each wave of newcomers was seen as being somehow inferior to the established residents. The Irish who judged the Italians so harshly had themselves been

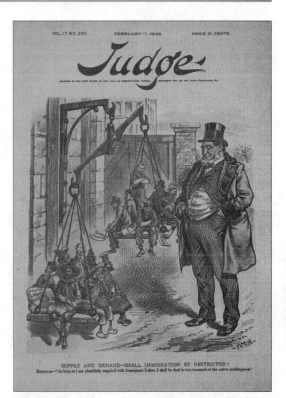

THE COMPETITION OF CHEAP LABOR
Big business looks on approvingly as cheap immigrant labor outweighs American workers in this political cartoon published in the weekly **Judge** *in 1888. "As long as I am plentifully supplied with Immigrant Labor," says the portly manufacturer, "I shall be deaf to the demands of the native working-man." Cartoons like this one underscored organized labor's concern with the number of foreign workers entering the country in the 1880s—nearly eight million, twice the number of the previous decade. Not only did the seemingly unlimited supply of immigrant laborers keep wages low, but the new recruits, who knew nothing of labor's struggles, often took work as strikebreakers.*
Judge, February 11, 1888.

www.bedfordstmartins.com/tap   SEE THE ONLINE STUDY GUIDE for more help in analyzing this image.

seen as a subhuman species just a generation before. Immigrants not only brought their own religious and racial prejudices to the United States but also absorbed the popular prejudices of American culture. Social Darwinism, with its strongly racist overtones, decreed that whites stood at the top of the evolutionary ladder. But who was "white"? The social construction of race is nowhere more apparent than in the testimony of an Irish dockworker, who boasted that he hired only "white men" to load cargo, a category that he insisted excluded "Poles and Italians."

Racism took its most blatant form in the treatment of African Americans and Asians. Like other migrants from the rural periphery, African American men in the South, former slaves and the children of slaves, found work as human machines. The labor gang system used in many industries was most extreme and brutal in the South, where private employers contracted prison labor, mostly African Americans jailed for such minor crimes as vagrancy. Shackled together by chains as they worked under the watchful eyes of armed guards, these workers formed the bottom rung on labor's ladder. A Georgia man who escaped the brutal chain gang system remarked, "Call it slavery, peonage, or what not, the truth is we lived in a hell on earth."

On the West Coast, Asian immigrants became the scapegoats of the changing economy. Workers vigorously attacked the Chinese and later the Japanese as the "tools of corporate interest" recruited by the bosses to undercut wages and threaten "white society." The labor movement played a key role in excluding Asians from American life. Labor unions practiced exclusionary policies against both Chinese and Japanese workers and championed the 1882 Chinese Exclusion Act, which prohibited the immigration of Chinese to the United States.

America's Diverse Workers

Throughout the nineteenth century, America's industrial workers toiled in a variety of settings. Skilled craftsworkers and artisans still worked in small workshops or alone. But with the rise of corporate capitalism, large factories, mills, and mines increasingly dotted the landscape. Sweatshops and outwork, the contracting of piecework performed in the home, provided a different work experience from that of the factory operative (machine tender) or the industrial worker. Pick-and-shovel labor, whether on the railroads or in the building trades, constituted another kind of work. The best way to get a sense of the diversity of workers and workplaces is to look at five distinct types of industrial work: common labor, skilled work, factory work, sweatshop labor, and mining.

Common laborers formed the backbone of the American labor force throughout the nineteenth century. They built the railroads and subways, tunneled under New York's East River to anchor the Brooklyn Bridge, and helped to lay the foundation of industrial America. In her book *China Men*, Maxine Hong Kingston tells the story of Ah Goong, one of the *gam saan haak* ("travelers to the gold mountain") who came to California in 1863 and went to work for the Central Pacific Railroad. For less than a dollar a day, Ah Goong hung in a basket on the cliffs above the American River, setting black powder in crevices and firing the fuses to blast a path through the mountains. In 1869, when the railroad experimented with nitroglycerin, he sometimes risked his life to earn an extra dollar by going back into the tunnel to investigate when the temperamental nitro failed to explode. Working in the dark tunnel, Ah Goong toiled on eight-hour shifts seven days a week. When the railroad tried to increase the shift to ten hours, Ah Goong and ten thousand of his fellow workers went on strike in 1867. They demanded the same wages paid to the white, mostly Irish gangs, who earned $40 a month compared with Ah Goong's $30. Construction superintendent Charles Crocker broke the strike, but in the end he raised the wages of the Chinese workers to $35 a month.

Common laborers built the railroads and subways, tunneled under New York's East River to anchor the Brooklyn Bridge, and helped to lay the foundation of industrial America.

Life was cheap on the Central Pacific. Men died on the cliffs when they failed to scramble out of the way before a blast or when the ropes to the baskets broke. Men died in the tunnels when the nitroglycerin exploded without warning. Ah Goong was one of the lucky ones; he lived to see the Central Pacific reach Promontory Point, Utah, where it joined the Union Pacific to form the first transcontinental railroad in 1869. In the celebration that followed, orators basked in the accomplishment of the "greatest monument of human labor," never mentioning the Chinese workers whose prodigious labor had built the railroad.

CHINESE RAILROAD WORKERS
Chinese workers like this section gang pictured at Promontory Point, Utah, in 1869 made up more than 80 percent of the workforce that built America's first transcontinental railroad. Charles Crocker of the Central Pacific hired them, reasoning that the race that built the Great Wall could build his road across the treacherous Sierra Nevada. Besides, the Chinese workers were a bargain: Crocker paid them $10 a month less than he paid his Irish section gangs.
Denver Public Library, Western History Collection, photo by J. B. Silvis.

Texting your understanding ①

At the opposite end of the economic ladder from common laborers were skilled craftsmen like iron puddler James J. Davis, a Welsh immigrant. When he was eleven years old, he went into the iron mills in Sharon, Pennsylvania, where his father was a puddler. Using brains along with brawn, puddlers took the melted pig iron in the heat of the furnace and, with long poles, formed the cooling metal into two-hundred-pound balls, relying on eye and intuition to make each ball uniform. Davis compared the task to baking bread: "I am like some frantic baker in the inferno kneading a batch of iron bread for the devil's breakfast. My spoon weighs twenty-five pounds, my porridge is pasty iron, and the heat of my kitchen is so great that if my body was not hardened to it, the ordeal would drop me in my tracks."

Possessing such a skill meant earning good wages, up to $7 a day, when there was work. But often no work could be found. Much industry and manufacturing in the nineteenth century remained seasonal; it was a rare worker who could count on year-round pay. In addition, two major depressions only twenty years apart, in 1873 and 1893, spelled unemployment and hardship for all workers. Puddling jobs often passed from father to son, and although Davis earned the title of master puddler by the time he was sixteen, his father was not ready to turn over his hearth to his son, so in the hard times of the 1890s Davis tramped the countryside looking for work. In an era before unemployment insurance, workers' compensation, or old-age pensions, even the best worker could not guarantee security for his family. "The fear of ending in the poor-house is one of the terrors that dog a man through life," Davis confessed. Davis escaped such a fate. He gained an education, became a labor organizer, was elected to Congress, and served as secretary of labor in the 1920s.

In the iron industry, puddlers controlled the pace of work, the organization of the job, and the rate of pay. Such worker control posed a challenge to employers. As the century wore on, they attempted to limit the workers' autonomy by replacing people with machinery, breaking down skilled work into ever smaller parts, and replacing skilled workers with unskilled operatives, often young women willing to work for low wages. The textile mills provide a classic example of mechanized factory labor in the nineteenth century. Mary, a weaver at the mills in Fall River, Massachusetts, told her story to the *Independent* magazine in 1903. She had gone to work in the 1880s at the age of twelve and

had begun weaving at fourteen. Mechanization of the looms had reduced the job of the weaver to watching for breaks in the thread. "At first the noise is fierce, and you have to breathe the cotton all the time, but you get used to it," Mary told her interviewer. "When the bobbin flies out and a girl gets hurt, you can't hear her shout—not if she just screams, you can't. She's got to wait, 'till you see her. . . . Lots of us is deaf," she confessed.

The majority of factory operatives in the textile mills were young, unmarried women like Mary who were paid by the piece rather than by the day or hour. Mary worked from six in the morning to six at night, six days a week, and took home about a dollar a day. The seasonal nature of the work also drove wages down. "Like as not your mill will 'shut down' three months," and "some weeks you only get two or three days' work, when they're curtailin'," Mary recounted. After twenty years of working in the mill, Mary's family had not been able to scrape together enough money to buy a house. "We saved some, but something always comes."

Mechanization transformed the garment industry as well. With the introduction of the foot-

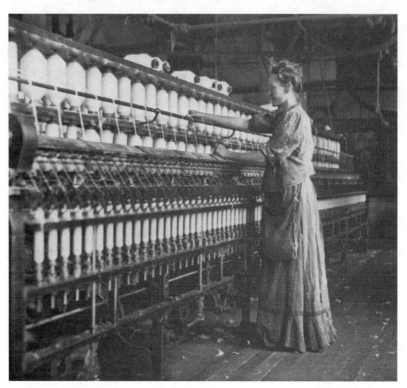

TEXTILE MILL WORKER
This woman weaver is typical of the factory operatives who worked in New England's textile mills. Young, unmarried women formed the majority of mill workers. The weaver's job was to watch the power looms to be sure the threads did not break. The work was both nerve-racking and unhealthy— note the lint on the floor. What can't be seen is the tremendous racket made by the huge machines—so loud that many women lost their hearing.
Courtesy George Eastman House.

womens rights?

COAL MINERS
Coal miners come up out of the shaft in the "cage" in Scranton, Pennsylvania. As one observer commented, "Although the mines are always cold and wet, the labor of drilling and handling the coal is so great that the miner, stripped to his shirt, soon becomes wet with sweat while the dust from the coal is at times almost stifling. The work is thirst-provoking and each miner carries with him a bottle or can, often a quart or more of strong, black coffee for the purpose of washing the dust from his throat."
Picture Research Consultants & Archives.

pedaled sewing machine in the 1850s and the use of mechanical cloth-cutting knives in the 1870s, independent tailors were replaced with workers hired by contractors to sew pieces of cloth into clothing. Working in sweatshops, small rooms hired for the season, or even the contractor's own tenement, women and children formed an important segment of garment workers.

Sadie Frowne, a sixteen-year-old Polish Jew, went to work in a Brooklyn sweatshop in the 1890s. Frowne sewed for eleven hours a day in a room twenty feet long and fourteen feet wide containing fourteen machines. "The machines go like mad all day, because the faster you work the more money you get," she recalled. Paid by the piece, she earned about $4.50 a week and, by rigid economy, tried to save $2. Young and single, Frowne typified the woman wage earner in the late nineteenth century. The largest percentage of women worked in the nee-

dle trades, but factory work ranked a close second. In 1890, the average working woman had started to work at age fifteen and was now twenty-two, working twelve hours a day, six days a week, and earning less than $6 a week. Discriminated against in the marketplace, where they earned less than men, and largely ignored by the labor unions during this period, women generally worked only eight to ten years, until they married. These women formed a unique subculture. Their youth, high spirits, and camaraderie made the hard, repetitive work they did bearable, and after hours they relished the "cheap amusements" of the day—the dance halls, social clubs, and amusement parks.

The most hazardous work and the worst working conditions existed in metal and coal mining, along with extractive industries such as lumbering. To look closely at conditions in the mines, mills, and forests, in the words of one historian, is to enter a "chamber of horrors." Ross Moudy, a miner in Cripple Creek, Colorado, recounted the dangers he faced, first in a chlorination mill. For nine or ten hours a day, he worked for $1.50 to $2, breathing sulfur dioxide or chlorine fumes and working in dust so thick that "one cannot see an object two feet away." He soon quit and went to work in a Cripple Creek gold mine. There, according to Moudy, "dangers do not seem so great to a practiced miner, who is used to climbing hundreds of feet on . . . braces put about six feet apart . . . and then walking the same distance on a couple of poles sometimes not larger than fence rails, where a misstep would mean a long drop." When a group of stockholders came to tour the mine, Moudy recounted how one man, white as a ghost after a near fall, told the miner beside him "that instead of being paid $3 per day they ought to have all the gold they could take out."

Miners died in explosions, cave-ins, and fires. New technology eliminated some dangers but often added others, for machinery could maim and kill. In the hard-rock mines of the West in the 1870s, accidents annually disabled one out of every thirty miners and killed one in eighty. Moudy's biggest worry was the carbon dioxide that often filled the tunnels because of poor ventilation. "Many times," he confessed, "I have been carried out unconscious and not able to work for two or three days after." Those who avoided accidents still breathed air so dangerous that respiratory diseases eventually disabled them. After a year on the job, Moudy joined the union "because I saw it would help me to keep in work and for protection in case of accident or sickness." The union provided good sick benefits and hired nurses, "so if one is alone and sick he is sure to be taken care of." Moudy acknowledged that there were some "hotheads" in the union, the militant Western Federation of Miners. But he insisted that most union men "believe the change will come about gradually and not by revolution."

The Family Economy: Women and Children

Although real wages (pay measured in terms of buying power) rose by 15 percent between 1873 and 1893, workers did not share equally in the improvement. African American men, for example, continued to be paid at a much lower rate than white men, as did immigrant laborers and white women. And the protracted depressions following the panics of 1873 and 1893 undercut many of labor's gains. In 1890, the average worker earned $500 a year. Many working-class families, whether native-born or immigrant, lived in poverty or near poverty; their economic survival depended on the contributions of all, regardless of sex or age. One statistician estimated that in 1900, as many as 64 percent of working-class families relied on income other than the husband's wages to make ends meet. The paid and unpaid work of women and children were thus essential for family survival and economic advancement.

Child labor had been common in the mines and textile mills since midcentury. As other industries mechanized in the 1880s and 1890s, they hired children, girls as well as boys, who often could tend machines as efficiently as adults yet received wages considerably lower. One worker recalled his youth in the textile mills of Massachusetts: "When I began as a boy in the mill, I worked fifteen hours a day. I used to go in at a quarter past four in the morning and work until a quarter to eight at night, having thirty minutes for breakfast and the same for dinner, drinking tea after ringing out at night. . . . This I did for eleven years."

Attempts to abolish child labor began before the Civil War. By 1863, seven states had passed laws limiting the hours of child workers to forty-eight a week, but often the laws were not strictly enforced. Most southern states refused to regulate child labor, and children as young as six or seven years old continued to be widely employed in southern mills. In the nation's mines, particularly in Appalachia, young boys were recruited to pick out the slate and waste from coal as it passed along chutes. Suspended on wooden boards over the moving coal, these "breaker boys" engaged in dangerous, physically demanding work. A boy who slipped into the coal had little chance of surviving without serious injury. When a child labor committee investigated conditions in Pennsylvania, it found that more than ten thousand children were illegally employed in the coalfields. Child labor increased decade by decade, with the percentage of children under fifteen engaged in paid labor not dropping until after World War I. The 1900 census showed that 1,750,178 children ages ten to fifteen were employed, an increase of more than a million since 1870. Children in this age range constituted over 18 percent of the labor force and 7 percent of all nonagricultural workers.

"BREAKER BOYS"
Child labor in America's mines and mills was common at the turn of the century, despite state laws that attempted to restrict it. Here "breaker boys" in the 1890s take a rest from their twelve-hour day in the coal mines of Appalachia. Their unsmiling faces bear testimony to their hard and dangerous work. A committee investigating child labor found more than ten thousand children illegally employed in the Pennsylvania coalfields.
Brown Brothers.

Many working-class families, whether native-born or immigrant, lived in poverty or near poverty; their economic survival depended on the contributions of all, regardless of sex or age.

Even children who did not work for wages contributed to the family economy by scavenging firewood and coal. Gangs of children patrolled the railroad tracks, picking up whatever fell from the coal cars that fueled the locomotives. Other children worked as street vendors, newsboys, and bootblacks. Although laws in many states mandated school attendance, harried truant officers found it hard to collar children whose parents insisted they work rather than go to school.

In the late nineteenth century, the number of women workers rose sharply, with their most common occupation changing slowly from domestic service to factory work and then to office work. The typical factory operative in the late nineteenth century was a teenage girl. In 1870, the census listed 1.5 million women working in nonagricultural occupations. By 1890, more than 3.7 million women earned wages, although they were paid less than men (Figure 18.1). Women's working patterns varied considerably according to race and ethnicity. White married women, even among the working class, rarely worked outside the home; in 1890, only 3 percent were employed. Nevertheless, married women found ways to contribute to the family economy. Families often took in boarders, which meant extra housework. In many Italian families, piecework such as making artificial flowers allowed married women to contribute to the family economy without leaving their homes. Black women, married and unmarried, worked for wages outside their homes at a much higher rate than white women. The 1890 census showed that 25 percent of African American married women worked outside the home, often as domestics in the houses of white families.

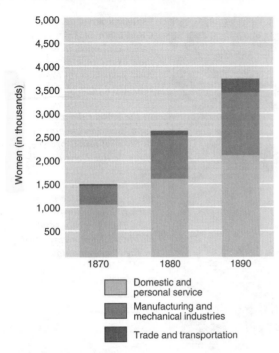

FIGURE 18.1

Women and Work, 1870–1890
In 1870, close to 1.5 million women worked in non-agricultural occupations. By 1890, that number had more than doubled to 3.7 million. The total number of women workers rose sharply while the most common occupation changed from domestic work to industry and later to office work.

Managers and White Collars

In the late nineteenth century, business expansion and consolidation led to a managerial revolution, creating a need for a new class of managers. As skilled workers saw their crafts replaced by mechanization, some moved into management positions. At the same time, new white-collar jobs in offices and department stores attracted a growing number of women workers.

The New Managerial Class

"The middle class is becoming a salaried class," a writer for the *Independent* magazine observed, "and is rapidly losing the economic and moral independence of former days." As large business organizations consolidated and created national markets, they replaced what the eighteenth-century economist Adam Smith had called "the invisible hand" of market forces with the "visible hand" of salaried managers.

At the same time, corporate development separated management from ownership, and the job of directing the firm became the province of salaried managers and executives. The majority of these new middle managers were white men drawn from the 8 percent of Americans who held high school diplomas. In 1880, the middle managers at the Chicago, Burlington, and Quincy Railroad earned between $1,500 and $4,000 a year, while senior executives, generally recruited from the college-educated elite, took home $4,000 or more, and the company's general manager made $15,000 a year, approximately thirty times what the average worker earned.

In the late nineteenth century, business expansion and consolidation led to a managerial revolution, creating a need for a new class of managers.

Until late in the century, when engineering schools began to supply recruits, skilled workers trained on the job often moved from the shop floor to positions of considerable responsibility. The career of Captain William "Billy" Jones provides a glimpse of a skilled ironworker turned manager. Jones, the son of a Welsh immigrant, grew up in the heat of the blast furnaces, where he started working as an apprentice at the age of ten. During the Civil War, he served in the Union army and earned the rank of captain, a title he used for the rest of his life. When Andrew Carnegie opened his steelworks on the outskirts of Pittsburgh in 1872, he hired Jones as his plant superintendent. By all accounts, Jones was the best steel man in the industry. "Good wages and good workmen" was his motto. Carnegie constantly tried to force down wages, but Jones fought for his men: In 1881, he succeeded in shortening the shift from twelve to eight hours a day by convincing Carnegie that shorter hours would reduce absenteeism and accidents. Jones himself demanded and received a "hell of a big salary." Carnegie paid him $25,000—the same salary as the president of the United States—a stupendous sum in 1881 and one that testified to the value the tightfisted Carnegie placed on his superintendent. Captain

Jones did not have long to enjoy his newfound wealth. He died in 1889 when a blast furnace exploded, adding his name to the estimated thirty-five thousand killed each year in industrial accidents.

Office Work and Women "Typewriters"

As businesses became larger and more far-flung in the decades after the Civil War, the need for more elaborate and exact records as well as the greater volume of correspondence led to the hiring of more office workers. Mechanization soon transformed business as it had industry and manufacturing. The adding machine, the cash register, and the typewriter came into general use in the 1880s. Employers seeking literate workers soon turned to women. Educated men had many other career choices, while for middle class, white women secretarial work constituted one of the few areas where they could put their literacy to use for wages.

Sylvie Thygeson was typical of the young women who went to work as secretaries. Thygeson grew up in an Illinois prairie town. When her father died in 1884, she went to work as a country schoolteacher at the age of sixteen, immediately after graduating high school. Quickly learning that teaching school did not pay, she mastered typing and stenography and found work as a secretary to help support her family. According to her account, she made "a fabulous sum of money." Nevertheless, she gave up her job after a few years when she met and married her husband.

Far from seeing their work as dehumanizing, women "typewriters" viewed it with pride and relished the economic independence it afforded them.

Called "typewriters," women workers like Thygeson were quite literally identified as indistinguishable from the machines they operated. Far from seeing their work as dehumanizing, women "typewriters" viewed it with pride and relished the economic independence it afforded them. By the 1890s, secretarial work was the overwhelming choice of white, native-born women, who constituted over 90 percent of the female clerical force. Not only considered more genteel than factory work

CLERICAL WORKER
A stenographer takes dictation in an 1890s office. Note that the apron, a symbol of feminine domesticity, has accompanied the woman into the workplace. In the 1880s, with the invention of the typewriter, many women were able to put their literacy skills to use for wages in the nation's offices.
Brown Brothers.

or domestic labor, office work also meant more money for shorter hours. Boston's clerical workers made more than $6 a week in 1883, compared with less than $5 for women working in manufacturing. For Sylvie Thygeson and thousands of women like her, the office provided a welcome alternative to the limited options available to women workers.

The Department Store

A new consumer culture came to dominate American life in the late nineteenth century as men and women increasingly sought security, comfort, material well-being, and pleasure. Department stores became the symbol of this new consumer culture. Boasting ornate facades, large plate-glass display windows, marble and brass fixtures, and elegant skylights and galleries, department stores like Macy's in New York, Wanamaker's in Philadelphia, and Marshall Field in Chicago stood as monuments to the material promise of the era.

Within these palaces of consumption, one could find cash girls, stock clerks, and wrappers who earned as little as $3 a week. At the top of the scale,

THE LURE OF THE DEPARTMENT STORE
Grand department stores like Marshall Field in Chicago, pictured here in the 1890s, became monuments to the new art of consumption. Occupying an entire city block and featuring as many as seven to ten stories of goods, not counting the main floor and the bargain basement, the stores attracted shoppers to their lavishly decorated display windows. Notice how men in straw "boaters" and women in elaborate hats are drawn like magnets to the displays, where they indulge in a favorite new pastime—window shopping.
Chicago Historical Society.

buyers like Belle Cushman of the fancy goods department at Macy's earned $25 a week, an unusually high salary for a woman in the 1870s. But the gender segregation that kept women's wages low in the office and the factory also prevailed in the department stores. Male supervisors, called floorwalkers, commanded salaries of $10 to $16 per week at a time when the typical Macy's saleswoman received $5 to $6. In all stores, saleswomen were subject to harsh and arbitrary discipline. Sitting was forbidden, and conversation with other clerks led to instant dismissal. Fines for tardiness or gum chewing pared down already meager wages. Yet white-collar workers counted themselves a cut above factory workers, even when their pay envelopes were thinner and did not justify the sense of superiority.

At Home and at Play

The growth of American industrial capitalism not only dramatically altered the workplace but also transformed home and family life and gave rise to new forms of commercialized leisure. Industrialization redefined the very concepts of work and home. Increasingly, men went out to work for wages, while most white married women stayed home, either working in the home without pay—cleaning, cooking, and rearing children—or supervising paid domestic servants who did the housework. The growing separation of workplace and home led to a new ideology, one that sentimentalized the home and women's role in it.

Domesticity and "Domestics"

The separation of the workplace and the home that marked the shift to industrial society in the early nineteenth century redefined the home as a "haven in the heartless world," presided over by a wife and mother who made the household her "separate sphere." The cultural ideology that dictated woman's place to be in the home has been called the "cult of domesticity," a phrase used to prescribe an ideal of womanhood that dominated the period from 1820 to the end of the nineteenth century.

In the decades after the Civil War, the typical middle-class dwelling in which women were to find their place became more embellished architecturally and its interiors more cluttered. Possession of such a home, indeed of any home at all, marked the gulf between the working poor and the middle class. Home owners constituted only 36 percent of the U.S. housing population in 1900, compared with 66 percent today.

SUNDAY DINNER
Sunday dinner at the home of the S. H. Fairfield family of Topeka, Kansas, is served by their African American domestic servant. Middle-class families as well as the wealthy relied on domestic help in the nineteenth century. Unlike white women, who rarely worked after marriage, more than 25 percent of African American married women worked for wages outside their homes, many as domestics. Often they had to leave their own homes and children and live in the homes of their white employers.
The Kansas State Historical Society, Topeka, Kansas.

The cult of domesticity and the elaboration of the middle-class home in the nineteenth century led to a major change in patterns of hiring household help in the North. (The South continued to rely on black female labor, first slave and later free.) Domestic labor changed over the course of the nineteenth century; the so-called hired girl, who worked beside the housewife/employer, became the live-in servant, or domestic, who increasingly carried the main burden of the housework. In American cities by 1870, from 15 to 30 percent of all households included live-in domestic servants, more than 90 percent of whom were women. As the cult of domesticity and growing consumerism raised the expectations of the urban middle and upper classes, domestic servants not only worked longer hours than any other women workers but also spent their supposedly free time on call. "She is liable to be rung up at all hours," one study reported. "Her very meals are not secure from interruption, and even her sleep is not sacred."

The growing separation of workplace and home led to a new ideology, one that sentimentalized the home and women's role in it.

By the mid-nineteenth century, native-born women increasingly took up other work and left domestic service to immigrants. The maid was so often Irish that "Bridget" became a generic term for female domestics. Domestic servants by all accounts resented their lack of privacy and their limited opportunities for socializing. Furthermore, going into service carried a social stigma. As one young woman observed, "If a girl goes into the kitchen she is sneered at and called 'the Bridget,' but if she goes behind the counter she is escorted by gentlemen." No wonder domestic service was the occupation of last resort, a "hard and lonely life" in the words of one servant girl.

PULLMAN, ILLINOIS
An early photograph of a street scene in the town of Pullman, taken when the town was so new its trees were no more than saplings, illustrates the order and comfort of the company's housing, with wide streets, white wooden fencing, front steps, and window awnings. Note the neat wooden walkways over the drainage ditches on each side of the street. George Pullman's model town took into account everything but the desire of the workers to own their own houses and to have some say in the design of their community.
Chicago Historical Society.

For women of the white middle class, domestics were a boon, freeing them from household drudgery and giving them more time to spend with their children or to pursue club work or reform. Thus, while it supported the cult of domesticity, domestic service created for those women who could afford it opportunities that expanded their horizons outside the home.

Mill Towns and Company Towns

In the mill towns and company towns that sprang up across America, industrial capitalism redefined the concept of the home for the working class. Homestead, the Carnegie mill town outside Pittsburgh, grew up haphazardly. By 1892, eight thousand people lived in Homestead, transforming what had been a rural village into a bustling mill town that belied its pastoral name. As the Carnegie steelworks expanded, they encroached on the residential area, pushing the homes out of the flatlands along the Monongahela River. Workers moved into the hills and ravines. In an area called the Hollow, shanties hung precariously on the hillsides. These small, boxlike dwellings—many no larger than two rooms—housed the unskilled laborers from the mills.

Elsewhere, particularly in New England and the South, the company itself planned and built the town. The Amoskeag textile mill in Manchester, New Hampshire, was a self-contained world laid out according to a master plan conceived in the 1830s. Such planned communities rested on the notion of benevolent corporate paternalism. Viewing the workers as the "corporation's children," Amoskeag's owners sought to socialize their increasingly immigrant workforce to the patterns of industrial work and to instill loyalty to the company, curb labor unrest, and prevent unionization.

Perhaps the most famous company town in the United States was built by sleeping-car magnate George M. Pullman nine miles south of Chicago on the shores of Lake Calumet. In the wake of the Great Railroad Strike of 1877, Pullman determined to remove his plant and workers from the "snares of the great city." In 1880, he purchased forty-three hundred acres of bare prairie and built his model town according to the principle on which he built the Pullman Palace cars that made his fortune—to be orderly, clean, and with the appearance of luxury. It was "to the employer's interest," he determined, "to see that his men are clean, contented, sober, educated, and happy."

When the first family moved in on January 1, 1881, the model town of Pullman boasted parks, artificial lakes, fountains, playgrounds, an auditorium, a library, a hotel, shops and markets, a men's club, and eighteen hundred units of housing. Noticeably absent was a saloon. One worker lamented that he frequently walked by and "looked at but dared not enter Pullman's hotel with its private bar." The intimidation the workers felt underscored a major flaw in Pullman's plan. In his eagerness to inculcate what he referred to as the "habits of respectability," Pullman consulted his own wishes and tastes rather than those of his workers. The town offered housing that was clearly superior to that in neighboring towns, but workers paid for the eye appeal. Pullman intended the town to support itself and expected a 6 percent return on his investment. As a result, Pullman's rents ran 10 to 20 percent higher than housing costs in nearby communities. And a family in Pullman could not own its own home. George Pullman refused to "sell an acre under any circumstances" because as long as he controlled the town absolutely, he held the powerful whip of eviction over his employees and could quickly get rid of troublemakers. Although observers were at first dazzled by its beauty and order, critics were soon comparing Pullman's model town to a "gilded cage" for workers. In 1884, the economist Richard T. Ely went to the heart of what most concerned workers and critics alike: "The idea of Pullman is un-American. . . . It is benevolent, well wishing feudalism, which desires the happiness of the people, but in such way as shall please the authorities."

The autocracy that many feared in Pullman was realized both in textile mill towns south of the Mason-Dixon line and in mining towns in the West. "Practically speaking," a federal investigator travel-

Pullman's Model Town
"Pullman's Company Town."
NG MAPS/NGS Image Collection.

trol over workers. Paid in company currency, or scrip, workers had no choice but to patronize the company store, where high prices led to a mounting spiral of debt that reduced the workers to virtual captives of the company. By 1890, 92 percent of southern textile workers' families lived in company towns.

The autocracy that many feared in Pullman was realized both in textile mill towns south of the Mason-Dixon line and in mining towns in the West. "Practically speaking," a federal investigator observed, "the company owns everything and controls everything, and to a large extent controls everybody in the mill village."

In western mining towns, companies exerted control not only over the housing of the employees but over their religious and social lives as well. In Ludlow, a mining town in Colorado controlled by the Rockefeller family, the local minister was hired and supported by the company. Such ironfisted control was designed to prevent labor unions from gaining a foothold. Rockefeller hired paid spies to infiltrate the town, hang out at the local saloons, and report on any union activity.

The mill towns and company towns of America provide only the most dramatic examples of the ways in which industrialization and the rise of corporate capitalism changed the landscape of the United States and altered traditional patterns of work and home life. After the Civil War, communities where men and women of different classes knew and dealt with one another personally became more and more rare. In the face of increasing business consolidation and impersonality, traditional ideas about equal competition in the marketplace and the relative independence of employers and employees lost much of their hold.

Cheap Amusements

Growing class divisions manifested themselves in patterns of leisure as well as in work. The poor and working class took their leisure, when they had it, in the streets, the dance halls, the music houses, the ballparks, and the amusement arcades, which by the 1890s formed a familiar part of the landscape. (See "The Promise of Technology," page 669.) Saloons

A PULLMAN CRAFTSWORKER
Pullman palace cars were known for their luxurious details. Here a painter working in the 1890s applies elaborate decoration to a Pullman car while in the foreground we see examples of carved doors and hand detailing. Pullman workers struck in 1894 (see page 697) to protest the company's efforts to undermine their status as craftsworkers and put them on piecework for lower wages.
Chicago Historical Society.

ing in the South observed, "the company owns everything and controls everything, and to a large extent controls everybody in the mill village." These largely nameless southern company towns, with their company-controlled stores, churches, schools, and houses, provide a classic example of social con-

new technology

THE PROMISE OF TECHNOLOGY

The Nickelodeon

Corbis-Bettmann.

THE ADVENT OF PROJECTED MOTION PICTURES marked the culmination of the efforts of many inventors to present lifelike moving pictures on the screen. During the second half of the nineteenth century, a host of inventions, including the kinematoscope, the choreutoscope, the phasmatrope, and the zoopraxiscope, were designed to make pictures move. But it was Thomas Alva Edison's invention in 1889 of the motion picture camera (kinetograph) and a peephole device to display the moving pictures (kinetoscope) that led to the commercial development of the cinema and the rise of the first moving picture theaters, the nickelodeons.

Edison presented the first of his kinetoscope "peep shows" in 1894 and they quickly became popular in hotel lobbies, amusement parks, and arcades where viewers peered into the machine one at a time. By the century's close projectors replaced peep shows and audiences watched moving pictures together in nickelodeons. The name came from combining *nickel*, the price of admission, with *melodeon*, the old reed organ sometimes played to accompany the silent films. By 1907, there were some five thousand nickelodeons across the United States. A viewer described the early shows: "A picture about 2 × 4 feet was projected from an Edison machine and a reel of film 300 to 400 feet in length was a complete show, lasting for four or five minutes. After each show the house was cleared and filled again."

At first viewers marveled at the moving images—horses, dancers, waves on a beach. But the novelty soon wore off and audiences wanted a story. In 1903, *The Great Train Robbery*, an eleven-minute movie with a simple cops-and-robbers plot, proved such a hit that silent movies soon challenged the popularity of music halls, vaudeville houses, and penny arcades. To supply the public's growing taste for films, Edison opened a motion picture studio in West Orange, New Jersey. By 1900 about a dozen producers operated out of New York and Chicago.

Edison's hope that the motion picture could be coordinated with the phonograph proved frustrating. Most theaters and all major studios remained uninterested in experimenting with "talkies" until radio technology developed in the 1920s.

Yet it is not too much to say that modern cinema began with the nickelodeons, for their sudden growth stimulated a motion picture industry that soon became one of the fastest growing industries in the nation.

played a central role in workers' lives, often serving informally as political headquarters, employment agencies, and union halls. But not all the working class thronged to the saloons. Recreation varied according to ethnicity, religion, gender, and age. For many new immigrants, social life revolved around the family; weddings, baptisms, birthdays, and bar mitzvahs constituted the chief celebrations. Generally, older-stock American men spent more time away from home in neighborhood clubs, saloons, and fraternal orders than did their immigrant counterparts. German beer gardens, for example, included the whole family. But more often, men and women took their leisure separately, except during youth and courtship.

The growing anonymity of urban industrial society posed a challenge to traditional rituals of courtship. Adolescent working girls, immigrant and old stock, no longer met prospective husbands only through their families. Fleeing crowded tenements, the young sought each other's company in dance halls and other commercial retreats. Reformers worried that the dance halls served as a breeding ground for drunkenness and prostitution. In 1884, millionaire heiress Grace Dodge, determined to help young working women find respectability, set up a Working Girl's Club in New York City. Members contributed twenty-five cents a month to rent and furnish a comfortable club room where young women could relax and entertain. Designed as an alternative to dance halls and amusement resorts, the Working Girl's Club sought to replicate patterns of middle-class courtship, where the young met under the watchful eye of older adults. By 1885, branches had sprung up in Brooklyn, Philadelphia, and Boston. But by far the majority of young working women seemed to prefer the pleasure (and danger) of the dance halls.

Speiling, a form of dancing in which a tightly clinched couple spun around and around, promoted a sexually charged atmosphere. "Vulgar dancing exists everywhere," observed one social reformer, noting "the easy familiarity in the dance practiced by nearly all the men in the way they handle the girls." Scorning proper introductions, working-class youth "picked up" partners at the dance halls, where drinking and smoking were part of the evening's entertainment. Young working women, who rarely could afford more than trolley fare when they went out, counted on being "treated" by men, a transaction that often implied sexual payback. The need to negotiate sexual encounters if they wished to participate in commercial amusements blurred the line between respectability and promiscuity, and made the dance halls a potent symbol for reformers who feared they lured girls into prostitution.

For men, baseball became a national pastime in the 1870s—then, as now, one force in urban life that was capable of uniting a city across class lines. Cincinnati mounted the first professional team, the Red Stockings, in 1869. Teams proliferated in cities across the nation, and Mark Twain hailed baseball as "the very symbol, the outward and visible expression, of the drive and push and rush and struggle of the raging, tearing, booming nineteenth century."

CONEY ISLAND
Coney Island became a pleasure resort in the 1870s, but it was not until the turn of the century, with the development of elaborate amusement parks like Steeplechase, Luna, and Dreamland, that Coney Island came into its own as the capital of commercialized leisure. This official guide highlighted the beach, the vaudeville hall, and the midway with its rides and its risqué harem dancers. In the foreground a barker gesticulates and a hawker urges a young man in a straw hat to buy souvenir photographs for his companion.
Brooklyn Historical Society.

The increasing commercialization of entertainment in the late nineteenth century can best be seen at Coney Island. A two-mile stretch of sand close to Manhattan by trolley or steamship, Coney Island in the 1870s and 1880s attracted visitors to its beaches, dance pavilions, and penny arcades—all connected by its famous boardwalk. In the 1890s, Coney Island was transformed into the site of some of the largest and most elaborate amusement parks in the country. Promoter George Tilyou built Steeplechase Park

For men, baseball became a national pastime in the 1870s—then, as now, one force in urban life that was capable of uniting a city across class lines.

in 1897, advertising "10 hours of fun for 10 cents." With its mechanical thrills and funhouse laughs, the amusement park encouraged behavior one schoolteacher aptly described as "everyone with the brakes off." By 1900, as many as half a million New Yorkers flocked to Coney Island on any given weekend. Other cities rushed to build their own playgrounds—Boston's Paragon Park and Revere Beach, Philadelphia's Willow Grove, Cleveland's Euclid Beach—but none rivaled Coney Island. Its popularity signaled the rise of mass entertainment, making the New York amusement park the unofficial capital of a new mass culture.

The Labor Movement

By the late nineteenth century, workers were losing control in the workplace. In the fierce competition to lower prices and cut costs, industrialists like Andrew Carnegie invested heavily in new machinery that enabled managers to replace skilled workers with unskilled workers. The erosion of skill and the redefinition of labor as mere "machine tending" left the worker with a growing sense of individual helplessness that served as a spur to collective action. Alone, the worker might be helpless in the face of the anonymous corporation, but together, workers could challenge the bosses and reassert their power in the workplace.

The Great Railroad Strike of 1877

Labor flexed its muscle with notable results during the summer of 1877 in the Great Railroad Strike. The strike, which began on the Baltimore and Ohio Railroad in West Virginia on July 16, quickly swept across the nation's rails until it involved nearly 100,000 railroad workers (Map 18.3). The strikers, whose wages had been repeatedly cut, aroused a good deal of public sympathy, even among the militia sent to put them down. In Reading, Pennsylva-

nia, militiamen refused to fire on the strikers, saying, "We may be militiamen, but we are workmen first." Rail traffic ground to a halt, and the nation lay paralyzed by the strike.

Violence erupted as the strike spread. In Pittsburgh, striking Pennsylvania Railroad workers were joined in the streets by steel rollers, mechanics, the unemployed, and women and children who were determined to make a common fight against the corporations. Militiamen recruited from Philadelphia marched into Pittsburgh arrogantly boasting that they would clean up what they described as "the workingmen's town." Opening fire on the crowd, they killed twenty people. Predictably, angry workers retaliated, and the resulting conflagration reduced an area of two miles along the track to smoldering rubble. Before the day ended, twenty more workers had been shot and the railroad had sustained property damage totaling $2 million.

Within the space of eight days, the governors of nine states, acting at the prompting of the railroad owners and managers, defined the strike as an insurrection and called for federal troops. President Rutherford B. Hayes (who, according to the New York *World*, owed his contested election in 1876 to the influence of Pennsylvania Railroad president Tom Scott) hesitated briefly and then called up the troops. By the time federal troops arrived, the violence had run its course. The army did not shoot a single striker in 1877. Its primary task consisted of acting as strikebreaker—opening rail traffic, protecting nonstriking "scab" train crews, and maintaining peace along the line.

Although the Great Railroad Strike was spontaneous and unorganized, it frightened the authorities and upper classes like nothing before in U.S. history. They quickly tried to blame the tiny, radical Workingman's Party and predicted a bloody uprising. "Any hour the mob chooses it can destroy any city in the country—that is the simple truth," wrote future secretary of state John Hay to his wealthy father-in-law. The *New York Times* editorialized about the "dangerous classes," and the *Independent* magazine offered the following advice on how to deal with "rioters":

> If the club of a policeman, knocking out the brains of the rioter, will answer, then well and good; but if it does not promptly meet the exigency, then bullets and bayonets, canister and grape[shot] . . . constitutes the one remedy and one duty of the hour.

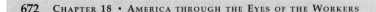

MAP 18.3

The Great Railroad Strike of 1877
Starting in West Virginia and Pennsylvania, the Great Railway Strike of 1877 spread as far north as Buffalo and as far west as San Francisco, bringing rail traffic to a standstill.

Although large numbers of middle-class Americans had initially sympathized with the conditions that led the workers to strike, they turned against the strikers, blaming them for the violence and property damage that occurred.

In the end, the strikers, whose united action had raised the specter of revolution, won few concrete gains. Wage cuts remained in force on most railroads, hundreds of strikers were fired, and strikers' names were circulated on a blacklist to prevent them from ever being rehired. But the workers were far from demoralized. They had learned the power of concerted action and would use it in the future. As labor leader Samuel Gompers acknowledged fifty years later, "The railroad strike of 1877 was the tocsin [alarm bell] that sounded a ringing message of hope to us all."

The Knights of Labor and the American Federation of Labor

The Knights of Labor, the first mass organization of America's working class, proved the chief beneficiary of labor's newfound consciousness. The Noble and Holy Order of the Knights of Labor had been founded in 1869 by Uriah Stephens, a Philadelphia garment cutter. A secret but peaceable society of workers, the Knights envisioned a "universal brotherhood" of all laborers, from the common laborer to the master craftsman. Although the Knights played no active role in the 1877 strike, membership swelled as a result of the growing interest in unionism. In 1878, the organization dropped the trappings of secrecy and launched an ambitious campaign to organize workers regardless of skill, sex, race, or nationality.

Under the direction of Grand Master Workman Terence V. Powderly, the Knights of Labor became the dominant force in labor during the 1880s. The Knights advocated a kind of workers' democracy that embraced reforms including free land, income tax, public ownership of the railroads, equal pay for work by women, and the abolition of child labor. The Knights sought to remove class distinctions and encouraged local assemblies to welcome all comers, employees and employers alike. "I hate the word 'class' and would drive it from the English language if I could," Powderly stated. Only the "parasitic" members of society—gamblers, stockbrokers, lawyers, bankers, and liquor dealers—were denied membership.

In theory, the Knights of Labor opposed strikes. Powderly championed arbitration and preferred to use boycotts. But in practice, much of the organization's appeal came from the successful strike the Knights mounted in 1885 against three railroads controlled by Jay Gould. The Knights won a sweeping victory, including the revocation of a 15 percent pay cut. Despite the reservations of its leadership, the Knights of Labor was quickly becoming a militant labor organization that excited passionate support from working people.

The Knights advocated a kind of workers' democracy that embraced reforms including free land, income tax, public ownership of the railroads, equal pay for work by women, and the abolition of child labor.

The Knights of Labor was not without rivals. Other trade unionists disliked the broad reform goals of the Knights and sought to focus on workplace issues. Samuel Gompers, a cigar maker born in London of Dutch Jewish ancestry, promoted what he called "pure and simple" unionism. Gompers founded the Organized Trades and Labor Unions in 1881 and reorganized it in 1886 into the American Federation of Labor (AFL), which coordinated the activities of craft unions throughout the United States. His plan was simple: Organize skilled craftworkers like machinists, locomotive engineers, and iron puddlers—those with the most bargaining power—and use strikes to gain immediate objectives such as higher pay and better working conditions. Gompers at first drew few converts. The AFL had only 138,000 members in 1886, compared with 730,000 for the Knights of Labor. But events soon brought down the Knights and enabled Gompers to take control of the labor movement.

Haymarket and the Specter of Labor Radicalism

While the AFL and the Knights of Labor competed for members, radical socialists and anarchists offered different visions of labor's true path. The rad-

SAMUEL GOMPERS
Samuel Gompers, pictured here in 1895, founded the American Federation of Labor in 1886 and served as its president continuously (except for 1895) until his death in 1924. Unlike the Knights of Labor, who supported the Populist Party in the 1890s, the AFL advocated "pure and simple unionism." Gompers, convinced that workers could gain little from politics, organized only skilled workers and focused on bread-and-butter issues.
The George Meany Memorial Archives.

icals, many of whom were immigrants steeped in the tradition of European socialism, believed that reform was futile; they called instead for social revolution, in theory if not in practice. Anarchists also wanted revolutionary change but envisioned a smaller role for the state than the socialists did. Both groups, sensitive to criticism that they preferred revolution in theory to improvements here and now, rallied around the popular issue of the eight-hour day.

Since the 1840s, labor had sought to end the twelve-hour workday, which was standard in industry and manufacturing. By the mid-1880s, it seemed clear to many workers that labor shared too little in the new prosperity of the decade, and once again pressure mounted for the eight-hour day. The radicals seized on the popular issue and launched major rallies in cities across the nation. Supporters of the movement set May 1, 1886, as the date for a nationwide general strike in support of the eight-hour day.

The radicals believed that reform was futile; they called instead for social revolution, in theory if not in practice.

All factions of the nascent labor movement came together in Chicago on May Day, for what was billed as the largest demonstration in history in support of the eight-hour day. A group of radicals led by anarchist Albert Parsons, a *Mayflower* descendant, and August Spies, a German immigrant, spearheaded the eight-hour movement in Chicago. Chicago's Knights of Labor rallied to the cause even though Powderly and the union's leadership, worried by the increasing activism of the rank and file, refused to champion the movement for shorter hours.

Samuel Gompers was on hand, too, to lead the city's trade unionists, although he privately urged the AFL assemblies not to participate in a general strike. Gompers's skilled workers were labor's elite. Many still worked in small shops where negotiations between workers and employers took place in an environment tempered by personal relationships. Well dressed in their Prince Albert coats and starched shirts, they stood in sharp contrast to the dispossessed workers out on strike across town at Chicago's huge McCormick reaper works. There, strikers watched helplessly as the company brought in strikebreakers to take their jobs and marched the scabs to work under the protection of the Chicago police and security guards supplied by the Pinkerton Detective Agency. Cyrus McCormick Jr., son of the inventor of the mechanical reaper, viewed labor organization as a threat to his power as well as to his profits; he was determined to smash the union.

During the May Day rally, forty-five thousand workers paraded peacefully down Michigan Avenue in support of the eight-hour day, many singing the song that had become the movement's anthem:

> We mean to make things over;
>   we're tired of toil for naught
> But bare enough to live on: never
>   an hour for thought.

> We want to feel the sunshine; we
>   want to smell the flowers;
> We're sure that God has willed it,
>   and we mean to have eight hours.
> We're summoning our forces from
>   shipyard, shop, and mill:
> Eight hours for work, eight hours for rest,
>   eight hours for what we will!

Trouble came two days later, when strikers attacked scabs outside the McCormick works and police opened fire, killing or wounding six men. Angry radicals rushed out a circular urging workers to "arm yourselves and appear in full force" at a rally in Haymarket Square. On the evening of May 4, the turnout at Haymarket was disappointing. No more than two or three thousand gathered in the drizzle to hear Spies, Parsons, and the other anarchist speakers. Mayor Carter Harrison, known as a friend of labor, mingled conspicuously in the crowd, pronounced the meeting peaceable, and went home to bed. A short time later, police captain John "Blackjack" Bonfield, who had made his reputation cracking skulls, marched his men into the crowd, by now fewer than three hundred people, and demanded that they disperse.

Suddenly, someone threw a bomb into the police ranks. After a moment of stunned silence, the police drew their revolvers. "Fire and kill all you can," shouted a police lieutenant. When the melee ended, seven policemen and an unknown number of civilians lay dead. An additional sixty policemen and thirty or forty civilians suffered injuries. News of the "Haymarket riot" (a misnomer for what was more properly called the Haymarket affair) provoked a nationwide convulsion of fear, followed by blind rage directed at anarchists, labor unions, strikers, immigrants, and the working class in general. The hysteria ran deepest in Chicago. The police rounded up Spies and the other Haymarket speakers and jailed hundreds of radicals. Parsons managed to escape but later turned himself in to stand trial with his fellows.

Eight men went on trial in Chicago, although witnesses could testify that none of them had thrown the bomb. It was clear from the start that the men were on trial for their ideas, not their actions. "Convict these men," cried State's Attorney Julius S. Grinnell, "make examples of them, hang them, and you save our institutions." Although the state could not link any of the defendants with the

THE CHICAGO RIOT
Inflammatory pamphlets like this one published in the wake of the Haymarket affair presented a one-sided view of the incident and stirred public passion. The anarchist speakers were tried and convicted for the bombing, even though the identity and motivation of the bomb thrower remained undiscovered.
Chicago Historical Society.

Haymarket bomb, the jury nevertheless found them all guilty. Four were executed, one committed suicide, and three received prison sentences. On the gallows, August Spies spoke for the Haymarket martyrs: "The time will come when our silence will be more powerful than the voices you throttle today."

In 1893, Governor John Peter Altgeld, after a thorough investigation, pardoned the three remaining Haymarket anarchists. He denounced the trial as a shameless travesty of justice and concluded that Captain Bonfield was "the man really responsible for the death of the police officers." The governor's action brought on a storm of protest and cost him his political career. But through the entire process, Altgeld never wavered. "If I decide they are innocent, I will pardon them," he promised, "even if I never hold office another day." He did, and he didn't.

The bomb blast at Haymarket had lasting repercussions. To commemorate the death of the Haymarket martyrs, labor would make May 1 an international celebration of the worker. But the Haymarket bomb, in the eyes of one observer, proved "a godsend to all enemies of the labor movement." It effectively scotched the eight-hour day and dealt a fatal blow to the Knights of Labor.

With the labor movement everywhere under attack, many workers severed their radical connections, and many skilled workers turned to the American Federation of Labor. Under the leadership of Samuel Gompers, the AFL soon became the dominant voice of American labor. In the aftermath of Haymarket, Gompers urged workers to focus on concrete gains—higher wages, shorter hours—and use strikes and boycotts judiciously to win its demands. Gompers's narrow economic strategy made sense at the time and enabled one segment of the workforce—the skilled—to organize effectively and achieve tangible gains. But the majority of unskilled workers remained largely untouched by the AFL's brand of "pure and simple" trade unionism.

Visions of a Better Life

Fear of social upheaval generated by the uprisings of workers in the 1870s and 1880s led to a search for social solutions. Liberal reformers, sympathetic to labor's plight but fearful of violence, sought schemes that would mitigate economic injustice without threatening bloodshed or class warfare. Two journalists, Henry George and Edward Bellamy, put forward visions of a better life that captured the imagination of their times. The utopian plans of George and Bellamy expressed both fears about the present and hopes for a better future.

Henry George and the Single Tax

The Great Railroad Strike of 1877 inspired San Francisco journalist Henry George to write a book that

read

HISTORICAL QUESTION

From Rags to Riches: What Is "Making It" in America?

THE RAGS-TO-RICHES FABLES of novelists like Horatio Alger fueled the dreams of countless young people at the end of the nineteenth century. Alger's formulaic novels feature fatherless young men who through the right combination of "pluck and luck" move ahead in the world. Yet despite the myth, few Americans rose from rags to riches. Even Alger's heroes, like his popular Ragged Dick, more often traded rags for respectability.

Without exception, Alger's characters came from old stock and were not the new immigrants who poured through the "golden door" into the United States at the turn of the century. What were *their* chances of success? Literature written by the new immigrants themselves tells different stories. Abraham Cahan's *The Rise of David Levinsky* (1917) describes the experience of an eastern European Jewish immigrant who, as the title indicates, rises to gain material success. But while the theme of success is distinctively American, the treatment is not. The author laments that Levinsky's "rise" is paralleled by a spiritual loss. "I cannot escape from my old self," Levinsky confesses at the end of the novel. "David, the poor lad swinging over a Talmud volume at the Preacher's Synagogue, seems to have more in common with my inner identity than David Levinsky the well-known cloak manufacturer." Having sacrificed all to material gain, Levinsky acknowledges, "At the height of my business success I feel that if I had my life to live over again I should never think of a business career."

Mike Gold tells a darker story of immigrant life in *Jews without Money* (1930), an autobiographical tale of the implacable economic forces that devastated Gold's fictional family and turned its young protagonist to communism. Gold's characters inhabit a world of grinding poverty and ignorance, a landscape so bleak that one character comes to doubt the existence of a benevolent God, asking plaintively, "Did God make bedbugs?" Determined to "write a truthful book of Poverty," Gold pledged, "I will mention bedbugs":

It wasn't a lack of cleanliness in our home. My mother was as clean as any German housewife; she slaved, she worked herself to the bone keeping us fresh and neat. The bedbugs were a torment to her. She doused the beds with kerosene, changed the sheets, sprayed the mattresses in an endless frantic war with the bedbugs. What was the use; nothing could help. It was Poverty; it was the Tenement.

Yet Gold's own success belied the grim economic determinism of his fiction. He made it out of the ghetto and into the world of literature and social activism.

Historians have been fascinated by the question of "making it" in America. Repeatedly they have attempted to measure economic and social mobility, from colonial times to the twentieth century. Looking at the lives of common folk, scholars have struggled to determine who made it, who did not, and why. Was America a land of boundless opportunity where the poor could rise? Or did the rich stay rich and the poor stay poor-to-middling, as pioneering studies of social mobility in the 1950s indicated?

By the 1960s, quantitative methods made possible by advances in computer technology promised to move history away from the "impressionistic," anecdotal evidence of fiction and memoirs and provide a statistical framework in which to measure success. But just what could historians measure with their new tools? Comparing Jewish and Italian immigrants in New York City at the turn of the century, one historian concluded that the Jews had done a better job of making it. By employing a table that categorized occupations, ranking them from professional, white-collar jobs to unskilled labor, the historian duly noted the movement from one category to another, concluding from his data that Jews moved more quickly than Italians into the white-collar class.

Studies of occupational mobility, however, contained major flaws. In a country where money has been and continues to be the common measure of success, historians' decision to use occupational categories and not income as the yardstick of mobility and success seemed to beg the question. Yet the choice was not surprising, given that census data, the staple of quantitative studies, provide information on occupation but not on income. Even occupational mobility proved difficult to measure accurately. For example, in the study cited, peddlers somewhat arbitrarily ranked at low-white-collar

RAGS TO RICHES
Horatio Alger's novels like **Ragged Dick** *(1868) invariably end with the young hero on the road to success. Contrast Alger's cheerful message with the bathos of the 1900 song "No One Cares for Me," in which the young newsboy in his rags replicates Alger's hero. Instead of getting ahead, the newsboy is portrayed as a victim of cruel neglect. Which portrait is more accurate? Historians for decades have wrestled with the question of social mobility and success.*
Culver Pictures; Picture Research Consultants & Archives.

status because they were self-employed. Yet the pushcart peddler and the Italian street vendor could hardly be said to have enjoyed white-collar status in the larger society in which they moved. Students must look carefully at what historians are measuring, recognizing that occupational mobility may not equate with social mobility or economic success.

The larger questions remain: What is "making it" in America? How best can it be measured—in dollars and cents, job satisfaction, occupational status, comparison with the lives of one's parents or neighbors? And what of the immigrants themselves? How did they define it? If becoming a bricklayer spelled success to the Italian immigrant and

his family, do studies of occupational mobility based on statisticians' categories and job rankings distort his lived reality? In dealing with the issue of "making it" in America, historians have increasingly come to recognize that each immigrant group had its own unique definition of success. Not all immigrants sought upward mobility, whether economic or occupational. Cultural factors, such as the value Italians placed on loyalty to the family, also played a key role. Ultimately, questions of success and mobility cannot easily be quantified, and they demand attention to the larger cultural context that shaped individual economic and occupational choices.

(margin handwritten notes: 1865 - c/w ended; 1863 - emancipation proclamation; Henry George)

soon became a classic of American political economy: *Progress and Poverty* (1879). George knew poverty firsthand and harbored a deep sympathy for the underdog. In this spirit, he dedicated his book "to those who, seeing the vice and misery that spring from the unequal distribution of wealth and privilege, feel the possibility of a higher social state and would strive for its attainment." In *Progress and Poverty*, George explored the paradox central to American life: Why, in a land so rich, was there such inequality? (See "Historical Question," page 676.) He elaborated a theory that tied increasing inequality and growing monopoly to the scarcity of land caused by speculation (the practice of buying land and holding it until the price went up). Land speculators, he charged, contributed nothing to the economy yet made huge profits in "unearned increment."

George championed a single tax on unimproved land as a cure-all for the nation's industrial problems. Once speculators could no longer turn large profits on the land they held, George reasoned, the way lay open to utopia. Land would become available for farming. Industrial workers would leave the factories for the farms. Wages would naturally increase, and the life of industrial laborers would become more secure. Government, and with it the political corruption of the Gilded Age, would virtually disappear.

Liberal reformers, sympathetic to labor's plight but fearful of violence, sought schemes that would mitigate economic injustice without threatening bloodshed or class warfare.

To underscore the urgent need for change, George ended his book with an apocalyptic vision of what would befall the United States if action were not taken: disease, pauperism, and an atmosphere of "brooding revolution." His single tax offered a way out, an alternative to class warfare. In George's view, venturesome capitalists and honest laboring people were not class enemies. The real villain was the grasping land speculator. The single tax, then, promised to bring America back from the brink of disaster and usher in a golden age.

George's message found many ready adherents who made the single tax a rallying cry for reform. George moved east after the publication of *Progress and Poverty* and in 1886, in the aftermath of the Hay-

market affair, ran for mayor of New York City on the United Labor Party ticket. A member of the Knights of Labor, George appealed to laborers, who saw him as one of their own. Tammany Hall attempted to buy him off, promising to run him for Congress on the Democratic ticket. "You cannot be elected," a Tammany pol told George, "but your running will raise hell." To which George replied, "I do not want the responsibility and the work of the Mayor of New York, but I do want to raise hell."

At first, George's opponents dismissed him as a "humbug" and a "busybody" with no real chance. But when thirty-four thousand laborers signed a petition endorsing him, Democrats and Republicans began to take him seriously. Samuel Gompers himself became the chair of George's city organization and headed the speakers' bureau. Staunch Republican liberals, fearful of class war, threw their support to the Democrats and tarred George as "an apostle of anarchy and destruction." At the prompting of Tammany Hall, the Catholic archbishop of New York warned his flock not to "be deluded by men who advocate revolutionary doctrines." In what George accurately described as "one of the fiercest contests that ever took place in this or any other city," he lost the election by twenty thousand votes, despite strong working-class support. The Democratic candidate beat George, who in turn nosed out his Republican rival, a political newcomer named Theodore Roosevelt.

Edward Bellamy's Nationalist Utopia

While Henry George campaigned for mayor of New York and the country awaited the execution of the Haymarket anarchists, Edward Bellamy took up his pen to write a novel that ranks with Harriet Beecher Stowe's antislavery novel *Uncle Tom's Cabin* in terms of sales and influence. In 1888, Bellamy, a Massachusetts newspaper writer forced by tuberculosis to give up his editorial career, published *Looking Backward: 2000–1887*, a combination of utopian fantasy and genteel romance that spoke to the concerns of millions in the United States who were looking for a peaceful solution to the labor problem.

In *Looking Backward*, Bellamy's upper-crust hero, Julian West, falls asleep in Boston in 1887 and wakes in the year 2000 to find the world transformed. No labor strife, no class antagonism, no extremes of poverty and wealth exist in the twenty-first century. Instead, the people are organized into an efficient industrial army in which all men and women between the ages of twenty-one and forty-five work for the same guaranteed annual income. In Bellamy's highly centralized state, the disharmony, corruption, and party strife of the Gilded Age have vanished, replaced by benevolent bureaucracy.

Bellamy's utopia came complete with visions of technological marvels that were unheard of in the 1880s—the radio and moving sidewalks. But although the material conditions of the people have improved, Bellamy makes it clear that the new world came about from a spiritual and not a material transformation. The Religion of Solidarity, or "nationalism," transformed society, eliminating the destructive energies of both capitalist greed and proletarian envy and hatred. All society had to do was recognize and cooperate in the inevitable evolutionary process from competition to cooperation.

Julian himself experiences a conversion and, by the book's end, overcomes the smug selfishness that was the hallmark of his class. Looking back at his old life, he compares society in the late nineteenth century to "a prodigious coach which the masses of humanity were harnessed to and dragged toilsomely along a very hilly and sandy road." The driver of the coach is hunger, and his whips cut deep into the backs of the struggling team below. On top of the coach, "well up out of the dust," perch the passengers, who occasionally call down encouragement to the toilers below, "exhorting them to patience, and holding out hopes of possible compensation in another world for the hardness of their lot." Such inhumanity, Julian patiently explains to his twenty-first-century audience, could be explained by the conviction that "there was no other way in which Society could get along, except that the many pulled at the rope and the few rode." Besides, the riders suffer from the hallucination that "they [are] not exactly like their brothers and sisters" but are made "of finer clay." "This seems unaccountable," Julian confesses, "but, as I once rode this very coach and shared that very hallucination, I ought to be believed."

In the parable of the stagecoach, Bellamy offered a scathing critique of social Darwinism and a call to action. The book caused a sensation. Within three years, over a million copies had been sold, and enthusiastic readers launched more than 160 Bellamy Clubs devoted to discussing nationalism and implementing the social goals expressed in *Looking Backward*. While neither George's single tax nor Bellamy's nationalist utopia produced the kind of mass movement for social change envisioned by the two authors, the enthusiastic response to both books indicated that many Americans feared social cataclysm and were ready to take action.

Conclusion: The Workers' Own Struggle

The late nineteenth century witnessed many competing visions of a better life as Americans sought solutions to the problems attending urban industrialization and corporate capitalism. Henry George's single tax won supporters across the country and rallied New York's laborers to support him for mayor. Bellamy's nationalist utopia attracted followers drawn largely from the "sensible middle class." President Hayes called for "education" and a "wise judicious policy" to avoid labor upheavals like the Great Railroad Strike of 1877. American workers themselves had their own vision of what a better life might be—a life in which the independence eroded by industrialization could be countered by collective action, workers could regain some control of the workplace, and a shorter day and a higher wage promised escape from a brutal life of toil. Their vision and their willingness to fight for it made them active agents of social change, willing to risk their livelihood and sometimes their very lives in the struggle.

Looking at the impact on his life occasioned by industrialization, a Massachusetts machinist declared in the 1890s:

> The workers of Massachusetts have always been law and order men. We loved our country and respected the laws. For the last five years the times have been growing worse every year, until we have been brought down so far that we have not much farther to go. What do the Mechanics of Massachusetts say to each other? I will tell you: "We must have a change. Any thing is better than this. We cannot be worse off, no matter what the change is."

Mounting anger and frustration would lead American workers and farmers to join forces in the 1890s and create a grassroots movement to fight for change under the banner of a new People's Party.

www.bedfordstmartins.com/tap SEE THE ONLINE STUDY GUIDE to assess your mastery of the material covered in this chapter.

680   CHAPTER 18 • AMERICA THROUGH THE EYES OF THE WORKERS

1870–1890

CHRONOLOGY

1869	Uriah Stephens founds Knights of Labor.		1884	Grace Dodge organizes Working Girl's Club in New York City.
	Cincinnati mounts first professional baseball team, the Red Stockings.		1886	Organized Trades and Labor Unions reorganized as the American Federation of Labor (AFL).
1870	Wage earners account for over half of those employed in 1870 census.			Massive rally in support of eight-hour workday takes place in Chicago on May 1; Haymarket bombing on May 4 results in widening fear of anarchy and a blow to the labor movement.
1872	Andrew Carnegie opens his steelworks outside Pittsburgh.			
1873	Panic on Wall Street touches off depression.			Henry George campaigns for mayor of New York City on United Labor Party ticket and loses in close election.
1877	Great Railroad Strike paralyzes nation.			
1878	Knights of Labor campaigns to organize workers regardless of skill, sex, or race.		1888	Edward Bellamy publishes *Looking Backward: 2000–1887.*
1879	Henry George publishes *Progress and Poverty.*		1890	Average worker earns $500 per year.
1880	George M. Pullman builds model town near Chicago.		1893	Illinois Governor John Peter Altgeld pardons three remaining Haymarket anarchists.
1881	Samuel Gompers founds Organized Trades and Labor Unions.		1893	Panic on Wall Street touches off major depression.
1882	Chinese Exclusion Act prohibits immigration of Chinese to the United States.		1897	Steeplechase amusement park opens on Coney Island.

(handwritten note in left margin:) Immigrants came over 1865–1910. Jobs hard to find

BIBLIOGRAPHY

GENERAL

Edward L. Ayers, *The Promise of the New South: Life after Reconstruction* (1992).

John B. Boles, *The South through Time*, vol. 2 (1995).

Alan Dawley, *Struggles for Justice: Social Responsibility and the Liberal State* (1991).

Sara M. Evans, *Born for Liberty: A History of Women in America* (1989).

Alice Kessler-Harris, *Out to Work: The History of Wage-Earning Women in the United States* (1982).

Julie A. Matthaei, *An Economic History of Women in America: Women's Work, the Sexual Division of Labor, and the Development of Capitalism* (1982).

David Montgomery, *The Fall of the House of Labor: The Workplace, the State, and American Labor Activism, 1865–1925* (1987).

Nell Irwin Painter, *Standing at Armageddon: The United States, 1877–1919* (1987).

AMERICAN WORKERS

William Adelman, *Touring Pullman: A Study in Company Paternalism* (1977).

Stephen E. Ambrose, *Nothing Like It in the World: The Men Who Built the Transcontinental Railroad, 1863–1869* (2000).

Paul Avrich, *The Haymarket Tragedy* (1984).

David Haward Bain, *Empire Express: Building the First Transcontinental Railroad* (1999).

BIBLIOGRAPHY 681

1870–1890

Charles Albro Barker, *Henry George* (1991).

Gunther Barth, *Bitter Strength: The History of the Chinese in the United States, 1850–1870* (1964).

Henry F. Bedford, ed., *Their Lives and Numbers: The Condition of Working People in Massachusetts, 1870–1900* (1995).

Susan Porter Benson, *Counter Cultures: Saleswomen, Managers, and Customers in American Department Stores, 1890–1940* (1986).

David Brody, *Workers in Industrial America: Essays on the Twentieth-Century Struggle* (1980).

Robert V. Bruce, *1877: Year of Violence* (1959).

Stanley Buder, *Pullman: An Experiment in Industrial Order and Community Planning, 1880–1930* (1967).

Patricia A. Cooper, *Once a Cigar Maker: Men, Women, and Work Culture in American Cigar Factories* (1987).

Henry David, *The History of the Haymarket Affair* (1963).

Margery W. Davies, *Woman's Place Is at the Typewriter: Office Work and Office Workers, 1870–1930* (1982).

James J. Davis, *The Iron Puddler: My Life in the Rolling Mills and What Became of It* (1922).

Melvyn Dubofsky, *Industrialism and the American Worker, 1865–1920* (1975).

Faye E. Dudden, *Serving Women: Household Service in Nineteenth-Century America* (1983).

Lani Ah Tye Farkas, *Bury My Bones in America: The Saga of a Chinese Family in California, 1852–1996: From San Francisco to the Sierra Gold Mines* (1998).

Philip S. Foner, *The Great Labor Uprising of 1877* (1977).

Philip S. Foner, *Women and the American Labor Movement: From the First Trade Unions to the Present* (1979).

William E. Forbath, *Law and the Shaping of the American Labor Movement* (1991).

Michael H. Frisch and Daniel J. Walkowitz, eds., *Working-Class America: Essays on Labor, Community, and American Society* (1983).

John S. Garner, *The Company Town: Architecture and Society in the Early Industrial Age* (1992).

Sherna Gluck, *From Parlor to Prison: Five American Suffragists Talk about Their Lives* (1976).

David M. Gordon, Richard Edwards, and Michael Reich, eds., *Segmented Work, Divided Workers: The Historical Transformation of Labor in the United States* (1982).

Herbert C. Gutman, *Work, Culture, and Society in Industrializing America: Essays in American Working-Class and Social History* (1976).

Jacquelyn Dowd Hall, James Leloudis, Robert Korstad, Mary Murphy, Lu Ann Jones, and Christopher B. Daly, *Like a Family: The Making of a Southern Mill World* (1987).

Tamara K. Hareven, *Family Life and Industrial Time: The Relationship between the Family and Work in a New England Industrial Community* (1982).

Tamara K. Hareven and Randolph Langenbach, *Amoskeag: Life and Work in an American Factory-City* (1978).

Robert Hendrickson, *The Grand Emporiums* (1979).

Jacobson, Matthew Frye, *Whiteness of a Different Color: European Immigrants and the Alchemy of Race* (1998).

Elizabeth Jameson, *All That Glitters: Class, Conflict, and Community in Cripple Creek* (1998).

Jacqueline Jones, *The Dispossessed: America's Underclasses from the Civil War to the Present* (1992).

David M. Katzman, *Seven Days a Week: Women and Domestic Service in Industrializing America* (1978).

David M. Katzman and William M. Tuttle Jr., eds., *Plain Folk: The Life Stories of Undistinguished Americans* (1982).

Larry Lankton, *Cradle to Grave: Life, Work, and Death at Lake Superior Copper Mines* (1991).

Janet Lecompte, ed., *Emily: The Diary of a Hard-Worked Woman* (1987).

Sidney Lens, *The Labor Wars: From the Molly Maguires to the Sitdowns* (1974).

Huping Ling, *Surviving on the Gold Mountain: A History of Chinese American Women and Their Lives* (1998).

Cathy L. McHugh, *Mill Family: The Labor System in the Southern Cotton Textile Industry, 1880–1915* (1988).

Milton Meltzer, *Bread and Roses: The Struggle of American Labor, 1865–1915* (1967).

Joanne J. Meyerowitz, *Women Adrift: Independent Wage Earners in Chicago, 1880–1930* (1988).

Daniel Nelson, *Farm and Factory: Workers in the Midwest, 1880–1900* (1995).

Lynn Pan, *Sons of the Yellow Emperor: The Story of the Overseas Chinese* (1990).

Cornelia Stratton Parker, *Working with the Working Women* (1922).

Samuel H. Preston and Michael R. Haines, *Fatal Years: Child Mortality in Late-Nineteenth-Century America* (1991).

Richard B. Rice, William A. Bullough, and Richard J. Orsi, *The Elusive Eden: A New History of California* (1988).

Edward J. Rose, *Henry George* (1968).

Leon Stein and Philip Taft, eds., *Workers Speak* (1971).

David O. Stowell, *Streets, Railroads, and the Great Strike of 1877* (1999).

Sharon Hartman Strom, *Beyond the Typewriter: Gender, Class, and the Origins of Modern American Office Work, 1900–1930* (1992).

Ronald Takaki, *Strangers from a Different Shore: A History of Asian Americans* (1989).

Leslie Woodcock Tentler, *Wage-Earning Women: Industrial Work and Family Life in the United States, 1900–1930* (1979).

John L. Thomas, *Alternative America: Henry George, Edward Bellamy, Henry Demarest Lloyd and the Adversary Tradition* (1983).

Christopher L. Tomlins, *The State and the Unions: Labor Relations, Law, and the Organized Labor Movement in America, 1880–1960* (1985).

Carole Turbin, *Working Women of Collar City: Gender, Class, and Community in Troy, New York, 1864–1886* (1992).

Jules Tygiel, *Workingmen in San Francisco, 1880–1901* (1992).

Richard White, *"It's Your Misfortune and None of My Own": A New History of the American West* (1991).

Samuel Yellen, *American Labor Struggles* (1936).

Irwin Yellowitz, *Industrialization and the American Labor Movement, 1850–1900* (1977).

POPULAR CULTURE

Elaine Abelson, *When Ladies Go A'Thieving: Middle-Class Shoplifters in the Victorian Department Store* (1989).

Charles Albro Barker, *Henry George* (1991).

Sylvia E. Bowman, *Edward Bellamy* (1986).

Lewis A. Erenberg, *Steppin' Out: New York Nightlife and the Transformation of American Culture, 1890–1930* (1981).

Michael Kammen, *American Culture, American Tastes* (1999).

William Leach, *Land of Desire: Merchants, Power, and the Rise of a New American Culture* (1993).

Kathryn J. Oberdeck, *The Evangelist and the Impresario: Religion, Entertainment, and Cultural Politics in America, 1884–1914* (1999).

Kathy Peiss, *Cheap Amusements: Working Women and Leisure in Turn-of-the-Century New York* (1986).

Ellen M. Plante, *Women at Home in Victorian America: A Social History* (1997).

Thomas J. Schlereth, *Victorian America: Transformations in Everyday Life, 1876–1915* (1992).

Daniel E. Sutherland, *The Expansion of Everyday Life, 1860–1876* (1989).

Practicing Your Textbook Reading Skills

1. Which of the following sentences from the chapter introduction best explains the connection between the chapter-opening story (p. 651) and the rest of the chapter?

   a. "In three weeks it was over."

   b. "The unprecedented industrial growth that occurred after the Civil War came about as a result of the labor of millions of men, women, and children who toiled in workshops and factories, in sweatshops and mines, on the railroads and construction sites across America."

   c. "Their stories provide a different perspective from that of the great industrialists and the politicians."

   d. "Through their eyes it is possible to gauge how corporate capitalism transformed old work patterns and affected the social and cultural—as well as the economic and political—life of the United States."

2. Examine Map 18.1 (p. 653) to identify the most significant coal mining region in late-nineteenth-century America.

   a. Wyoming

   b. Minnesota and Wisconsin

   c. Illinois, Kentucky, Ohio, West Virginia, and Pennsylvania

   d. Washington, Oregon, California, and Nevada

3. Where can you find help interpreting the cover of *Judge* pictured on page 655?

   a. in the printed study guide for *The American Promise*

   b. online at www.bedfordstmartins.com/tap

   c. in the library

   d. in the section of the chapter titled "America's Diverse Workers" (p. 654)

4. Which of the following sentences from the section "Immigration, Ethnic Rivalry, and Racism" (pp. 655–56) is a fact?

   a. "'There should be a law . . . to keep all the I-talians from comin' in and takin' the bread out of the mouths of honest people.'"

   b. "Throughout the nineteenth century, members of the educated elite as well as workers viewed ethnic and even religious differences as racial characteristics—referring to the Polish 'race' or the Jewish 'race.'"

   c. "But who was 'white'"?

   d. "The social construction of race is nowhere more apparent than in the testimony of an Irish dockworker, who boasted that he hired only "white men" to load cargo, a category that he insisted excluded 'Poles and Italians.'"

5. The photograph of a New England weaver on page 658 illustrates
   a. nineteenth-century fashion.
   b. the cloth-making process.
   c. working conditions in nineteenth-century textile mills.
   d. women's role in labor politics.

6. According to Figure 18.1 (p. 662), what was the most common source of employment for women from 1870 to 1890?
   a. trade and transportation
   b. manufacturing and mechanical industries
   c. domestic and personal service
   d. agriculture

7. What inference about nineteenth-century laborers can be drawn from the following song lyrics? "We're summoning our forces from / shipyard, shop, and mill: / Eight hours for work, eight hours for rest, / eight hours for what we will!"
   a. They were lazy.
   b. They believed that if they worked together they could win reform.
   c. They didn't want to improve conditions for miners.
   d. They wanted more money.

8. What significant outcome of the attack on the labor movement followed the Haymarket bombing?
   a. Just punishment was dealt to the guilty parties and further strikes were prevented for nearly ten years.
   b. Many workers severed their radical connections, and many skilled workers turned to the American Federation of Labor.
   c. Additional bombings were planned.
   d. None of the above.

9. Throughout the chapter, passages from the text are reprinted in larger, italicized type between lines. Why?
   a. to make the book longer
   b. to provide comments and observations from the people discussed in the chapter
   c. to highlight the chapter's main ideas
   d. to indicate when a new topic is being raised

10. According to the main character's stagecoach analogy in Edward Bellamy's novel *Looking Backward: 2000–1887,* the wealthy classes of the late nineteenth century were
    a. hunger personified.
    b. treated too harshly.
    c. like arrogant passengers who benefited from the toil of others.
    d. social Darwinists. Pg 177

Testing Your Understanding

Identify the following statements as true or false.

1. America's first transcontinental railroad was built largely by Chinese men.

   T __X__   F _____

2. Child labor was rare in the 1800s.

   T _____   F __X__

3. In the years after the Civil War, female office workers were thought of as mechanical equipment.

   T __X__   F _____

4. A greater percentage of Americans owned their own homes in 1900 than today.

   T _____   F __X__

5. On an average weekend in 1900, as many as 500,000 people went to Cleveland's Euclid Beach.

   T _____   F __X__

Select the best answer to each of the following questions.

6. By the 1870s, the world's industrial core was
   a. western Europe.
   b. western Europe and the northeastern United States. pg 176
   c. North America, eastern Europe, and Russia.
   d. Australia and New Zealand.

7. Which of the following was *not* a type of industrial worker?
   a. skilled artisan worker
   b. common laborer   pg 178
   c. factory worker
   d. miner

8. All of the following were life-threatening dangers of mining except:

    a. explosions

    c. cave-ins

    b. new technologies

    (d.) union hotheads

9. What percentage of Americans finished high school in the late nineteenth century?

    (a.) less than 10 percent

    b. approximately 25 percent

    c. a little less than 60 percent

    d. a little more than 85 percent

10. Of the following popular sources of recreation, which was considered least respectable for young women?

    pg 192

    a. beer gardens

    c. baseball parks

    (b.) dance halls

    d. amusement parks

11. The Great Railroad Strike of 1877 resulted in

    pg 193

    a. the deaths of more than twenty militiamen.

    (b.) increased tensions between workers and the middle and upper classes.

    c. middle-class sympathy for the strikers.

    d. substantially improved working conditions for railroad employees.

12. Terence V. Powderly was

    pg 194

    a. the owner of the Pennsylvania Railroad.

    b. the founder of the Knights of Labor.

    (c.) the Grand Master Workman of the Knights of Labor.

    d. the president of the American Federation of Labor.

13. The eight-hour workday was a primary goal of

    a. Samuel Gompers.

    pg 196

    (b.) radical socialists and anarchists. - Albert Parson

    c. Terence V. Powderly.

    d. the Pinkerton Detective Agency.

14. In his book *Progress and Poverty*, Henry George argued in favor of

    (a.) a tax on unimproved land bought and sold by speculators for profit.

    b. disease, pauperism, and an atmosphere of "brooding revolution."

    c. his campaign to be mayor of New York City.

    d. the election of Theodore Roosevelt.

15. Which of the following events happened first?

    a. Illinois Governor John Peter Altgeld pardoned three remaining Haymarket anarchists.

    b. Grace Dodge organized the Working Girl's Club in New York City.

    c. Henry George published *Progress and Poverty.*

    (d.) Uriah Stephens founded the Knights of Labor. pg 202

Use context clues and word analysis to define the following terms as they are used in the chapter.

16. *puddlers*

_____

_____

_____

17. *cult of domesticity*

_____

_____

_____

_____

18. *company town*

_____

_____

_____

19. *nickelodeon*

_____

_____

_____

_____

20. *utopia*

_____

_____

_____

_____

Answer each of the following questions using the space provided.

21. Describe the nineteenth-century industrial workforce.

_____

_____

_____

_____

_____

22. Why was the emergence of department stores like Marshall Field in Chicago, Macy's in New York, and Wanamaker's in Philadelphia significant?

pg 186

_____

_____

_____

_____

23. Briefly explain the differences between the Knights of Labor and the American Federation of Labor.

pg 194

_____

_____

_____

24. What was the Haymarket "riot," and how did it affect the labor movement?

pg 196-197

_____

_____

_____

_____

_____

_____

_____

_____

25. Can statistical data give historians an accurate measure of the success of different immigrant groups? Why or why not?

So many immigrants, not legal that it makes it hard to keep accurate measures.

Making Thematic Connections

The business chapter reprinted in Unit 1, "Human Resource Management," describes what modern companies do to hire and keep the best possible employees for their businesses. What lessons from U.S. labor history might they be responding to? How might the course of American history have been different if nineteenth-century businesses had followed contemporary human resources practices?

Glossary of Terms

acculturative stress   The stress that results from the pressure of adapting to a new culture. [Unit 2]

American Federation of Labor   A labor group, founded in the nineteenth century, that emphasized the power of unions and strikes to gain specific benefits and improvements in the workplace. *See also* Knights of Labor. [Unit 5]

attrition   Policy of reducing an organization's work force through normal turnover and voluntary terminations. [Unit 1]

benefits   Noncash compensation, such as health insurance, paid vacations, or retirement plans, which employees select or receive by virtue of being members of the organization. [Unit 1]

biopsychosocial model   The belief that physical health and illness are determined by the complex interaction of biological, psychological, and social factors. [Unit 2]

bonus   A cash payment that rewards employees for achieving an organizational goal. [Unit 1]

career development   The process of planning and coordinating the progress of employees through positions of increasing responsibility within an organization. [Unit 1]

career path   A succession of jobs that employees hold as they move upward through an organization to positions of increasing responsibility and pay. [Unit 1]

carnivore   Predator that obtains its nutrients and energy by eating meat. [Unit 4]

catecholamines   Hormones secreted by the adrenal medulla that cause rapid physiological arousal; include adrenaline and noradrenaline. [Unit 2]

Note: The definitions are derived from the five units of this book and referenced accordingly. The units are as follows: Unit 1, Business: "Human Resource Management"; Unit 2, Psychology: "Stress, Health, and Coping"; Unit 3, Mass Communication: "Public Relations and Framing the Message"; Unit 4, Biology: "Interactions in Communities"; and Unit 5, History: "America through the Eyes of the Workers, 1870–1890."

character displacement   A phenomenon in which species that live together in the same environment tend to diverge in those characteristics that overlap; exemplified by Darwin's finches. [Unit 4]

Chinese Exclusion Act of 1882   U.S. law that prohibited the immigration of Chinese to the United States. [Unit 5]

commensalism   *See* symbiosis. [Unit 4]

commission   Pay based on a percentage of the money an employee brings into a business. [Unit 1]

community   All the populations of organisms inhabiting a common environment and interacting with one another. [Unit 4]

company town   A self-contained residential neighborhood built by a company to house its workers, provide socialization, instill company loyalty, curb unrest, and prevent unionization. [Unit 5]

comparable worth   The payment of equal compensation to women and men in different positions that require similar levels of education, training, and skill. [Unit 1]

compensation   The payment—pay and benefits—that employees receive for their work. [Unit 1]

competition   Interaction between individual organisms of the same species or of different species using the same resource, often present in limited supply. [Unit 4]

conflict   A situation in which a person feels pulled between two or more opposing desires, motives, or goals. [Unit 2]

contingent work force   Part-time, temporary, and self-employed workers who do not conform to the traditional model of the 9-to-5, full-time employee. [Unit 1]

coping   Behavioral and cognitive responses used to deal with stressors; involves efforts to change circumstances, or your interpretation of circumstances, to make them more favorable and less threatening. [Unit 2]

corticosteroids   Hormones released by the adrenal cortex that play a key role in the body's response to long-term stressors. [Unit 2]

cult of domesticity   The nineteenth-century view of the home as a feminine sanctuary or escape from the masculine working world; this view stressed that woman's place was in the home. [Unit 5]

daily hassles   Everyday minor events that annoy and upset people. [Unit 2]

demotion   Movement of an employee to a position of lesser responsibility, usually as a result of poor performance in a higher-level position. [Unit 1]

diversity training   Training in awareness of and respect for individual, social, and cultural differences among co-workers and customers. [Unit 1]

ecological niche   A description of the roles and associations of a particular species in the community to which it belongs; the way in which an organism interacts with all of the biotic (living) and abiotic (nonliving) factors in its environment. [Unit 4]

ecological succession   The gradual process by which the species composition of a community changes. [Unit 4]

emotion-focused coping   Coping efforts primarily aimed at relieving or regulating the emotional impact of a stressful situation. [Unit 2]

employee leasing   Purchasing the long-term services of a worker from another company. [Unit 1]

employee orientation   Training that brings new employees up to speed on how the business and its industry work. [Unit 1]

employee referral   A current employee's recommendation of friends or acquaintances. [Unit 1]

employee stock option plan   Program that attempts to motivate employees to maintain high levels of performance by allowing them to buy company stock at discount prices. [Unit 1]

employment at will   An employer-employee relationship in which either party may, in the absence of a contract, terminate the arrangement at any time and for any reason. [Unit 1]

Family and Medical Leave Act   Federal law requiring firms with 50 or more employees to grant up to 12 weeks of unpaid leave following the birth or adoption of a child or the placement of a foster child, or during the serious illness of the employee or a member of his or her family. [Unit 1]

fight-or-flight response   A rapidly occurring chain of internal physical reactions that prepare people either to fight or take flight from an immediate threat. [Unit 2]

fixed benefits   Benefits that all employees receive by virtue of being a member of the organization. [Unit 1]

flack   A derogatory term that journalists use to refer to a public relations agent. [Unit 3]

flexible benefits   Benefits that employees choose according to their wants and needs; also called *cafeteria benefits*. [Unit 1]

flextime   Program that allows employees to work during hours of their choice as long as they work their required number of hours and are present during prescribed core periods. [Unit 1]

gain sharing   The granting of periodic (quarterly, semiannual, or annual) bonuses to employees based on organizational performance, not individual performance. [Unit 1]

general adaptation syndrome   Endocrinologist Hans Selye's term for the three-stage progression of physical changes that occur when an organism is exposed to intense and prolonged stress. The three stages are alarm, resistance, and exhaustion. [Unit 2]

Great Railroad Strike of 1877   A strike that began on the Baltimore and Ohio Railroad in West Virginia and quickly swept across the nation's rails until it involved nearly 100,000 railroad workers and 500,000 workers from other industries. Although large numbers of middle-class Americans initially sympathized with the railroad workers' demands for fair wages, they eventually turned against the strikers. [Unit 5]

Haymarket affair   Also known as the "Haymarket riot," this 1886 incident started as a rally to protest police actions toward strikers in Chicago. A bomb thrown at the police resulted in a bout of violence that left seven policemen and scores of civilians dead. In the aftermath, several radicals and labor organizers were sentenced to death. The affair prompted blind rage directed at anarchists, labor unions, strikers, immigrants, and the working class in general. [Unit 5]

health psychology   The branch of psychology that studies how biological, behavioral, and social factors influence health, illness, medical treatment, and health-related behaviors. [Unit 2]

herbivore   An animal that eats plants or other photosynthetic organisms to obtain its food and energy. [Unit 4]

human resource management   Ensuring that a business has an adequate supply of skilled, trained, and motivated employees to meet the organization's objectives. [Unit 1]

immune system   Body system that produces specialized white blood cells that protect the body from viruses, bacteria, and tumor cells. [Unit 2]

job analysis   A general overview of all aspects of a particular job. [Unit 1]

job description   A statement of the tasks and responsibilities of a particular job. [Unit 1]

job posting   A notice advertising available positions within an organization. [Unit 1]

job requisition   A request for hiring submitted to the human resource department. [Unit 1]

job rotation   The practice of moving employees through a series of jobs for set periods of time to give them an understanding of a variety of business functions. [Unit 1]

job sharing   Arrangement in which two employees share a full-time job, each working part time. [Unit 1]

job specification   A statement of the qualifications, skills, and previous experience a person needs to perform a given job. [Unit 1]

keystone species   A species that is of exceptional importance in maintaining the species diversity of a community; when a keystone species is lost, the diversity of the community decreases and the structure of the community is significantly altered. [Unit 4]

Knights of Labor   A labor group formed in the nineteenth century that advocated broad-ranging reforms, such as an income tax and equal pay for women, to benefit working-class people. Unlike the American Federation of Labor, the Knights of Labor did not officially condone strikes. *See also* American Federation of Labor. [Unit 5]

layoff   Dismissal of an employee because of financial constraints on the firm. [Unit 1]

leave   Time away from the job, with or without pay. [Unit 1]

lobbying   In government public relations, the process of attempting to influence the voting of lawmakers to support a client's or an organization's best interests. [Unit 3]

lymphocytes   Specialized white blood cells that are responsible for immune defenses. [Unit 2]

mentoring   An informal relationship in which a more experienced employee guides and sponsors a less experienced employee in a similar work role. [Unit 1]

mutualism   *See* symbiosis. [Unit 4]

nickelodeon   A theater or hall where people watched short movies in the late nineteenth century. The word comes from *nickel* (the price of a ticket) and *melodeon* (a kind of organ that sometimes provided music for silent films). [Unit 5]

on-the-job training   Training in which employees learn by doing a job or by receiving one-on-one instruction—usually from a manager or co-worker—in how to do a job. [Unit 1]

optimistic explanatory style   Accounting for negative events or situations with external, unstable, and specific explanations. [Unit 2]

parasitism   *See* symbiosis. [Unit 4]

pay   Cash compensation in the form of wages, salary, or incentive bonuses. [Unit 1]

pay for performance   Linking pay increases directly to an employee's level of performance. [Unit 1]

performance appraisal   A periodic written evaluation of an employee's performance compared with specific goals, which are often stated in a performance plan. [Unit 1]

pessimistic explanatory style   Accounting for negative events or situations with internal, stable, and global explanations. [Unit 2]

predator   An organism that eats other living organisms. [Unit 4]

press agent   The earliest type of public relations practitioner, who sought to advance a client's image through media exposure. [Unit 3]

press release   In public relations, an announcement, written in the style of a news report, that gives new information about an individual, a company, or an organization and pitches a story idea to the news media. [Unit 3]

probation period   An initial trial period, often of three to six months, in which newly hired employees may be terminated if their job performance is unsatisfactory. [Unit 1]

problem-focused coping   Coping efforts primarily aimed at directly changing or managing a threatening or harmful stressor. [Unit 2]

profit sharing   An incentive system that gives some or all employees a percentage of the profits earned by a business. [Unit 1]

promotion   In the context of human resources, advancement to a position of greater responsibility and higher compensation. [Unit 1]

propaganda   In advertising and public relations, a communication strategy that tries to manipulate public opinion to gain support for a special issue, program, or policy, such as a nation's war effort. [Unit 3]

pseudo-event   In public relations, any circumstance or event created for the purpose of gaining coverage in the media. [Unit 3]

psychoneuroimmunology   An interdisciplinary field that studies the interconnections among psychological processes, nervous and endocrine system functions, and the immune system. [Unit 2]

publicity   In public relations, the positive and negative messages that spread controlled and uncontrolled information about a person, corporation, issue, or policy in various media. [Unit 3]

public relations   The total communication strategy conducted by a person, a government, or an organization attempting to reach and persuade its audiences to adopt a point of view. [Unit 3]

public service announcements (PSAs)   Reports or announcements, carried free by radio and TV stations, that promote government programs, educational projects, voluntary agencies, or social reform. [Unit 3]

real wages   Pay measured in terms of buying power. [Unit 5]

resumé   A brief summary of an applicant's relevant experience, ideally one or two pages in length. [Unit 1]

retirement   An employee's voluntary departure from a job on reaching a certain age. [Unit 1]

salary   Pay provided to professional employees in weekly, monthly, or yearly amounts. [Unit 1]

separation   The severing of an employee's relationship with an employer through layoff, termination, or retirement. [Unit 1]

social Darwinism   The racist belief—which emerged in the nineteenth century and was based on the theories of naturalist Charles Darwin—that whites stood at the top of the evolutionary ladder. [Unit 5]

social support   The resources provided by other people in times of need. [Unit 2]

stress   A negative emotional state occurring in response to events that are perceived as taxing or exceeding a person's resources or ability to cope. [Unit 2]

stressors   Events or situations that are perceived as harmful, threatening, or challenging. [Unit 2]

succession planning   A formal evaluation to determine which individuals within an organization are capable of future moves into key positions. [Unit 1]

symbiosis   An intimate and protracted association between two or more organisms of different species. Includes *mutualism,* in which the association is beneficial to both; *commensalism,* in which one benefits and the other neither is harmed nor benefits; and *parasitism,* in which one benefits and the other is harmed. [Unit 4]

telecommuting   A form of work-at-home program in which employees communicate with the office by computer or fax machine. [Unit 1]

termination   A voluntary or involuntary permanent departure from a job. [Unit 1]

transfer   A lateral, or sideways, move from one job to another with a similar level of authority and compensation. [Unit 1]

Type A behavior pattern   A behavioral and emotional style characterized by a sense of time urgency, hostility, and competitiveness. [Unit 2]

unemployment insurance   Program that pays workers who have lost their jobs a basic level of compensation for a limited time while they look for new work. [Unit 1]

video news releases (VNRs)   In public relations, the visual counterpart to a press release; it pitches a story idea to the TV news media by mimicking the style of a broadcast news report. [Unit 3]

wages   Pay provided to hourly employees. [Unit 1]

work-at-home programs   Benefit that allows employees to work all or some of their scheduled hours at home. [Unit 1]

Answer Key

1. Business: "Human Resource Management"

Preparing to Read the Textbook Chapter
Answers will vary.

Practicing Your Textbook Reading Skills

1. b (pp. 371–72)	6. c (p. 365)
2. c (pp. 373–74)	7. d (p. 365)
3. a (p. 357)	8. c (p. 371)
4. d (p. 359)	9. b (p. 378)
5. b (p. 360)	10. b (p. 380)

Testing Your Understanding

1. T (p. 353)	9. a (p. 361)
2. F (pp. 357–59)	10. d (pp. 362–68)
3. T (p. 366)	11. d (pp. 366–68)
4. T (p. 373)	12. b (pp. 371–72)
5. F (p. 376)	13. a (pp. 372–73)
6. c (pp. 351–52)	14. d (p. 374)
7. d (pp. 357–59)	15. b (pp. 374–78)
8. b (p. 359)	

Answers to questions 16–25 will vary.

16. Textbook's definition: Purchasing the long-term services of a worker from another company (p. 353).

17. Textbook's definition: Part-time, temporary, and self-employed workers who do not conform to the traditional model of the 9-to-5, full-time employee (p. 351).

18. Textbook's definition: A periodic written evaluation of an employee's performance compared with specific goals, which are often stated in a performance plan (p. 366).

19. Textbook's definition: A form of work-at-home program in which employees communicate with the office by computer or fax machine (p. 374).

20. Textbook's definition: Dismissal of an employee because of financial constraints on the firm (p. 376).

21. Possible answer: The first stage, *research,* involves determining what changes and employment needs an organization might expect; *forecasting* considers what kinds of employees are available to meet those needs; *job analysis* identifies what positions are needed and what employee skills are required (pp. 354–55).

22. Textbook's answer: When a job requisition is submitted, the human resource manager begins a search for applicants. The first and preferred source of applicants is the company's own employees. Other sources include employee referrals, as well as advertising in local newspapers, contacting employment agencies, and recruiting on college campuses (pp. 357–59).

23. Possible answer: Some people argue that the tests used by employers are unfair because they are biased in favor of white American men (p. 360).

24. Possible answer: Well-trained employees are more efficient and enable companies to be more competitive. The cost of employee training is paid off by increased productivity; Motorola, for example, gained $30 in increased productivity for every $1 spent on employee education (pp. 361–66).

25. Possible answer: *Commissions* are a percentage of the money that a worker generates for a business; *bonuses* are payments awarded to employees if a company reaches particular goals; *gain sharing* is the payment of periodic bonuses based on company performance; *profit sharing* pays employees a percentage of a company's profits; *employee stock option plans* offer employees an opportunity to purchase company stock at a discount (pp. 370–71).

Making Thematic Connections
Answers will vary.

2. Psychology: "Stress, Health, and Coping"

Preparing to Read the Textbook Chapter
Answers will vary.

Practicing Your Textbook Reading Skills

1. b (p. 537)
2. d (pp. 537–39)
3. b (p. 537)
4. a (p. 540)
5. b (p. 541)

6. c (p. 545)
7. c (pp. 543–44)
8. c (pp. 551, 569)
9. b (p. 565)
10. a (p. 567)

Testing Your Understanding

1. T (p. 540)
2. F (pp. 541–42)
3. T (pp. 553–54)
4. F (pp. 554–55)
5. T (p. 559)
6. b (p. 541)
7. c (pp. 542–43)
8. d (pp. 543–44)

9. a (pp. 549–50)
10. d (pp. 555–56)
11. a (p. 556)
12. d (p. 559)
13. b (p. 563)
14. a (p. 564)
15. c (pp. 563–65)

Answers to questions 16–25 will vary.

16. Textbook's definition: A situation in which a person feels pulled between two or more opposing desires, motives, or goals (p. 543).

17. Textbook's definition: The stress that results from the pressure of adapting to a new culture (p. 545).

18. Textbook's definition: A rapidly occurring chain of internal physical reactions that prepare people either to fight or take flight from an immediate threat (p. 546).

19. Textbook's definition: Hormones released by the adrenal cortex that play a key role in the body's response to long-term stressors (pp. 548–49).

20. Textbook's definition: Behavioral and cognitive responses used to deal with stressors; involves efforts to change circumstances, or your interpretation of circumstances, to make them more favorable and less threatening (p. 561).

21. Possible answers: (1) Accept that not all decisions are easy; (2) try to use a *partial approach strategy* in which you consider a decision or commitment but leave yourself the option of changing your mind; (3) research your options thoroughly; (4) seek advice (p. 544).

22. Possible answers: fast breathing, rapid heart rate, elevated blood pressure, increased blood flow to muscles, poor digestion, enlarged pupils (p. 547).

23. Possible answer: The *alarm stage* occurs as an immediate response to a stressor; it is characterized by intense arousal. The next stage is *resistance,* in which the body fights or tries to adjust to the stressor. The final stage, *exhaustion,* occurs if the stress continues for a long period of time and can result in illness and even death (pp. 548–49).

24. Possible answer: In terms of *social support,* women tend to be caregivers more than men, so they carry the added stress of supporting others. Also, because women tend to have larger and more intimate social networks, they are affected negatively by the stresses of others more than men are. Because men tend to have smaller social networks, they are more prone to isolation. In terms of *coping,* women generally reach out to others for support, whereas men under stress tend to withdraw (pp. 560–62).

25. Possible answers: Americans are less likely to seek social support than Asians are; Americans tend to favor problem-solving strategies whereas Asians tend to prefer emotion-focused coping strategies (p. 566).

Making Thematic Connections
Answers will vary.

3. Mass Communication: "Public Relations and Framing the Message"

Preparing to Read the Textbook Chapter
Answers will vary.

Practicing Your Textbook Reading Skills

1. d (pp. 422–25)
2. c (p. 428)
3. b (p. 429)
4. c (pp. 430–31)
5. a (p. 431)

6. c (p. 432)
7. c (p. 438)
8. b (pp. 446–47)
9. a (pp. 449–51)
10. d (p. 450)

Testing Your Understanding

1. F (p. 425)
2. T (p. 426)
3. T (p. 430)
4. T (pp. 433–34)
5. F (p. 435)
6. b (p. 425)
7. d (pp. 426–27)
8. c (p. 428)

9. c (p. 431)
10. a (p. 432)
11. b (p. 433)
12. c (p. 435)
13. a (p. 436)
14. b (pp. 436–37)
15. b (p. 439)

Answers to questions 16–25 will vary.

16. Textbook's definition: Publicity is one type of PR communication: positive and negative messages that spread controlled and uncontrolled information about a person, corporation, issue, or policy in various media (p. 425).

17. Textbook's definition: Any circumstance or event created for the purpose of gaining coverage in the media (p. 430).

18. Textbook's definition: Communication strategically placed, either as advertising or publicity, to gain support for a special issue, program, or policy, such as a nation's war effort (p. 433).

19. Textbook's definition: The process of attempting to influence the voting of lawmakers to support a client's or an organization's best interests (p. 439).

20. Textbook's definition: For journalists, the word *flack* has come to mean PR people who insert themselves between their employers/clients and members of the press; used derogatorily (p. 440).

21. Possible answer: They pioneered some public relations strategies to persuade both the public and the government to help pay their expenses. Illinois Central hired lobbyists to help convince members of the government that rail service would improve the economy and prevent the Civil War. Some railroads bribed reporters to write stories in their favor; others gave out free passes to the press to encourage them to use the rail service and write positive reviews. The hope was that these reviews would get others to ride trains as well. Once they succeeded in obtaining government funds, the railroads further lobbied for government regulation of rates and fares, which drove many smaller lines out of business (p. 427).

22. Possible answers: vote buying, hiring editorial services to write and distribute favorable articles about a client, attaching famous and respected names to articles written by someone else, planting favorable histories in textbooks (pp. 427–428).

23. Possible answer: Because local news is usually broadcast live during that time slot, politicians like to create these kinds of pseudo-events in the hope that the networks will air their views as part of the evening news programs (pp. 430–31).

24. Possible answer: *Independent agencies* are companies whose entire purpose is to provide public relations services to their clients. *In-house services* are departments within a company (such as a large corporation or a medical services provider) that handle that company's own public relations needs (pp. 431–33)

25. Possible answers: Journalism depends on public relations as a source of story ideas and news leads, but many journalists resent the interference of PR workers when they try to reach interviewees. Some journalists also believe that public relations people routinely distort the truth in the service of clients. Understaffing in journalism outlets forces writers to rely on PR workers for information, but a primary function of public relations is to limit or control reporters' access to sensitive or damaging information about a client. Many journalists resent how public relations people allow corporations and individuals to get free publicity through the news media, reducing the credibility of newswriters. These journalists believe that such publicity should be purchased through ads (pp. 440–45).

Making Thematic Connections

Answers will vary.

4. Biology: "Interactions in Communities"

Preparing to Read the Textbook Chapter

Answers will vary.

Practicing Your Textbook Reading Skills

1. b (p. 793)
2. a (pp. 793, 799, 802, 807)
3. a (pp. 793–94)
4. b (p. 795)
5. a (p. 796)
6. c (p. 798)
7. d (p. 809–11)
8. a (pp. 801–2)
9. c (pp. 806–7)
10. d (pp. 811–12)

Testing Your Understanding

1. F (p. 795)
2. T (p. 795)
3. F (p. 797)
4. T (p. 798)
5. T (p. 799)
6. b (p. 793)
7. d (p. 794)
8. c (pp. 794–95)
9. b (p. 794)
10. d (pp. 795–96)
11. d (pp. 800–1)
12. b (pp. 802–3)
13. d (pp. 803–5)
14. a (pp. 807–8)
15. a (pp. 808–9)

Answers to questions 16–25 will vary.

16. Textbook's definition: The phenomenon in which species that live together in the same environment tend to diverge in those characteristics that overlap (p. 797).

17. Textbook's definition: The consumption of live organisms, including plants by animals, animals

by animals, and even animals by plants or by fungi (p. 799).

18. Textbook's definition: Organisms that are of exceptional importance in maintaining the species diversity of a community (p. 801).

19. Textbook's definition: A close and long-term association between organisms of two different species; "living together" (p. 802).

20. Textbook's definition: The term refers not only to true islands but also to fragmented terrestrial areas (pp. 807–8).

21. Possible answer: An organism's fundamental niche is determined by the environment and what the organism itself can physiologically withstand; a realized niche is determined not only by physical factors but also by what other organisms are competing for resources (pp. 798–99).

22. Possible answer: *Parasitism* is a relationship in which one species benefits and the other is harmed; *mutualism* is a relationship in which both species benefit; *commensalism* is beneficial to one species and neither beneficial nor harmful to the other (p. 802).

23. Possible answer: Ants burrow out holes in the thorns of acacia plants and live there. The ants receive shelter and food (in the form of nectar as well as small herbivores that prey on the trees); the acacia trees receive protection from predators such as caterpillars, which the ants eat (p. 805).

24. Possible answer: The *facilitation hypothesis* suggests that succession happens regularly and predictably, with each stage "preparing the way" for the next; the *inhibition hypothesis* argues that early species prevent—rather than assist—colonization by other species; and according to the *tolerance hypothesis,* the species dominant at any given time are those that can best tolerate the existing physical conditions and the availability of resources (pp. 810–11).

25. Possible answers: Joan Arehart-Treichel, "Science Helps the Bluebird"; Jared M. Diamond, K. David Bishop, and S. Van Balen, "Bird Survival in an Isolated Javan Woodland: Island or Mirror?"; James R. Karr, "Avian Extinction on Barro Colorado Island, Panama: A Reassessment"; John Terborgh, "Why American Songbirds Are Vanishing" (p. 813).

Making Thematic Connections
Answers will vary.

5. History: "America through the Eyes of the Workers, 1870–1890"

Preparing to Read the Textbook Chapter
Answers will vary.

Practicing Your Textbook Reading Skills

1. d (pp. 651–52)	6. c (p. 662)
2. c (p. 653)	7. b (p. 674)
3. b (p. 655)	8. b (p. 675)
4. b (pp. 655–56)	9. c
5. c (p. 658)	10. c (p. 679)

Testing Your Understanding

1. T (pp. 656–57)	9. a (p. 662)
2. F (pp. 660–61)	10. b (pp. 668–71)
3. T (p. 663)	11. b (pp. 671–72)
4. F (p. 665)	12. c (pp. 672–73)
5. F (p. 671)	13. b (pp. 673–74)
6. b (pp. 653–55)	14. a (pp. 675–78)
7. a (p. 656)	15. d (p. 680)
8. d (pp. 659–60)	

Answers to questions 16–25 will vary.

16. Possible answer: Skilled workers who transformed melted raw iron into uniformly sized and shaped balls for the use of other ironworkers (pp. 657–58).

17. Possible answer: A phrase used to describe the sentimentalized view of the home as a feminine sanctuary or escape from the masculine working world. This new ideology stressed that woman's place was in the home, and women were expected to make their households "a haven in the heartless world" for their husbands and children (p. 665).

18. Possible answer: Self-contained residential neighborhood planned and built by a company to house its workers, provide socialization, instill company loyalty, curb unrest, and prevent unionization (pp. 667–68)

19. Possible answer: The word comes from *nickel* (the cost of a ticket) and *melodeon* (the kind of organ that sometimes provided music for silent films). It was a theater or hall where people watched short movies in the late nineteenth century (p. 669).

20. Possible answer: An idealized vision of a future society in which everybody is treated fairly and nobody suffers (pp. 675–79).

21. Possible answer: The industrial workforce was diverse. Immigrants, ethnic minorities, women, and children constituted a large percentage of workers in factories, mills, and mines. Many (if not most) workers moved to industrial centers from rural agricultural areas both in the United States and around the world. Pay was low and work was unreliable, so most industrial workers were very poor (pp. 652–61).

22. Possible answers: Department stores served as centers of consumerism. Their elaborate designs and decorations highlighted the value of material goods and encouraged both men and women to shop for entertainment. At the same time, salary differences and employee regulations highlighted the period's gender inequalities (pp. 664–65).

23. Possible answer: The Knights of Labor advocated broad-ranging reforms, such as an income tax and equal pay for women, to benefit working-class people; although this organization did not officially condone strikes, many of its achievements were the result of an 1885 strike against railroads. The American Federation of Labor emphasized the power of unions and strikes to gain specific benefits and improvements in the workplace (pp. 672–73).

24. Possible answer: The 1886 Haymarket "riot" started as a rally to protest police actions toward strikers at Chicago's McCormick works. The turnout was disappointingly small, but an unexpected bomb thrown at the police resulted in a bout of violence that left seven policemen and an unknown number of civilians dead. Although there was no evidence of who was responsible for the bomb, the Illinois state attorney decided to use the incident to make an example, and a number of radicals and labor organizers were convicted and executed. The attack on the labor movement that this event started essentially frightened workers from involvement with unions (pp. 673–75).

25. Possible answers: Although historians can interpret contemporary fiction, compare census figures, examine tables that show job mobility, or use income information to assess financial prosperity, the definition of "success" or "making it" is too subjective to be measured quantitatively (pp. 676–77).

Making Thematic Connections

Answers will vary.

Acknowledgments (continued)

Illustrations

UNIT 1

Page 348 Skjold/The Image Works **352** Ed Kashi **363** Jon Feingersh/Stock, Boston **368** Burke Uzzle/Zuma Images **378** Scott Harvey

UNIT 2

Page 536 Phoebe Beasley **538** (*top left and right*) Carmen Taylor/AP; (*bottom*) Paul Hawthorne/AP **539** (*top*) Mario Tama/Getty Images; (*bottom*) Ed Bailey/AP **540** Courtesy of Myrleen Ferguson/PhotoEdit **542** (*top*) Tony Freeman/PhotoEdit; (*bottom*) Courtesy of Richard S. Lazarus/University of California, Berkeley **543** (*top*) Billy E. Barnes/Stock Boston; (*bottom*) Bebeto Matthews/AP **545** Steve Liss/The Gamma-Liaison Network **546** Tina Fineberg/AP **547** Edgar Fahs Smith Collection, University of Pennsylvania Library **548** (*top*) © 1974 John Olson/People Weekly; (*bottom left and right*) Petrovic, P., Kalso, E., Petersson, K. M., and Ingvar, M. Placebo and opioid analgesia—Imaging shared neuronal network, *Science,* 295, 1737–1740 **549** Omikron/Science Source/Photo Researchers **550** (*left*) Courtesy of Robert Ader, photo by James Montanus, University of Rochester; (*right*) Courtesy of Nicholas Cohen, University of Rochester **551** (*top*) Courtesy of Janice Kiecolt-Glaser, Ohio State University College of Medicine; (*bottom*) Gary A. Connor/PhotoEdit **553** Shaul Schwarz/Getty Images **554** David Lassman/Syracuse Newspapers/The Image Works **556** Robert Brenner/PhotoEdit **559** © Macduff Everton/The Image Works **560** (*top*) Jim Vecchione/The Gamma-Liaison Network; (*bottom*) Joe Carini/The Image Works **561** Tony Freeman/PhotoEdit **562** © 2002 The New Yorker Collection from cartoonbank.com. All rights reserved **563** Lester Sloan/The Gamma-Liaison Network **564** Joel Gordon **565** (*top*) Marko Shark/Corbis; (*bottom*) Joshua Griffler **567** Piers Cavendish/Zuma Press

UNIT 3

Page 423 Art Rogue/AP, Wide World Photos **424** Photofest **426** Library of Congress/Corbis **429** (*top*) Bettmann Archive-Corbis Pictures **432** Table 12.1: "The Top Public Relations Firms, 1999," reprinted by permission of the J.R. O'Dwyer Company, 2000. www.odwyerpr.com **433** Bettmann Archive-Corbis Pictures **437** Steve Lehman/Corbis-Saba **438** NBC/AP, Wide World Photos **439** Bob Daemmrich/Stock, Boston **441** "Shoe" by MacNelly, © Tribune Media Services, Inc. **443** Table 12.2: "PRSA Member Statement of Professional Values" section from the PRSA Ethics code posted on the PRSA website: www.prsa.org. Reprinted by permission of the Public Relations Society of America **444** John Gaps III/AP, Wide World Photos **446–47** James Leynse/Corbis-Saba **447** (*bottom*) courtesy, Levi Strauss & Co., Inc.

UNIT 4

Page 792 Heather Angel **796** (*top*) after MacArthur, 1958; (*bottom*) R. Carr/Bruce Coleman, Inc. **797** (*left*) after D. Lack, *Darwin's Finches,* Harper and Row, Publishers, Inc., New York, 1961; (*right*) adapted from R. E. Ricklefs, *Ecology,* 2d ed., Chiron Press, Inc., New York, 1979 **799** William E. Townsend, Jr./Photo Researchers, Inc. **800** Australian Department of Lands **801** (*bottom*) E. S. Ross **802** Joe Lubchenco **803** (*right*) Australian News and Information Service **804** (a) Max Gibbs/Oxford Scientific Films; (b) Guillermo Esteves/Waterhouse; (c) Kim Taylor/Bruce Coleman, Ltd.; (d) Lorna Stanton/ABPL/NHPA **805** (a) N.H. Cheatham/ DRK Photo; (b) Michael Fogden/DRK Photo **806–7** Townsend Dickenson/ Comstock **808** (*top*) after Ricklefs, *op. cit.;* (*bottom*) (a) Stephen Frink/ Waterhouse; (b) Fred Ward/Black Star **809** (*top*) adapted from J. H. Connell, *Science,* vol. 199, page 1303, 1978; (*bottom*) John Marshall **810** Wayne Sousa